An Intertextual Commentary
to the Psalter

An Intertextual Commentary to the Psalter

Juxtaposition and Allusion in Book I

DAVID EMANUEL

PICKWICK *Publications* · Eugene, Oregon

AN INTERTEXTUAL COMMENTARY TO THE PSALTER
Juxtaposition and Allusion in Book I

Pickwick Publications
An Imprint of Wipf and Stock Publishers
199 W. 8th Ave., Suite 3
Eugene, OR 97401

www.wipfandstock.com

PAPERBACK ISBN: 978-1-62032-185-0
HARDCOVER ISBN: 978-1-4982-8580-3
EBOOK ISBN: 978-1-7252-4745-1

Cataloguing-in-Publication data:

Names: Emanuel, David [author].

Title: An intertextual commentary to the Psalter : juxtaposition and allusion in book I / David Emanuel.

Description: Eugene, OR: Pickwick Publications, 2022 | Includes bibliographical references and index.

Identifiers: ISBN 978-1-62032-185-0 (paperback) | ISBN 978-1-4982-8580-3 (hardcover) | ISBN 978-1-7252-4745-1 (ebook)

Subjects: LCSH: Bible.—Psalms, I–XLI | Bible.—Psalms—Criticism, interpretation, etc. | Bible.—Psalms—Commentaries | Intertextuality in the Bible

Classification: BS1430.3 E43 2022 (print) | BS1430.3 E43 (ebook)

09/01/22

In Memory of Henri Vaucher
(1941–2022)

כִּי הֶנְרִי הֵכִין לְבָבוֹ לִדְרוֹשׁ אֶת־תּוֹרַת יְהוָה
וְלַעֲשֹׂת וּלְלַמֵּד בְּיִשְׂרָאֵל חֹק וּמִשְׁפָּט

For Henri devoted himself to study the law of the Lord
and to practice it, and to teach His statutes and ordinances in Israel
(adapted from Ezra 7:10)

Contents

Preface

THE PRESENT STUDY EXPLORES two dimensions of literary connections in Book I of the Psalter. The first concerns the arrangement of the psalms. Instead of seeking to uncover a broader plot or rationale for sequencing the entire Psalter, the present work focusses on literary connections between juxtaposed compositions, psalms placed next to each other. Assuming the underlying theory that editors and arrangers of individual psalms did not work haphazardly, the present study identifies and explores potential arrangement strategies employed by the editors. The second area of literary analysis addresses the question of biblical allusion. In addition to literary and lexical connections between juxtaposed psalms, many of the compositions in Book I bear further associations with other songs in the Psalter, together with a variety of texts in the Old Testament. The present work—adopting a diachronic approach, when possible—identifies these connections and discusses the various ways in which the psalmists rework literary texts from the Old Testament into their new compositions. Due to the notorious difficulty in dating psalms, it is not always possible to establish a lucid vector of allusion between the psalmists' work and potential sources. In these instances, the discussion veers towards intertextuality (synchronic) and echo.

All of the biblical references in the present work are listed according to English Bible translations, and where variations exist between the Hebrew and English text, I have placed the Hebrew verse number (and chapter where necessary) in brackets afterwards. Most of the English translations are taken from the New American Standard Version of the Bible (1995), and I have clearly indicated when deviating from this practice. The vowel points for Hebrew scripts are omitted unless their presence is necessary for interpretation. Variances between the written tradition (*ketiv*) and the read tradition (*qere*) are indicated by parenthesis and brackets: square brackets surround the *qere* and parenthesis surround the *ketiv*. References to the BHS refer to the critical apparatus found on the relevant page of the verse in question.

The present volume is, in many respects, intended to be foundational, and it is my hope that as students and scholars alike read it that they are inspired to pursue and examine further the relationships discussed within this book—those involving both juxtaposition and intertextuality. The field of Inner-biblical Allusion has enjoyed a great deal of attention in recent years, however, most of that attention has fallen on the low-hanging fruit of prophetic use of the Torah, and texts that are easily identifiable as late reusing popular early texts. However, the book of psalms has generally garnered less attention with respect to this line of investigation. In writing this book, my aim is to refocus a little more light on the psalms, in regards to Biblical Allusion. Similarly, with regards to the sequencing of individual psalms, much attention has fallen on macro structures and sequences concerning the whole Psalter, whereas attention to the positioning of individual psalms has, by and large, fallen by the wayside. This area, too, I would like to rectify in the present volume.

Abbreviations

1cs	First common singular
11QPs	*Psalms Scroll*
11QPsa	*Psalms Scroll-a*
2ms	Second masculine singular
3ms	Third masculine singular
b. Ber.	Babylonian Talmud, Berakot
AB	The Anchor Bible
ANE	Ancient Near East
BDB	E. Brown, C. Briggs and S. R. Driver, *A Hebrew and English Lexicon of the Old Testament*
BHS	*Biblia Hebraica Stuttgartensia*
CBQ	*Catholic Bible Quarterly*
CSB	Christian Standard Bible
EBH	Early Biblical Hebrew
EJ	*European Judaism*
EQ	*Evangelical Quarterly*
ESV	English Standard Version
ETL	*Ephemerides Theologicae Lovanienses*
HAR	*Hebrew Annual Review*
HTS	*Hervormde Teologiese Studies* (also known as *HTS Teologiese Studies/Theological Studies*)
HUCA	*Hebrew Union College Annual*
ICC	International Critical Commentary
JBL	*Journal of Biblical Literature*

JETS	*Journal of the Evangelical Theological Society*
JPS	Jewish Publication Society of America version
JQR	*Jewish Quarterly Review*
JSOT	*Journal for the Study of the Old Testament*
JSOTSup	Journal for the Study of the Old Testament: Supplement Series
JSS	*Journal of Semitic Studies*
JTISup	Journal of Theological Interpretation: Supplement Series
JTS	*Journal of Theological Studies*
LBH	Late Biblical Hebrew
LXX	The Septuagint [=70] Greek Old Testament
MT	Masoretic Text(s)
NASB	New American Standard Bible (1995)
NET	New English Translation
NIB	*The New Interpreter's Bible*
SBLDS	Society of Biblical Literature Dissertation Series
SBH	Standard Biblical Hebrew
SJOT	*Scandinavian Journal of the Old Testament*
SJSJ	Supplements to the Journal for the Study of Judaism
Tg.	Targum
Tg. Ps.-J	Targum Pseudo-Jonathan
VT	*Vetus Testamentum*
VTSup	Supplements to *Vetus Testamentum*
WBC	Word Biblical Commentary
ZAW	*Zeitschrift für die Alttestamentliche Wissenschaft*

Introduction

WHY THIS BOOK?

THE PRESENT VOLUME BLOSSOMED from an original desire soon after completing my doctoral dissertation to compile a detailed compendium of intertextual connections between individual psalms and their intertexts. The dissertation itself focused on a selection of historiographic exodus psalms that bore a significantly high number of intertexts from both within the Psalter and throughout biblical literature.[1] After completing this project, I became curious about other compositions in the Psalter: Were they as rich as the historiographic psalms with respect to their reuse of biblical texts?

To satisfy this curiosity, I began compiling a list of the Psalter's intertexts, beginning with Book I. After generating a rudimentary working list, it appeared that further analysis was necessary to establish the nature of each connection where possible. In many instances, what looked like an intertext, or an allusion marker constituted a false association generated from a common genre, or a common poetic expression. Similar obfuscations arise in contemporary English literature. If, for example, a columnist from the *New York Times* today adopts the expression "what goes around comes around," it is ill-advised to assume the writer drew material from a Welsh novel produced in the early 1900s that utilizes the same expression.

Ultimately, the present volume represents the initial stages of a revelatory process that probes and uncovers, for scholars and students alike, the rich literary intertextual crop within the Psalter that is ripe for harvest. Although I am not the first individual to discuss many of

---

1. Four chapters of the dissertation are published in Emanuel, *Bards to Biblical Exegetes.*

the allusions and echoes appearing in this book, few, if any, have collected and discussed evidence of allusion and purposeful juxtaposition in Book I of the Psalter into a single volume. From the wide variety of commentaries on the psalms, some, but not all, pass comment on the relationships between individual psalms and their neighbors, and others further discuss potential intertexts. As a result, data pertaining to intertexts and juxtaposition remains scattered throughout numerous commentaries, which challenges students and scholars alike to sift through individual volumes to uncover this precious information. By conducting independent research and analysis and synthesizing the views and observations of a select group of prominent commentaries,[2] the present study draws together in one place an introductory discussion and rudimentary analysis of each psalm's potential intertexts and juxtaposition strategies in Book I of the Psalter. In so doing, this study concentrates a diluted and dispersed subject matter into a single location.

JUXTAPOSITION THEORY

The form-critical approach to psalms introduced by Herman Gunkel dominated the study of psalms throughout the twentieth century. Although students of Gunkel's methodology adapted elements of his approach,[3] the fundamental goals of establishing each psalm's genre and setting remained the primary goal for most commentators over the last one hundred years. For that reason, form critics seldom addressed issues concerning the sequence and arrangement of psalms in the Psalter. In recent years, following a renewed interest in canonical criticism,[4] a growing number of scholars have devoted attention to the arrangement of the Psalter, recognizing intentional strategies employed in the positioning of individual compositions. Much of the discussion in this area, however, centers on explaining the Psalter's overall organization.

---

2. For the present study, I enlisted the assistance of a selection of commentators who are sensitive to close juxtaposition strategies. Among the more prominent: Clifford, *Psalms 1–72*; VanGemeren, *Psalms*; McCann, "Psalms."

3. Modern commentaries, such as Craigie and Tate, *Psalms 1–50*, and Allen, *Psalms 101–150*, still focus heavily on establishing the form and setting of each psalm, determining the *Sitz im Leben*. Kraus, *Psalms 1–59*, similarly adopts this approach. For a more detailed survey on psalms' research, see Clines, *On the Way to the Postmodern*.

4. For more on this idea, see Hayes, *Dictionary of Biblical Interpretation*, 1:164–67.

Within this rubric, various scholars have published numerous theories in the last thirty years.[5] Perhaps the most renowned proposal was presented by Gerald Wilson, who suggested a historical-theological agenda in which the Psalter's formation responds to the dilemma of the failed Davidic dynasty.[6] Typically, within this perspective, the concentration of the Davidic psalms in Books I–III reflects the failed monarchy, which subsequently ends with Psalm 89, a lament reflecting Jerusalem's destruction.[7]

With respect to the rationale or motivation behind juxtaposition of psalms, the present work veers away from approaches uncovering potential organizational principles for the entire Psalter, and instead focuses on the closer relationships between the psalms themselves. In other words, rather than theorizing about the organization of the pre-formed building blocks, i.e., larger groups of psalms, the present study concentrates on the relationships among smaller constructional units, the individual psalms. Accordingly, the primary question the present work addresses with regards to sequencing is: Why is Psalm X next to Psalm Y?

The important principle of association constitutes the most crucial key for identifying juxtaposition relationships between psalms. In modern scholarship, Keil and Delitzsch first draw attention to this technique for sequencing compositions. In their commentary on the Psalter, they state:

> It is the principle of homogeneousness, which is the old Semitic mode of arranging things: for in the alphabet, the hand and the hollow of the hand, water and fish, the eye and the mouth, the back and the front of the head have been placed together. In like the psalms follow one another according to their relationship as manifested by prominent external and internal marks.[8]

5. See, for example, Robertson, *The Flow*; Ho, "Design of the MT Psalter."

6. See Wilson, *Editing of the Hebrew Psalter*, and his later refinements in "Shaping the Psalter."

7. A more detailed survey of studies based on structural analysis of the Psalter appears in Howard, *Psalms 93–100*, 1–19. He dedicates most of his survey, however, to the shaping of the whole collection, as opposed to the close relationships, which is the present volume's focus.

8. For example, they assert that the Davidic Psalm 86 was inserted between Korahite Psalms 85 and 87, "because it is related both to Ps. lxxxv. 8 by the prayer: '*Shew me Thy way, O Jahve*' and '*give Thy conquering strength unto Thy servant*', and to Ps. lxxxvii by the prospect of conversion of the heathen to the God of Israel." Keil and Delitzsch, *Psalms*, 1:21. They were not the first to recognize that the psalms, along with other biblical texts, were purposefully arranged with a logical rationale behind the sequencing of textual units. Scattered throughout rabbinic literature, Jewish exegetes seek to explain why an editor or arranger placed one psalm next to another; see, for example,

In short, ancient editors and arrangers sequenced psalms according to common elements within the compositions. Although the work of Keil and Delitzsch forms the foundation of the present discussion, further refinement is necessary to perform a more detailed discussion of juxtaposition in the Psalter. Consequently, the present work classifies types of associations that exist between consecutive psalms.

A basic example consists of a simple lexical association between juxtaposed psalms, which involves either a single word, or combination of words replicated in contiguous psalms. In such instances, the common word or phrase rarely appears in the Psalter. Keil and Delitzsch adduce two examples that fall into this category. The first concerns Psalms 34 and 35, which, in their view, were juxtaposed on account of the phrase מלאך יהוה ("the angel of the Lord"). As an expression describing a messenger of God sent to protect or avenge the righteous, the words מלאך יהוה only appear in these contiguous psalms, with respect to the Psalter. This case represents a relatively rare and unequivocal example of association, where only two appearances of the keywords appear in the entire the Psalter. Such instances, however, do not detract from identifying other examples involving more common vocabulary, so long as they are not frequently distributed throughout the book of Psalms. Another example cited by Keil and Delitzsch concerns the word יונה ("dove"), which appears in Psalms 65 and 66. Apart from these two locations in the Psalter, the Hebrew word יונה only arises in one other location, Psalm 68. Therefore, because of the word's relative rarity, and its appearance in contiguous psalms, it is likely that an editor or arranger juxtaposed the two compositions because of this word.[9] As stated earlier, the lexical elements linking psalms together need not feature rare words if they combine uniquely in close proximity and appear in juxtaposed works. Thus, for example, the words חזק ("strong"), אמץ ("courageous") and ארץ ("land") all individually represent common words throughout the Hebrew Bible; however, when appearing together in juxtaposed texts, as in Deut 31:7, 23, and Josh 1:6, their presence suggests a purposeful attempt to connect the two books.

---

b. Ber 10a, which informs the reader that the need for exegesis through juxtaposition stems from the Torah itself.

9. Parunak also tackles the subject of transitional techniques in the Bible, though he references the principle of association in slightly different terms, employing the expression "keyword association." See, e.g., Parunak, "Transitional Techniques," 527–28.

In addition to lexical associations, semantic or thematic commonalities may generate a literary nexus. In such instances, common themes and/ or words with overlapping semantic domains influence arrangers when sequencing compositions. Keil and Delitzsch, for example, adduce the case of Psalms 50 and 51. Both psalms highlight the preference for spiritual sacrifice over animal sacrifice. Specifically, Ps 50:13–14 reads, "Shall I eat the flesh of bulls / Or drink the blood of male goats? / Offer to God a sacrifice of thanksgiving / And pay your vows to the Most High."[10] Psalm 51:16 follows with, "For You do not delight in sacrifice, otherwise I would give it; / You are not pleased with burnt offering." In addition to these cited verses, the primary content in each psalm addresses the same issue of sacrifice, defining appropriate and inappropriate offerings. As a result, the related material reflects an exceptionally specific theme in the Psalter that unifies the two psalms. Unlike the earlier examples, individual words or word combinations fail to unite the psalms; instead, they are bound by a common identifiable theme, which is addressed with different words.[11]

Although the aforementioned lexical and thematic associations contribute to answering the question, "Why are individual psalms juxtaposed," they fail to address the question of sequencing, "Why are they

10. All translations are from the New American Standard Bible (NASB 1995) unless otherwise stated.

11. These basic principles of association extend well beyond the psalms. Umberto Cassuto develops Keil and Delitzsch's identification of association, discussing numerous instances throughout biblical literature; see Cassuto, "Sequence and Arrangement," 1–6. He proposes that the principle of association serves as a technique "whose purpose was possibly to aid the memory" (p. 2). Cassuto recognizes Keil and Delitzsch's efforts on the topic but remains unconvinced concerning their faithful adherence to the principle in their commentary on the psalms. Additionally, Cassuto, "Sequence and Arrangement," 2, discusses instances where formulation of oral law reflects the principle of association, and further cites examples from the Law and the Minor Prophets. As an example, Joel follows Hosea due to the plea at the end of Hosea to "Return, O Israel, to the Lord Your God" (14:1) and the continuation of the theme of return in Joel 2:12. Cassuto also identifies examples from the Writings. More than just laying down the principle, however, Cassuto devotes a chapter to expounding on the role association plays in the arrangement of the book of Ezekiel; see Cassuto, "The Book of Ezekiel." Another important contributor to the field is Alexander Rofé, who applies the principle of association to his discussion of the arrangement of the laws in Deuteronomy; see Rofé, "The Laws in Deuteronomy." More importantly, Rofé further asserts association as the basic framework by which the Psalter is arranged; see Rofé, *Introduction to the Literature*, 314–15. Howard, *Psalms 93–100*, additionally recognizes the principle of association in his work (see p. 98 for example) in addition to less concrete thematic connections.

aligned in this specific order?"[12] If an assumed arranger bears responsibility for a short collection of psalms, and discovers common lexical
or even thematic elements between two psalms, he has two choices for
arranging the compositions, either in the sequence A→B, or the reversed
order, B→A. Nothing inherent within the shared themes or vocabulary
dictates the final sequencing of the psalms; typically, the theory of association, as understood by Keil and Delitzsch at least, simply explains
why an arranger juxtaposed two compositions in any order.

With this in mind, it is necessary to classify a third possibility involving both lexical and thematic association, one that determines the specific
ordering of the two psalms. The present work refers to such instances
as sequencing associations. One form of sequencing association occurs
when the common words or theme appear at the end of one composition
and the beginning of another, generating a literary adhesive that smooths
the reading between independent compositions. Outside of the Psalter, a
well-cited example occurs with the phrase, "The Lord roars from Zion
/ And utters His voice from Jerusalem," which appears at the end of Joel
(see 3:16), and at the beginning of Amos, the following book in the Minor Prophets (see 1:2). Because this type of linkage frequently surfaces
throughout the Old Testament, it is expected to emerge within the Psalter.[13]

Logical connections between psalms represent a fourth category of
sequencing that dictates the order of two or more compositions.[14] Examples of logical connections in this category include causation, temporal
sequence or overlap, question and answer, and promise and fulfillment.
A lucid example of temporal sequencing involves the ordering of Psalms
105 and 106. The former recounts events from Genesis, God's covenant
with Abraham, and surveys literary-historical events up to the Israelites'

---

12. At this point I should mention Keil and Delitzsch's category of community of
species, where psalm titles, such as Maskil, or Songs of Ascent, influence an arranger
in grouping psalms together. They further extend this notion to psalms beginning
with words such as הודו ("praise") as in Psalms 105–7, and those ending in הללו־יה
("Hallelu-Yah") as in Psalms 111–17, 146–50; see Keil and Delitzsch, *Psalms*, 1:22.

13. Parunak broaches the topic of transitional techniques in the Bible in both the
Old and New Testaments. He refers to this as a link, when a lexical element appears
at the end of one segment and the beginning of another; see Parunak, "Transitional
Techniques," 530.

14. Parunak, "Transitional Techniques," 528, recognizes this category and further adds possibilities of speech attribution and conditionality, though the scope of
his study extends well beyond the Psalter. See also Zakovitch, "Ordering of Psalms,"
214–18.

entrance into the promised land. Following Psalm 105's survey, Psalm 106 creates an overlap, recalling events from the crossing of the Sea of Reeds through to the exile. Logically, the content of the two psalms apparently dictated to an arranger their final sequence: a survey of Israel's history from God's covenant with Abraham to the exile.

A fifth sequential category of juxtaposition recognizes the possibility of sequencing that stems from interpretive motivations. Moving beyond simply juxtaposing texts on account of similar ideas or words, Zakovitch veers away from merely logical motivations for psalm arrangements and discusses how biblical editors purposefully sequenced texts to generate new layers of interpretation. He argues, "One type of inner-biblical interpretation is achieved through the juxtaposition of two units: the placement of two texts one after the other, one or both of which is meant to affect our reading of the other."[15] Consequently, he understands juxtaposition as an expression of inner-biblical interpretation.[16] Therefore, in the context of the Psalter, the editor or arranger of a sequence of texts additionally serves as an interpreter seeking to influence a reader's understanding of one composition through its juxtaposition with another.

Another consideration with regards to psalm sequencing, though admittedly difficult to establish, concerns arrangements stemming from liturgical needs.[17] The juxtaposition of two or more psalms may have originally facilitated a ceremony or event in a festal celebration. Influential religious figures may have arranged shorter collections of psalms to correspond with specific actions performed within an ordered service. Such collections may have subsequently been inserted into the Psalter together with the sequencing preserved. Scholars suggest this motivation for the ordering of the Psalms' scroll at Qumran in Cave 11. With regards to Books IV and V, the drastic differences between 11QPsa's ordering and MT's Psalter, as reflected in modern English Bibles, are difficult to ignore. Although some argue that 11QPsa reflects an alternative canonical version and arrangement of Books IV and V, others contend that it

15. Zakovitch, "Juxtaposition," 510.

16. Zakovitch cites from the Talmud, b. Ber. 10a, "Why is the chapter of Absalom [Psalm 3] juxtaposed to the chapter of God and Magog [Psalm 2]?" The rabbis assumed that textual proximity added a new layer of meaning; see Zakovitch, "Juxtaposition," 509–24, esp. 510. Zakovitch further dedicates a chapter of his volume on inner-biblical interpretation to the notion of interpretation through juxtaposition (see Zakovitch, *An Introduction*, 28–34).

17. For an example of this approach, see Goulder, "The Fourth Book," in which he theorizes a liturgical pattern for the organization of Book IV.

exhibits an arrangement ordered specifically for liturgical needs.[18] Psalms 113–18, termed the Egyptian Hallel in rabbinic literature, represent another example of sequencing stemming from liturgical function.[19]

Naturally, it is exceedingly problematic to prove unequivocally that instances of liturgical sequencing exist within the Psalter. To do so, one needs to adduce external evidence of a connection between a group of psalms and a specific festival or ceremony. Failing that, it is necessary to demonstrate at least a correlation between a sequence of psalms and a series of events in a prescribed order of service. For that reason, although the present study recognizes the possibility of liturgical sequencing, it applies extreme caution when suggesting this specific means for juxtaposition, and ultimately, all discussions surrounding this topic remain highly speculative.[20] However, because liturgical sequencing remains a real possibility, it deserves mention here.

At this juncture, two critical points necessitate further elaboration. First, none of the potential juxtaposition strategies mentioned above are mutually exclusive; thus, the nexus between contiguous psalms can exhibit two or more rationale behind their sequencing. Juxtaposed psalms, for example, may share vocabulary, generating an instance of association, and simultaneously reflect a further logical relationship between them. Second, the point at which individual psalms converge may fail to reveal any signs of the above strategies. Such instances are expected because the editors and arrangers did not have total control of where to insert specific compositions or groups of psalms. Instances like this demonstrate the proverbial exception that proves the rule. This second point serves a crucial role in the analysis of psalms' sequencing because it deters from the need to force the identification of a juxtaposition strategy where it is not warranted.

Considering the arrangement of the Psalter's compositions, one aspect seldom discussed in the literature concerns the probability of an

18. See, for example, Skehan, "A Liturgical Complex," which conclusively argues that 11QPsa was later than the canonized form of the Psalter reflected in MT.

19. For the thematic connections between the psalms and elements of the Passover celebration, see Schonfield, "Psalms 113–18." Furthermore, Yarchin, "Psalms Collections," presents compelling evidence that the ordering of books in the Psalter remains fluid even among medieval Hebrew manuscripts. The changes instigated in these instances were influenced through liturgical considerations.

20. Essentially, even if a group of psalms formed part of a liturgy, the need still arises to establish which elements inside each psalm correspond with the ceremonial elements. In short, the enigma remains, "Why was A next to B?"

arranger of psalms similarly functioning as a psalmist, which seems natural from a traditional standpoint. If one considers David as a psalmist, his role extends beyond writing psalms, and he would have similarly carried responsibility for their subsequent arrangement. Such a possibility holds two implications for the present analysis of juxtaposed psalms. First, two psalms may exhibit notable similarities with respect to shared vocabulary and theme simply because an editor composed a psalm purposefully to complement an earlier work. Alternatively, a psalmist-arranger may have adjusted or amended two otherwise unrelated psalms with the hope of creating greater unity between otherwise diverse compositions.[21] Second, a psalmist-editor would naturally adopt some of the same motivations for organizing stanzas within a psalm in his arrangement of independent psalms. For example, just as psalmists employ individual key words to link stanzas together within a psalm, a psalmist-editor may adjust wording between individual psalms to generate unity. Similarly, relationships such as contrast and continuity that often appear between juxtaposed stanzas may similarly arise between juxtaposed psalms. In this way, individual psalms themselves serve as enlarged stanzas in the hands of the editor.

The creation and gradual development of biblical psalms ultimately leads to a variety of themes within each individual composition, which subsequently leads to an unavoidable problem: uncovering an original author's presumed intention. Via creative exegetical ingenuity, it is possible for a reader to generate complex sequencing patterns that were far from an arranger's or editor's mind. By identifying certain individual words within psalms, for example, one could identify chiastic patterns that arise out of happenstance, as opposed to a purposeful arrangement. Naturally, no modern author is privy to the knowledge and motivations behind all psalmists and editors, so most of the conclusions concerning arrangement remain hypothetical. Regarding the present volume, it is worth noting that all conjecture of juxtaposition strategy leans towards a relatively conservative estimation.

INTERTEXTUAL THEORY

The second major topic for the present study concerns the psalms and intertextuality. Presently, two schools of thought regarding intertextuality

---

21. Likely, modifications like this affect psalm endings, as well as individual words within the body of the psalm.

exist: synchronic, and diachronic (also known as inner-biblical allusion).[22] Synchronic approaches remain oblivious to the temporal relationships between a text and its intertext(s). Thus, the exegete investigates levels of discourse between texts within the confines of Scripture, regardless of whether one author was aware of the other's existence. Within this interpretive framework, for example, a reader may uncover and discuss an inner-biblical discourse between excerpts from Genesis and the book of Esther. As part of the discussion, characters and events in Genesis may influence the exegete's interpretation of Esther, and similarly, events and characters in Esther, though written much later, may influence the interpretation of stories in Genesis. Operating under this rubric, the exegete remains free from the constraints of dating the two texts under discussion, and similarly free from the question of authorial intention.[23] It does not matter that Genesis' author bore no knowledge of Esther and the events surrounding her life in exile. The interpreter abandons any concern for a diachronic trajectory and depends primarily on imagination to link the two literary entities. Similarly, when adopting a synchronic approach, an exegete is empowered to discuss ways in which the book of Joshua sheds interpretive light on Ezra, despite Joshua being an earlier text.[24] The end result is a bidirectional inner-biblical discourse created and sustained by an exegetical imagination.

22. Due to the variation in which contemporary authors employ the term "intertextuality" within the realms of biblical studies, a compelling need arises to establish methodological clarity.

23. Concerning the question of authorial intention, on one hand, it is easy to dispel any notion of a twenty-first century reader knowing the mind of a biblical writer; after all, who among us today has been privileged to gaze over David's or Jeremiah's shoulder and into their thoughts as they composed their written documents? That said, however, one primary role of scholars and exegetes is to reconstruct the thought processes of these earlier writers as best they can. At times, one may be close to reconstructing a semblance of their original motivations, and at times, one will no doubt fall dismally short. Williamson, "Isaiah 62:4," 739, speaks well concerning this matter. Although he recognizes the validity of inner-biblical allusion, he also confesses, "In the case of inner-biblical allusions . . . it will never be possible finally to prove that a writer was consciously dependent on one source rather than another, especially when much of the vocabulary to which appeal is made is relatively common." This fact, however, should not deter scholars from any attempts to reconstruct the thinking processes of the original biblical authors. Contemporary scholars, as a response, must proceed with caution, and refrain from dogmatically clinging to untenable positions.

24. Tanner, *The Book of Psalms*, exemplifies this approach.

The alternative diachronic approach to intertextuality relates to inner-biblical interpretation and allusion,[25] identifying instances where an author refers back to a text, presumably known to his readers, and merges aspects of that source composition into his literary creation.[26] When adopting diachronic approaches, the exegete must first demonstrate, to some degree, a vector of allusion, or the direction of borrowing between the works, establishing the source text and later text that reuses it. The general assumption here is that an author, in our case the psalmist, identifies a well-known written composition, and engages with it for the enrichment of his text or to influence his audience's understanding of the source text. Only rarely in modern scholarship is this approach applied to the Psalter, where psalmists function as interpreters of earlier texts.[27]

Of the two approaches, the diachronic approach undoubtedly presents more exegetical challenges. Despite the inherent difficulties,[28] however, the present work leans slightly more towards the diachronic approach, that of inner-biblical allusion, as opposed to the synchronic approach of intertextuality. To analyze each psalm, the present volume relies on a three-step approach. It first establishes a point of connection between each psalm and an intertext, a marker,[29] which appears in a variety of forms, such as rare vocabulary shared between the psalm and

25. Strictly speaking, the term inner-biblical allusion, in the present context, covers two areas of study. Meek, "Intertextuality," 289, expresses the differences, stating, "In distinction from inner-biblical exegesis, inner-biblical allusion sets out to determine whether a receptor text has in some way referred to a source text, but the goal is not to demonstrate that the receptor text has modified the source text. Rather, with inner-biblical allusion the goal is simply to demonstrate that a later text in some way references an earlier text." For the sake of the present study, the term inner-biblical allusion, or just allusion by itself encompasses both of the aforesaid diachronic methodological approaches.

26. See Fishbane's seminal work, *Biblical Interpretation*, 1–19.

27. Fishbane, *Biblical Interpretation*, for example, seldom discusses interpretation from the perspective of the psalmist as interpreter. Apart from his work, however, a few notable exceptions exist, such as, Emanuel, "Psalm 105," and Kim, "Exodus 34.6."

28. Regarding diachronic approaches, questions quickly arise concerning evidence of one author knowing of, and accessing a written text reflected in MT. Further problems surface concerning the possibility of a psalmist accessing oral or variant written traditions. In such cases, differences between the source and borrower may arise from the psalmist's alterations or a degree of variance between the psalmist's source, written or oral, and the text reflected in MT. Tanner raises these, and other objections, but does not abandon the endeavor. See Tanner, "Allusion or Illusion," 24–35.

29. Regarding further discussion of the marker, see Sommer, *A Prophet Reads Scripture*, 11.

its connected passage to which it bears a literary association. Naturally, rarer vocabulary generates a more robust and reliable point of connection. When such words or phrases accumulate in number, the case for literary borrowing intensifies.[30] Another means of establishing a nexus between two texts stems from corresponding sequential arrangements. Regarding the Torah particularly, certain sequences were well known to the psalmists, such as the days of creation, or the events leading up to Israel's emancipation from Egypt. It is possible that events like these were employed to shape individual psalms. Naturally, the value and strength of intertextual associations are not all equal, and a need arises in the present volume to evaluate and discuss each marker on its own merits.[31]

Once the intertext(s) is established, the present volume determines which of the texts represents the source, and which reflects the later borrower. Often this process is easily resolved when psalms form literary connections with the Torah, or when concrete datable evidence arises from within the psalm, such as signs of an extant temple. Outside of establishing the Pentateuch as a source, however, the difficulty in identifying a vector of allusion increases exponentially. Ideally, one would establish the date of the source and borrowing texts; however, unlike most biblical literature, individual psalms frequently fail to exhibit concrete examples of datable people, events, and places, and are therefore notoriously difficult to date. Consequently, the present volume relies on additional means for ascertaining a relative date for the psalms and their proposed sources. [32] One method for determining a relative date relies on identifying the literary propensity of a given psalmist with regards to borrowing. For example, if a vector of allusion is discovered between two

30. For a detailed discussion of the strength and categories of words that connect compositions, see Leonard, "Inner-Biblical Interpretation," 112–17.

31. Numerous scholars have focused efforts on establishing rules for intertexts, such as Sommer, *A Prophet Reads Scripture*, and Hays, *Echoes of Scripture*. Leonard, "Inner-Biblical Interpretation," recently collected, synthesized, and presented a list of considerations for establishing inner-biblical allusion. His discussion, though useful to the present volume, fails to cater specifically to the psalms, which requires a modified approach. One necessary modification concerns the context in which a potential lexical marker appears. Due to the organic similarity between psalm genres, such as laments and hymns of praise, psalmists naturally adopt similar words and phrases that belong to a specific genre. This situation fails to reinforce the assertion of potential intertexts and weakens a case for intertextuality.

32. In this context, I employ the term "relative date" to describe the chronological relationship between two texts. Although both texts may originate from the preexilic era, it remains essential to establish which of the two is earlier.

texts, A and B, and text B contains three additional intertexts, whereas text A has none, then the probable vector of allusion runs from text B to text A. In this scenario, the author of text B exhibits a greater propensity for borrowing, and it is logical to suspect him of appropriating material from text A. Supplementing this, the present work consults modern commentaries[33] in addition to linguistic dating, when applicable.[34] Overall, though dating psalms represents a challenging endeavor, to say the least, it is by no means an impossible or unfruitful task. To achieve this goal, the present volume reflects appropriate degrees of caution, and clearly expresses levels of doubt that surround potential conclusions.[35]

The third phase of investigation depends on whether a diachronic trajectory is determinable. If so, the present work continues to hypothesize why the psalmist sought a connection to his source. At least three motivations recur throughout the study. The classical case for biblical allusion stems from an author's desire to supplement his work via a well-known intertext. For example, if a psalmist seeks to evoke deep-seated feelings of fear or sorrow, he may further allude to a widely recognized text that captures this sentiment. In doing so, he elicits an emotional response from his audience both from his own work and from his source. Thus, with an economic selection of words, the poet transfers an additional vigor to his composition.[36] In these situations, the author does not intend to influence the reader's interpretation of the source text but seeks to add depth and meaning to his own composition. A second reason for

33. Unfortunately, these frequently prove unreliable due to the wide variations of scholarly opinions and the general reluctance of many to settle on a final position concerning a psalm's date.

34. The possibility of using linguistic criteria for dating biblical texts has generated a firestorm in recent years. Traditionally, scholars divided the Hebrew language into three periods, EBH, SBH, and LBH. The work of Young and Rezetko, *Linguistic Dating*, challenges this view. Despite their objections, the present author adopts a conciliatory approach, using language and syntax in conjunction with traditional historical data, to determine the approximate date of a biblical text, whether it originated before or after the exile. Hurvitz, *A Concise Lexicon*, features a list and a discussion of late features in Biblical Hebrew, the volume aids in the location of late biblical vocabulary. Regarding methodology and potential pitfalls in linguistic dating, see Hendel and Joosten, *How Old*.

35. Unfortunately, exegetes frequently obfuscate the terms intertextuality and inner-biblical allusion/interpretation. See Leonard, "Inner-Biblical Interpretation," 101–5, for a discussion concerning the confusion. The present volume, however, maintains a clear distinction between these terms.

36. For this usage see, Watson, *Classical Hebrew Poetry*, 302–3.

allusion stems from an author's desire to add authority to his work. For example, a psalmist may adapt commandments from the Decalogue, and insert them into his own work to add further authority to his composition.[37] When reciting the psalm, the reader recalls the Decalogue in addition to the words of the psalmist. A third reason for allusion arises when a psalmist desires to comment on or add insight to another biblical text, generating an instance of inner-biblical interpretation. In these instances, psalmists potentially view inherent shortcomings in their source text that need subtle amendments or adaptations. Overall, when employing allusion in this way, the psalmist aims to alter the way his readers understand an earlier biblical text.[38] When attempting to identify inner-biblical interpretation, it is important to recognize the unavoidable changes that occur whenever a psalmist cites from a prose or legal source. When instances like this occur, words or phrases are often altered without any intention of influencing meaning.

That said, however, various instances arise in which a marker is undoubtedly identified, but the direction of borrowing between the two texts cannot be established with any degree of certainty. In such instances, rather than argue one way or the other, the present volume discusses the literary connection from both points of view. In this way, even though the diachronic approach forms the foundation for the present work, elements of synchronic analysis still creep into the discussions from time to time. In either event, the present volume argues for a definite literary connection between the works where the only outstanding issue concerns the direction of borrowing.[39]

In relation to the inner-biblical allusions in the Psalter, the question of psalm titles demands some attention. The descriptive subtitles ascribed to numerous psalms have long been recognized as later additions.

37. Other motivations exist, such as polemical and revisionist (see Leonard, "Inner-Biblical Interpretation," 126–27), but these seldom relate to the Psalter, or at least Book I. When such instances surface, however, the present volume discusses them.

38. The rationale presented here are not exhaustive; numerous other nuanced motivations spur psalmists to allude to biblical texts. The reasons presented here represent the more common strategies in the Psalter.

39. Although he deals with the Pentateuch, Carr, "Method in Determination," 110–11, proposes a few criteria for establishing the direction of borrowing between texts. He suggests that authors who borrow material are more likely to add to their sources and enrich them in the process. Thus, if identical material appears in two psalms, the author of the longer composition is more likely to be the borrower. Though it is not foolproof, this heuristic has some value as supporting evidence for establishing the direction of borrowing.

Despite the lateness of their origins,[40] however, they prove valuable to the present volume because they reflect an exegete's efforts to connect a psalm with an incident in Israel's literary and historical traditions, particularly those reflecting events in the life of David. For this reason, the present volume regards the interpretive titles as allusion markers and are thus treated as part of the psalm.

When identifying literary markers between intertexts, the ideal scenario occurs when a unique word, or word combination, links the two texts. Unfortunately, such robust examples of markers are not always forthcoming, and the need arises to settle for less unique word combinations that generate weaker associations, literary echoes. Biblical echoes occur when an author adopts an expression from memory without a specific text or context in mind. For example, a psalmist may adopt a poetic stock phrase or expression that frequently appears within a specific genre. In such instances, the psalm under investigation presents the illusion of a marker, linking two or three laments together, even though the author has no intention of drawing the reader's attention to the other texts. Because it is impossible to ascertain incontestably the inner thoughts of a psalmist's mind as he writes his composition, or to discern his library of resources, the possibility of echo remains an issue that obscures any final determinations of biblical allusion. Despite such challenges, the present volume endeavors, with caution and trepidation, to identify instances of echo, distinguishing them from true biblical allusion markers.

Although the present volume distinguishes two major study areas— close juxtaposition of psalms and inner-biblical allusion—an important degree of overlap exists between them, and they do not represent mutually exclusive phenomena. An editor-arranger of the Psalter could easily write a psalm specifically intending to juxtapose it with an existing composition within an established collection. In such instances, the psalm functions as both the object of intertextual and juxtaposition discussions. Finally, it is my hope that the present volume opens the eyes of students embarking on the road of biblical textual scholarship to the vast potential of material available in the field of biblical allusion and exegesis with particular regards to the Hebrew Psalter.

---

40. Scholars generally consider the contextual psalm titles, like those in Psalm 3, as late additions. See, for example, Futato, *Interpreting the Psalms*, 119–22. Even those with a more traditional view of psalms' authorship, such as Ross, *Psalms*, 42–47, recognize that despite the titles reflecting early traditions, they were not originally organic to the compositions in which they appear, and are therefore late.

Psalm Analysis

Book 1: *Psalms 1–41*

Psalm 1

BOOK I OF THE Psalter begins with an untitled composition most commonly, and accurately, defined as a wisdom psalm.[1] Two prominent and contrasting themes interweave throughout the psalm's fabric: the way of the wicked, and the way of the righteous. Overall, the psalm espouses the message that God ultimately rewards the righteous for their honorable deeds but punishes the wicked.

Verses 1–2, invoke a blessing on those who avoid all contact with wicked and perverse people and prefer meditating on the law of God. Building on this, the following two verses, vv. 3–4, direct the reader to the respective outcomes for those who pursue wickedness and those who choose righteousness. The righteous remain fruitful in all their endeavors, whereas the wicked fail to prosper. Furthering the description of their outcomes, v. 5 reveals their fate when they stand in the face of judgment: The righteous stand, but the wicked fall.[2] The final verse, and perhaps the most important, shifts the focus onto God, directly detailing his perspective. He knows the ways of both the righteous and wicked, and rewards or punishes each accordingly. Inevitably, though the wicked may temporarily evade the punishment for their actions, God still notices their works, and calls them into account for all their deeds.

1. For the association of this psalm to Israel's wisdom traditions, and its designation as a wisdom psalm, see McCann, "Psalms," 683; Avishur, "Chapter 1," 26; and Leslie, *Psalms*, 432.

2. Questions arise concerning the nature of this judgment, whether it implies an earthly or eschatological fulfillment, when God calls all the deeds of men into account. Neither interpretation affects the outcome of the present investigation.

Turning to Psalm 1's date, scholarly consensus predominantly inclines towards understanding the psalm as a postexilic composition.[3] The primary evidence supporting a late date stems from its definition as a wisdom psalm, focusing on the Torah. Though the genre alone does not constitute irrefutable evidence, scholars have long recognized that during the postexilic era, Israel gravitated more and more towards exposition of and meditation on the law of God.[4] Adopting this position lends weight to the probability that Psalm 1's author appropriated material from the texts discussed below, molding and shaping them to the purposes of his new composition.

Though Psalm 1 stands at the beginning of the Psalter, with no psalm preceding it, a few observations regarding its relationship to the preceding composition are still warranted. Despite the uncertainty of the preceding work, in this case Job, influencing the author of Psalm 1, the realistic probability of a canonical arranger recognizing the connection between the two compositions remains.[5] Psalm 1, as discussed above, depicts the characteristics of the righteous and the wicked; ultimately, it concludes that the righteous, when judged, will stand because God knows their deeds and vindicates them. Corresponding with this ideal, the preceding account of Job presents a practical example of the same principle. Job, portrayed as a pious man from the narrative's onset, finds himself persistently assailed by the verbal accusations of wicked men: his three friends.[6] Throughout the account, Job persistently maintains

3. With respect to dating, a few scholars avoid the issue entirely for this particular psalm (such as VanGemeren, *Psalms*; Clifford, *Psalms 1–72*; McCann, "Psalms"); others simply provide an overview of the range of possibilities (see Ross, *Psalms*, 183). Perhaps the most comprehensive survey, if a little dated, comes from Weiss, *The Bible from Within*, 135–42. Of those who ventured to suggest a date, Keil and Delitzsch, *Psalms*, 1:83, stand alone in arguing for a relatively early date, predating Jeremiah. Kraus, *Psalms 1–59*, 114–15, on the other hand, opts for a later postexilic date, adducing the word "congregation," as evidence, implying a distinct entity from Israel. He further suggests the concept of Torah study was a late phenomenon. Furthermore, Avishur, "Chapter 1," 27, asserts that the wisdom psalms were particularly prevalent during the late monarchy and Second Temple period. With specific regard to Psalm 1 interpreting Jeremiah, see Creach, "Like a Tree," 36, who, together with the present author, understands the psalmist borrowing from the prophet.

4. Here, the present author refers to meditation in the biblical sense of recitation, as opposed to a silent, mental contemplation commonly assumed today.

5. With specific regard to the Protestant Bible, or at least the version of the Septuagint from which its sequencing follows.

6. Though their wicked behavior remains obscure at the beginning of their

his innocence and righteousness in the face of relentless accusations disparaging his piety. At the end of the account, God himself judges Job and questions him concerning his righteousness. After conversing with God, Job is vindicated; though not proclaimed as entirely just in all his thoughts and actions, he is certainly viewed as more righteous than his companions. Thus, the logical relationship between the book of Job and Psalm 1 reflects a principle derived from a practical example. Job provides the reader with the practical example of God's vindication and reward of the righteous, whereas Psalm 1 adopts that principle and applies it to righteous people in general.

In the Leningrad Codex, represented by the *BHS*, Malachi immediately precedes the Psalter, yet a case for thematic juxtaposition can still be argued. In this instance, the notion of eschatological judgment, together with the injunction to remember the law of Moses, generates a link from one book to its neighbor. Towards the end of Malachi, the prophet proclaims that once more Israel will see the distinction between the righteous (צדיק) and the wicked (רשע) in 3:18. The same words repeat in Psalm 1. At the end of the composition the psalmist reminds the reader that the Lord knows the way of the righteous (צדיקים), but the way of the wicked (רשעים) is lost. Similarly, at the end of Malachi, designed to leave a lasting memory as the reader closes the book, the prophet further exhorts his readers to remember the law (תורה) of Moses (Mal 4:4 [3:22]). Recalling the Torah at the end of Malachi corresponds with Ps 1:2, where the righteous delight in the law (תורה) of the Lord, meditating on it daily.[7] This juxtaposed reading carries a notable interpretive nuance. The exact nature of the law, as mentioned in the psalm, remains obscure. If one reads the psalm devoid of any contextual influences, it is most logical to assume that the law mentioned refers to general instructions originating from God.[8] When read in the

---

discourse, the end of the book reveals God's displeasure with their representation of him. Job 42:7 says, "It came about after the Lord had spoken these words to Job, that the Lord said to Eliphaz the Temanite, 'My wrath is kindled against you and against your two friends, because you have not spoken of Me what is trustworthy as My servant Job *has*.'"

7. The connection between Psalm 1 and Malachi represents an instance of compositional linkage, where biblical editors and arrangers express a preference to juxtapose compositions where similar words or themes at the end of one text are repeated at the beginning of the following text. Signs of such an inclination arise between Malachi and the Psalter, as witnessed above, and additionally surface between Joel and Amos (as discussed in the Introduction).

8. Frequently in wisdom literature, Psalm 1 being a wisdom psalm, the word *torah*

context of the *BHS*, however, the understanding of the law adopts a more specific designation because it reminds the reader of the law of Moses, received at Sinai and recalled in Malachi. Thus, the specific designation of the law of Moses transfers to Psalm 1 in a sequential reading. The righteous meditate on the law of Moses day and night.[9]

Perhaps the most heralded intertextual association related to Psalm 1 concerns its connections to Jer 17:5–8.[10] In Jeremiah, the pericope's opening forms part of a larger section detailing God's words of condemnation leveled against Judah. God curses those who trust in men and consequently turn away from him. The table below compares the two texts:

Psalm 1:1–4	Jeremiah 17:5–8
How blessed [אשרי האיש] is the man who does not walk in the counsel of the wicked, / Nor stand in the path of sinners, / Nor sit in the seat of scoffers! / But his delight is in the law of the LORD, / And in His law he meditates day and night. / He will be like a tree *firmly* planted by [כעץ שתול על] streams of water [מים], / Which yields its fruit [פריו] in its season / And its leaf [עליהו] does not wither [יבול]; / And in whatever he does, he prospers. / The wicked are not so, / But they are like chaff which the wind drives away.	Thus says the LORD, "Cursed is the man who trusts in mankind / And makes flesh his strength, / And whose heart turns away from the LORD. / "For he will be like a bush in the desert / And will not see when prosperity comes, / But will live in stony wastes in the wilderness, / A land of salt without inhabitant. / "Blessed is the man [גבר] who trusts in the LORD / And whose trust is the LORD. / "For he will be like a tree planted by the water [כעץ שתול על מים], / that extends its roots by a stream / And will not fear when the heat comes; / But its leaves [עלהו] will be green, / And it will not be anxious in a year of drought / Nor cease to yield fruit [פרי].

In v. 6, Jeremiah compares those who trust in men to a bush in the desert that inhabits parched places in the wilderness. These individuals find themselves estranged from God, and unable to detect when good

bears this nuance; see, for example, Prov 1:8; 3:1.

9. The demise of the wicked similarly connects the end of Malachi with Psalm 1, the beginning of the Psalter. Both texts use agricultural terms to depict the downfall of evildoers: The wicked in Mal 4:1 [3:19] will be burned in an oven like stubble, and in a similar fashion, the wicked of Psalm 1 are blown away like grain husks (Ps 1:4).

10. Many commentators recognize this connection, such as Leslie, *Psalms*, 433; and McCann, "Psalms," 685.

comes. Contrasting this, in v. 7 the man who trusts in the Lord is subsequently blessed (ברוך הגבר), presumably, but not explicitly stated, by the Lord. Verse 8 develops the blessing with the simile of the righteous man compared to a tree planted by streams of water.

Connecting Psalm 1 to Jer 17:5–8 is a series of thematic and lexical associations. The psalm opens with the words אשרי האיש ("blessed is the man"),[11] a phrase reminiscent of Jer 17:7, which adopts a slightly different form (ברוך הגבר). Additionally, both compositions prefer agricultural imagery to emphasize their comparison, more specifically the image of a tree planted by water (כעץ שתול על מים; Ps 1:3; Jer 17:8). Because of its proximity to a constant water supply, the tree remains healthy and productive even in the face of drought. During such times of scarcity, the tree still produces its fruit, and its leaves remain healthy. Similarly, for both authors, the one who trusts God need not fear in troubled times. Like the tree, they prosper and continue to bear fruit because of their constant connection with God.[12] Thematically, Psalm 1, like Jeremiah, compares the righteous, those *trusting* in the Lord, with individuals who do not, the wicked. Both texts portray the righteous and the wicked as plants, and their deeds associated with production of fruit and usefulness.

Though the imagery is similar, the psalmist nevertheless adapts the context and meaning of his source, Jeremiah.[13] The psalmist rearranges the order of presentation, placing the image of the righteous first—a consideration, no doubt, to comply with the order of his composition— as opposed to second in Jeremiah.[14] For the psalm's writer, the notion of trusting in the Lord transforms into meditation on the Torah. Even though both represent related concepts, they still differ slightly, possibly as a reflection of the Psalm's later context. Apparently, Psalm 1's author

11. The synonyms גבר and איש appear in other contexts, such as Jer 23:9 and Mic 2:2.

12. Note the morphological similarity between יובל in Jer 17:8, meaning "stream," and יבול in Ps 1:3, meaning "wither." Although the words differ in meaning, their forms contribute towards the connection between the two passages.

13. The psalmist here may simply have adopted the same image as Jeremiah, without any intention of allusion. Countering this notion, however, are the additional literary connections the psalm shares with other biblical passages (see below).

14. Additionally, subtle adjustments exist between the modes of expression. For the psalmist, the tree "yields its fruit in its season," whereas Jeremiah employs the negative expression, "nor cease to yield fruit." Similarly, the psalmist's negative "foliage does not fade" contrasts Jeremiah's positive "Its leaves remain green." For further discussion of the "tree planted by streams" imagery, see Weiss, *The Bible from Within*, 130–63.

understands the two activities in the same light. By meditating on the Torah, he thus assumes that one learns more about God and trusts him as a result. Additionally, the image of the wicked sustains a slight adjustment. In Jeremiah, they are compared to a desert shrub located far from a water supply; as a result, it dehydrates, withers, and dies. In Psalm 1, the author compares the wicked to an unessential and dispensable part of a plant, chaff that the wind blows away. The psalmist instigates a further transformation of Jeremiah's work by widening the address from words of condemnation to a specific audience at a particular time to a general principle applicable to all people at all times.

In addition to the associations between Psalm 1 and Jeremiah, a lucid connection exists between the psalm and Joshua 1. The first chapter of Joshua recalls God's encouraging words to Moses' successor specifically before he leads the Israelites into battle against the inhabitants of Canaan. God tells him that the book of the law must not depart from his mouth, but he should meditate upon it day and night (והגית בו יומם ולילה, 1:8). As a direct consequence, Joshua would gain success and be prosperous in all his ways (תצליח את־דרכך). For Joshua, success equates to military victories in battle, leading the Israelites to conquer the land. Psalm 1 recognizes the same connection found in Joshua, where meditation on the law of the Lord leads to success. Unlike Joshua, however, the psalm restricts itself to the principle and not the specific situation. For the psalmist, the notion of an impending war could not be further from his thoughts. Instead, he presents a general notion of success and productivity as the reward for dedication to meditating on God's law. The principle applied to Joshua extends to all those seeking to adopt the psalmist's advice.

Another thematic connection between Psalm 1 and Joshua highlights the necessity of bravery and courage for obedience.[15] In Joshua 1:7, God implores Israel's new leader to be strong and courageous in his obedience to the law, suggesting the act of obedience necessitates bravery. Later in the book of Joshua, the author demonstrates the principle, when God directs Joshua to march around the walls of Jericho for seven days. Obeying this instruction does not immediately present itself as a logical course of action when facing an enemy, and Joshua must demonstrate courage to complete it. Accordingly, one can deduce that success, in Joshua's context, derives from brave obedience and adherence to God's words. The same idea, though not explicitly expressed, nevertheless

---

15. The *BHS* recognizes the connection via a gloss referencing Josh 1:8.

presents itself in Psalm 1. The psalmist apparently[16] maintains a belief in a final judgment that both the righteous and wicked must endure in the distant future, most probably after they die. Such a belief opens the possibility for longevity on earth when judgment remains ostensibly absent. During such times, an urgent need arises for the righteous to continue devoting themselves to the law of the Lord and upright living. Consequently, courage becomes a highly desirable and necessary trait to live consistently in obedience to the law, even if one's vindication is not immediately forthcoming.[17]

A comparison between Ps 1:1 and Deut 6:7 reflects a further connection to biblical literature, with Psalm 1 representing an earnest call to hear and obey the words of the Lord. The lexical connections listed below draw initial attention to the relationship between the texts.

Psalm 1:1	Deuteronomy 6:7
How blessed is the man who does not walk [הלך] in the counsel of the wicked, / Nor stand in the path [דרך] of sinners, / Nor sit in the seat of scoffers!	You shall teach them diligently to your sons and shall talk of them when you sit in your house and when you walk by the way [בלכתך בדרך] and when you lie down and when you rise up.

16. Many scholars understand the concept of judgment in Psalm 1 as an event(s) occurring during an individual's lifespan. Thus, when the righteous, who meditate on God's law, day and night, are brought to the courts, God intervenes for them, enabling them to prevail against their accusers. Craigie and Tate, *Psalms 1–50*, 58, maintain this view; Leslie, *Psalms*, 433, adheres to a variant of the same idea, where the judgment represents an event in the individual's lifespan. Notwithstanding this, a more eschatological understanding of v. 5 is possible, suggesting God judges the wicked and the righteous in the world to come. Dahood, *Psalms I*, 4–6, advocates this position, adducing additional verses in the Psalter that support the possibility of psalms adopting an eschatological viewpoint.

17. Futato, *Interpreting the Psalms*, 72, views Psalm 1's content as an orientation to the Psalter; similarly, McCann, "Psalms," 659–60, 666, emphasizes Psalm 1's theological importance at the beginning of the Psalter. Understanding Psalm 1 in this light, as a gateway to the Psalter, intensifies the urgency for courage. Of the psalms in Book I, individual laments by far constitute the dominant genre. Within this genre, psalmists frequently depict wicked men overpowering and assaulting the righteous. For the reader, therefore, Psalm 1's message encourages individuals, spurring them to continue devoting themselves to the law of the Lord and righteous deeds, even when facing oppression from evil individuals.

Beyond the lexical connections above—which by themselves, admittedly, fail to establish a convincing intertextual association—thematic ideas and stylistic elements further solidify the connection. Deuteronomy 6 emphasizes the need to speak constantly of God's law in every state of existence, whether sitting, walking, lying down or rising. Together, these verbs form a merismic list, reflecting activities performed by individuals throughout the day—the point of emphasis here is *all the time*. Psalm 1 similarly relies on merismus to emphasize perpetuity in recounting the law with the expression "day and night." Blessing as a reward for keeping his laws at the forefront of the mind also reflects in both texts. The promise of remaining in a fruitful land of milk and honey if Israel remembers God's laws and decrees lingers from Deut 6:3. Paralleling this is the hope of fruitfulness and productivity reflected in the imagery of the tree planted by streams of water in Ps 1:3. Furthermore, the threat of destruction looms in both texts. In Deuteronomy, Israel will be cut off the face of the earth should they neglect the law, and the wicked of Psalm 1, those who do not meditate on the law, face destruction because they will ultimately fall in the day of judgment.[18]

Notwithstanding the wealth of commonality between the works, subtle and nuanced adaptations were executed in the shaping of Psalm 1. Apparently, the psalmist transforms the broad message to the Israelite community into a personal message, aimed at individuals. With a little imagination, it is possible to argue that the psalmist reframes the context of Deut 6:4, "Hear, O Israel! The LORD is our God . . ." to, "How blessed is the man who . . ." (Ps 1:1)

A further transformation concerns the rewards for constant meditation on the law of the Lord. For Israel, the beneficial result concerns longevity in the land into which the Lord brought the people. If they obeyed, they would live long and prosperously in the land. Failing to adhere to the Lord's instruction ultimately ends with their expulsion from the land. The psalmist, however, develops this idea slightly differently. It begins with the promise of fruitfulness and success in one's endeavors, adapting national stability in the promised land into a personal degree of success, stability, and productivity.[19]

---

18. Note too Deuteronomy's word choice, opting for ודברת ("you shall talk," Deut 6:7), and its relationship to Psalm 1's choice of the root יהגה ("he meditates"). Both words appear elsewhere in biblical literature together as a recognized word pair; see, for example, Job 27:4; 37:30, 38:12 [13]; Isa 59:3.

19. Furthermore, the psalmist adds an eschatological benefit, Psalm 1 intimates that

Two more differences between the texts deserve attention. First, Deuteronomy positively frames its merismic verb list, mentioning walking, sitting, lying down, and rising up. At all times, during these activities, the law should be recited. Altering this, the psalm frames its merismic list—walking, standing, and sitting—in a negative context. It is not the righteous who perform these actions, but fools and evildoers. The righteous avoid walking, standing, and sitting with all who associate themselves with evil. Second, concerning Deuteronomy, the actions leading to blessing are more detailed compared to Psalm 1. Deuteronomy emphasizes obedience to his commands (v. 2), love for the Lord (v. 5), and teaching them to subsequent generations (v. 7). Contrasting this, Psalm 1 simply mentions meditation on the law, without offering further details regarding how one should meditate on the law.[20] A real possibility is that the psalmist relies on his readers' ability to connect his work with Deuteronomy 6, thus leading them to infer from his source text a detailed explanation of how to meditate on the law.

Another potential intertextual connection worth mentioning concerns the relationship between Ps 1:3 and Ezek 47:12. The markers between the two texts are as follows:

Psalm 1:3	Ezekiel 47:12
He will be like a tree [עץ] *firmly* planted by streams of water [מים], / Which yields its fruit [פריו] in its season / And its leaf does not wither [עלהו לא יבול]; / And in whatever he does, he prospers.	By the river on its bank, on one side and on the other, will grow all *kinds of* trees [עץ] for food. Their leaves will not wither [לא יבול עלהו] and their fruit [פריו] will not fail. They will bear every month because their water [מימיו] flows from the sanctuary, and their fruit will be for food and their leaves for healing.

In addition to the Hebrew words common to both pericopae, a notable similarity exists regarding fruit production, with Psalm 1 preferring the expression פריו יתן, ("It yields its fruit") versus the similar form

one's righteous acts enable him to stand in the final judgment. The privilege of enjoying such a reward serves as recompense for avoiding the company of wicked people.

20. Concerning Deuteronomy's relationship to Psalm 1, Liebreich's proposition deserves mention, he argues that the opening sections of the Prophets and Writings contain unavoidable thematic connections back to the Torah. Thus, Psalm 1 and Isaiah 1 serve as literary anchors securing the latter two divisions of the Old Testament to the Torah, and law of God; see Liebreich, "The Position of Chapter Six," 37n3.

and semantic nuance of the expression לא יתם פריו, ("Their fruit will not fail"). It is difficult to determine for sure whether allusion is at play in this example. Because of the vast differences between each passage's context, it appears both authors simply drew upon common imagery, as opposed to one borrowing from the other.[21]

Finally, the relationship between Psalms 1 and 112 deserves a brief mention. Both compositions begin and end with identical words, "How blessed is the man . . ." (אשרי האיש, Pss 1:1; 112:1); and "the wicked will perish" (רשעים תאבד, Pss 1:6; 112:10). Although the wording, for the most part, reflects vocabulary common to wisdom psalms, the genre of both psalms, and the specific positioning of the phrases above suggest a little more than a casual connection. Were there literary borrowing involved, however, Psalm 1 would in all likelihood represent the source text.[22]

21. Creach, "Like a Tree," 34–46, pursues the connection further, and develops the possibility of literary borrowing between Psalm 1 and Ezekiel 47. From the shared vocabulary, he asserts that the righteous mentioned in Psalm 1 relate not just to any tree, but specifically to a tree planted in the temple complex, as Ezekiel suggests. Such an image is not without precedent in biblical literature, and passages such as Ps 92:12–13 [13–14] adduce this position, "The righteous man will flourish like the palm tree, / He will grow like a cedar in Lebanon. / Planted in the house of the Lord . . ." Here, the image of the flourishing righteous man and the tree connects Psalm 92 to Psalm 1. Again, in Ps 52:8 [10], the psalmist likens himself to a tree, "But as for me, I am like a green olive tree in the house of God; / I trust in the lovingkindness of God forever and ever."

22. Allen, *Psalms 101–150*, 128, recognizes that the author of Psalm 112 borrowed from Psalm 111, indicating a propensity to reuse other psalms. Furthermore, Thomas, "Psalms 1 and 112," 21–22, understands a purposeful reuse of Psalm 1 by Psalm 112's author. He states, "Thus it may be seen that the author of Psalm 112 takes up in an abbreviated fashion the positive aspects of A (the introductory statement of Psalm 1), greatly expands upon the positive aspects of B (the body of Psalm 1)." Also supporting the notion of Psalm 1 as the source text is Kraus, *Psalm 60–150*, 363, who argues that Psalm 112 is a product of the late postexilic era.

Psalm 2

FOLLOWING PSALM 1, THE Psalter continues with a starkly disparate untitled composition in Psalm 2, a royal psalm.[1] The opening three verses adopt a distinctly aggressive tone, portraying world leaders and rulers rebelling against God and his anointed king. Because Psalm 1 ends by depicting the fate of the wicked, a consecutive reading subtly applies that label to the nations mentioned in Psalm 2's opening. Thus, from the start of the composition, the psalm's arrangement induces a negative perception of the assembling nations. Switching perspectives, vv. 4–9 provide the reader with God's view of the plans and schemes that the nation's rulers have plotted against him. Such schemes fail to disturb God. Instead, he attends to his chosen one,[2] and affirms the selection of his king and chosen leader,[3] ultimately promising him the ends of the earth (vv. 7–9), which encompasses the property of the nations who rise against him. Following this affirmation, God addresses the scheming rulers in vv. 10–12a, who rage against him. His response to them manifests itself in a stern warning: If they fail to pay homage and respect to his anointed one, then his wrath would be aroused and leveled against them. Tempering this warning in v. 12, the psalmist closes with words of hope for those

1. For this designation of the genre, see Clifford, *Psalms 1–72*, 42; moreover, Craigie and Tate, *Psalms 1–50*, 64, suggest it is a coronation psalm.

2. The notion of the king being God's son echoes throughout numerous scriptures, including 2 Sam 7:14 and Ps 89:27. Consequently, it is somewhat quixotic to assume an allusion because the image represents a common depiction of kingship in the Bible and ancient Near East.

3. Psalm 2 belongs in a group together with psalms such as 81 and 95 that contain a prophetic voice speaking on behalf of God.

who heed the divine admonition. All who seek refuge in the anointed one receive a blessing.

Various lexical markers link Psalm 2 with Psalm 1, as demonstrated in the table below:

Psalm 1	Psalm 2:1–2, 10–12
How blessed [אשרי] is the man who does not walk in the counsel of the wicked, / Nor stand in the path of sinners, / Nor sit in the seat of scoffers! / But his delight is in the law of the LORD, / and in His law he meditates [יהגה] day and night. / He will be like a tree *firmly* planted by streams of water, / Which yields its fruit in its season, / And its leaf does not wither; / And in whatever he does, he prospers. / The wicked are not so, / But they are like chaff which the wind drives away. / Therefore the wicked will not stand in the judgment, / Nor sinners in the assembly of the righteous; / For the LORD knows the way of the righteous, / But the way [דרך] of the wicked will perish [תאבד].	Why are the nations in an uproar / And the peoples devising a vain thing [יהגו]? / The kings of the earth take their stand / And the rulers take counsel together / Against the LORD and against His Anointed . . . Now therefore, O kings, show discernment; / Take warning, O judges of the earth. / Worship the LORD with reverence / And rejoice with trembling. / Do homage to the Son, that He not become angry, and you perish *in* the way [תאבדו דרך], / For His wrath may soon be kindled. / How blessed [אשרי] are all who take refuge in Him!

Creating an inclusion encompassing both compositions is the word אשרי ("blessed"), which opens Psalm 1, invoking a blessing on the one who avoids associating with wicked people. The same word appears at the end of Psalm 2, in v. 12, where it contributes towards a blessing for those seeking refuge in God's anointed one. More than just creating the inclusion, however, the lexical marker here additionally associates the one who delights in the law of the Lord (Ps 1:1–2) with he who finds shelter in God's anointed leader (Ps 2:12). Implicitly, the connection further associates those walking in wicked ways with the conspiring kings of the earth in Psalm 2, who reject the anointed one's authority. In addition to the above, the phrase תאבד . . . דרך ("the way . . . perishes") creates an extended chiasmus between the psalms; the words appear at the end of each composition.[4] In Ps 1:6 the words enforce the ultimate doom of the

---

4. It is important to note this phrase's distribution throughout the Psalter. Apart from appearing in Psalms 1 and 2, the phrase is absent from the Psalter. They only

wicked men, "For the LORD knows the way of the righteous, / But the *way* of the wicked will *perish*" (italics added). The final words of Psalm 2 reveal a similar warning: "Do homage to the Son, that He not become angry, and you *perish* in the *way*" (italics added).

Explaining the lexical associations between the two compositions, and the direction of borrowing, presents a complex problem.[5] Both compositions could, theoretically, have existed entirely independently of each other, and penned during diverse eras in Israel's literary historical tradition. Then, with the final, or near final, stages in the Psalter's compilation, a redactor noticed their corresponding lexical elements and, accordingly, sequenced them in their present order. Although such an explanation exists as a possibility, such a high number of rare words and word combinations appear within the proximity of two independently composed works seems extraordinary. Another explanation for the word similarity is that the editor himself altered words from one, or both, of the compositions to solidify the lexical bonds between the two psalms. A third possibility is that the author of Psalm 1—likely a later composition than Psalm 2[6]—purposefully composed his work to complement Psalm 2; thus, he would have adopted words from his source, strategically placing them in his composition and forging the present lexical layout between the two psalms.

Thematically, Psalm 2's closing words recall Psalm 1's ending because both texts finish with a depiction of two paths: one leading to

---

appear again in Job 6:18 and Jer 15:7, but in these locations the verb "to perish" is unconnected to the noun "way."

5. The Talmud, b. Ber 9b–10a, suggests Psalms 1 and 2 constitute a single composition. At least one New Testament Greek manuscript recording Acts 13:33 supports the Talmud's perspective (see Craigie and Tate, *Psalms 1–50*, 59). In my opinion, not enough evidence exists to support this argument. Primarily, the dates of the individual psalms contradict any notion of a single composition. Clifford, *Psalms 1–72*, 46, implies—rightfully in my opinion—that Psalm 2 originates from the preexilic era, whereas Psalm 1 finds its origins after the exile (see earlier note on dating). The two compositions may have been joined erroneously before their insertion as an introduction to the Psalter. The absence of a title in each work—unlike the overwhelming majority of Books I–III—facilitates a misreading of the two compositions as a single entity in at least one Hebrew manuscript.

6. Far less ambiguity exists among scholars concerning the date of Psalm 2. Postexilic estimates, such as Oancea, "Psalm 2," 173, fail to garner much traction. Scholarly opinion markedly favors a preexilic date for the psalm (see, e.g., VanGemeren, *Psalms*, 89; Avishur, "Chapter 2," 30; Craigie and Tate, *Psalms 1–50*, 64–68). The only tangible area of dispute concerns the precise period within the monarchy.

destruction, and the other leading to life and blessing. Psalm 1 ends declaring that the Lord knows the way of the righteous, implying he spares them for their upright living, and that the way of the wicked perishes. Similarly, Psalm 2 finishes with words of destruction to those failing to honor God's chosen king, but those who take refuge in him receive a blessing.

By juxtaposing the first two psalms consecutively, the arranger of the Psalter forges a principle-example relationship.[7] In principle, the whole of Psalm 1 contrasts the way of the wicked with the way of the righteous, and each section within the composition alternates between the two behavioral paths, mapping their actions and their consequences. These actions are depicted within a theoretical complex in the opening psalm, which fails to provide concrete examples for identifying the counsel of the wicked. Who are these people, and what exactly do they do? In Psalm 2, however, the reader experiences a concrete representation of the principles outlined in the opening composition.[8] Rather than simply mentioning the wicked, the psalm specifically depicts them as the kings of the world who seek counsel together, plotting against the Lord and his anointed. Similarly, in place of the righteous, the psalmist presents the Lord's anointed, who is chosen by God himself and performs his desires on the earth. Thus, the righteous correspond, to a certain degree, to those kings who seek refuge in the son.[9]

Furthermore, it is possible to detect, from a consecutive reading of the texts, a connection between the anointed king of Psalm 2 and the need to study the Torah. Association between the two echoes the injunction connecting the king's obedience to the law found in Deuteronomy 17, "Now it shall come about when he [the king] sits on the throne of his kingdom, he shall write for himself a copy of this law on a scroll in the presence of the Levitical priests. It shall be with him and he shall read it all the days of his life, that he may learn to fear the LORD his God,

7. Waltke refers to this type of relationship as "a didactic generalization followed by a practical enactment"; see Waltke, "Ask of Me," 3.

8. McCann, "Psalms," 688, touches on this idea.

9. Cole, "An Integrated Reading," 78–79, recognizes a further thematic connection between Psalms 1 and 2, and Josh 1:8. As noted earlier, Joshua 1 connects to Psalm 1 via the notion of meditating on the Torah; however, the idea of military success generates a further connection if Psalm 2 is read together with Psalm 1. Both Joshua and Psalm 2 imply a degree of military success. Along similar lines, Waltke, "Ask of Me," 3, suggests both psalms were read together during a coronation service, thus encouraging the king to obey the law (cf. Deut 17:18–19).

by carefully observing all the words of this law and these statutes" (vv. 18–19). From the combined readings of the psalms, together with the context of Deuteronomy 17, one can extrapolate that the king's protection is contingent upon meditating on divine instruction.

The combined themes of Psalms 1 and 2 create an apt gateway into the Psalter generally,[10] and the opening of Psalm 3 specifically.[11] Psalm 1 alerts readers to the knowledge that God is patently aware of individual behavior, whether good or bad, and that he ultimately calls them into judgment. Ultimately, the wicked cannot escape his judgment, despite outward appearances. This message counteracts the overbearing, oppressive tone of the Psalter's first three books, where individual laments prevail.[12] For most laments, the evil men ostensibly exact their selfish will and ambition against the righteous with impunity. Psalm 1 presents the reader with a moral balance to the situation, affirming that the wicked are held accountable for their actions. Similarly, the situation portrayed at the start of Psalm 2 resonates throughout Books I–III of the Psalter. Psalm 2's opening questions why the nations of the world and their leaders oppose and contend against God, and more importantly, his anointed king. The laments of Books I–III similarly depict various individuals and nations revolting against the psalmists, one of whom is none other than David himself—accepting a traditional understanding of Psalm authorship—the Lord's anointed king. Thus, the opening books of the Psalter reflect and exemplify the theme of the second psalm: individuals and nations revolting against the Lord's anointed, which additionally equates to opposing the plans and purposes of God himself. Despite this situation, Psalm 2 teaches that God notices this predicament too, and he will vindicate his anointed one. Together these two compositions, because of the thematic resonance with the following works, form a perfect introduction to the Psalter. Furthermore, regardless of how one understands

10. The joint function of Psalms 1 and 2 as a gateway to the whole Psalter has not escaped the notice of contemporary scholarship. See, for example, Whiting, "Psalms 1 and 2."

11. Combining the psalms like this, according to Cole, "An Integrated Reading," 80, further affects how the genres are interpreted. He suggests that together, they should be understood as a composition reflecting the ideal king who meditates on the Torah.

12. Characteristically, within the context of individual compositions, laments seldom reveal judgment meted out against the wicked. Usually, laments close with a promise or vow to offer praises, or a statement of praise; see Brueggemann and Bellinger, *Psalms*, 46.

their original creation dates and *Sitz im Leben*, as they stand together in the Psalter, Psalms 1 and 2 were intended to complement each other in their present ordering.[13]

13. Robertson, *The Flow*, 15–16, notes an interesting phenomenon here. Three times within the Psalter (Pss 1–2, 18–19, and 118–19), Torah psalms juxtapose royal or messianic psalms (as he refers to them). Although the sample pool within the Psalter is relatively small, this potential juxtaposition strategy regarding the placement of Psalms 1 and 2 should not be ignored.

Psalm 3

FOLLOWING PSALM 2 IS an individual lament[1] revealing a psalmist's desperate plea for divine assistance in battle. Unlike the opening two psalms, Psalm 3 bears a specific title linking the song's contents to an event in King David's life: When he fled from his son, Absalom, who revolted against him. In the cry of vv. 1–2 [1–3], the psalmist despairs at the sheer multitude of enemies assailing him,[2] which drives him to hopelessness and desperation because nobody arises to deliver him. The chant of the enemy, "There is no deliverance for him," flies in the face of Psalm 2's closing words, "How blessed are all who take refuge in him";[3] apparently, the promise in Psalm 2 failed to materialize in this instance. In an abrupt turn, vv. 3–6 [4–7] find the psalmist focusing more on God's ability to save, and less on the enemy's taunts. For the psalm's author, the Lord is a shield about him, and in the past, God had encouraged him, lifted his

1. See, for example, Clifford, *Psalms 1–72*, 47; and Craigie and Tate, *Psalms 1–50*, 71, who recognize it as an individual lament, but further define it as a protective psalm, a lament in which the imagined fears have yet to occur.

2. Note the conflict between the contents of the psalm, and the title. The title states that David's enemy is his son, but the words within the psalm suggest numerous enemies pursuing David, "Many are rising up against me" (3:1b), "Many are saying of my soul" (3:2a). Futato, *Interpreting the Psalms*, 121, further mentions the tension concerning David's attitude towards his son. The psalm implies that David sought his enemy's destruction, striking them on the jaw and breaking their teeth (see v. 7 [8]). Contrasting such harsh feelings of hatred and destruction, 2 Sam 18:5 expresses David's deep love for his son, "*Deal* gently for my sake with the young man Absalom." As it turns out, David's concern for his son even outweighs his compassion for his own men.

3. Concerning the thematic conflict between the opening compositions' themes and Psalm 3, McCann, "Psalms," 693, astutely observes that prosperity for those trusting in God does not necessarily equate to a struggle-free life.

head, and sustained him. With thoughts of how God previously prevailed over his enemies,[4] the psalmist finds encouragement (vv. 7–8 [8–9]) to exhort God once again to arise and deliver him. The final verse of the psalm almost seems out of place, as the psalmist draws the composition to a close by wishing a generic blessing on the people of God. Despite the psalm predominantly reflecting elements of an individual lament, it finishes with a communal reference.

Psalm titles in certain instances generate avenues for identifying inner-biblical allusions and exegesis. The present composition presents an example. Although no obvious markers appear between Psalm 3's main body and 2 Samuel 15, words from the psalm's incipit invite readers to initiate connections between the texts.[5] The editor or redactor who connected the texts via the incipit cleverly constructed a literary bridge, generating an instance of biblical allusion, as demonstrated below:

Psalm 3:1	2 Samuel 15:14
A Psalm of David [דוד] when he fled [בברחו] from Absalom [אבשלום] his son. / O LORD, how my adversaries have increased! / Many are rising up against me.	David [דוד] said to all his servants who were with him at Jerusalem, "Arise and let us flee [נברחה], for *otherwise* none of us will escape from Absalom [אבשלום]. Go in haste, or he will overtake us quickly and bring down calamity on us and strike the city with the edge of the sword."

In cases like this, even though it is difficult to ascertain which came first—the psalm itself or the narrative of Samuel—the editor's or redactor's superscription post-dates them both.[6]

---

4. Translation of the perfect verb's tense, הִכִּיתָ ("you struck"), is not a simple matter. Some translations, such as the NASB, opt for a past tense, whereas others, such as the ESV, depict a present progressive act. Ultimately, the tense remains irrelevant for the purposes of this volume because with either interpretation, the psalmist gains confidence with the surety of knowing that God confronts and judges his enemies.

5. Regarding the literary nexus between the accounts, Fishbane, *Biblical Interpretation*, 404, states, "Two disparate contexts are synoptically brought into association."

6. Questions arise concerning the originality of these psalm titles, i.e., incipits directly linking the contents of a psalm with specific instances in David's life. The mention of "your people" in v. 9 suggests that the original composition appears unrelated to the context suggested by the psalm title. For more on this issue, see Childs, "Psalm Titles."

The words and expressions indicated above create a unique link between the two passages. Through the psalm's title, an editor recalls 2 Sam
15:14, where David (דוד) orders his servants to arise and escape (ונברחה)
from Absalom (מפני אבשלום). Furthermore, with the initial lexical connection established, readers are additionally drawn to a variety of thematic correlations between the psalm and David's war with Absalom in 2
Samuel, as the table below demonstrates.[7]

Psalm 3	2 Samuel
I was crying to the LORD with my voice, / And He answered me from His holy mountain. Selah. (v. 4)	And David went up the ascent of the *Mount of* Olives, and wept as he went, and his head was covered and he walked barefoot. Then all the people who were with him each covered his head and went up weeping as they went. (15:30)
I will not be afraid of ten thousands of people Who have set themselves against me round about. (v. 6)	Furthermore, Ahithophel said to Absalom, "Please let me choose 12,000 men that I may arise and pursue David tonight. (17:1)

With the allusion to David's flight from Absalom in 2 Samuel forced
upon the reader via the incipit, further unavoidable associations arise
between the content of the psalm and the Samuel narrative.[8] The abstract and undefined enemies of the psalmist, "Many are saying of my
soul, / 'There is no deliverance for him in God'" (v. 2 [3]), take on new
significance considering the connection to David's expulsion narrative.
The amorphous "many" in the psalm suggests inclusion of Shimei from
2 Sam 16:5–8. Here, in 2 Samuel, Shimei curses David, and speaks evil
against him for what he did to the house of Saul. Shimei contends that
God initiated David's humiliation at the hands of his son, driving him
out of Jerusalem. As a result, because God instigated David's expulsion,
David apparently is unable to plead to this same God for assistance. In

7. See Craigie and Tate, *Psalms 1–50*, 73.

8. Were it not for the superscript, the connection to David's escape from Absalom
remains hidden from a casual reader.

effect, David's situation recalls the sentiment in Ps 3:2 [3], stating that there is no deliverance from God.[9]

Another intertextual association arises from the notion of sleeping and waking. Immediately after David flees Jerusalem, Absalom seeks advice from his counselors on how to pursue David. Ahithophel, a respected and renowned adviser, suggests an attack while David is still weary and in desperate need of sleep. To counter Ahithophel's advice, Hushai, while surreptitiously serving David, suggests that David will not sleep with the main company of refugees, but will seclude himself.[10] Again, the notion of sleep emerges as part of a deception working in David's favor. Both texts present David's need for sleep as a potential source of danger. From the psalm's perspective, David recognizes this apparent danger, and yet ultimately trusts that God will protect him while he sleeps, enabling him to rise again in the morning, "I lay down and slept; / I awoke, for the LORD sustains me" (v. 5 [6]). Though the presence of God in 2 Samuel's escape narrative remains conspicuously absent, reading this text together with the psalm intonates divine activity empowering Hushai's advice.[11]

Psalm 3's specific connection to concrete events in King David's life extends beyond the individual psalm, carrying an interpretive influence linked to the Psalter's introduction. Undoubtedly, a tangible degree of tension arises between Psalm 3's incipit and the contents of the psalm itself. The incipit speaks of an individual enemy, whereas the body of the psalm depicts many foes. A contrasting picture emerges when Psalm 3's

9. Whether David or a later author penned Psalm 3, it is important to recognize a notable omission from its contents. The psalm and title focus on David's (or the psalmist's) suffering at the hand of many enemies who have risen against him, seeking his life. Naturally, the notion of a threat to an individual's life dominates both sections. Missing, however, from the psalm's context, but an important component of the 2 Samuel narrative, is the reason for the enemy's threat against an individual. According to 2 Samuel 12, Absalom's rebellion against David is not attributed purely to his desire for power, but is framed within the larger context of a prophetic word against David as part of his punishment for murdering Uriah the Hittite and taking his wife. Understandably, this aspect of divine retribution conflicts with a prophetic plea for divine assistance against an enemy, thus all traces of punitive elements remain absent from the psalm.

10. "So Hushai said to Absalom, 'This time the advice that Ahithophel has given is not good.' Moreover, Hushai said, 'You know your father and his men, that they are mighty men, and they are fierce, like a bear robbed of her cubs in the field. And your father is an expert in warfare, and will not spend the night with the people" (2 Sam 17:7–8).

11. See Johnson, *David in Distress*, 14–19.

title is viewed in light of Psalms 1–3. Within this larger context, a degree of remarkable correspondence arises. The multiple enemies in Psalm 3's body correspond with the multiple nations conspiring against the Lord and his anointed one in Psalm 2. A consecutive reading of the psalms lends weight to the association of the two ideas. Similarly, the anointed one of Psalm 2 corresponds specifically with David in Psalm 3. Via this link, Psalm 3 furthers the thematic development from Psalm 1. The opening psalm establishes a principle whereby the righteous are ultimately vindicated. Psalm 2 develops the notion with a general example of the Lord defending the righteous, his anointed king, against his enemies. Developing this notion further, Psalm 3 defines a specific king and situation. Reading Psalm 3 in this context implies or highlights the righteousness of David during his escape from Absalom; because he was righteous, the Lord protected him.

God's holy mountain (הר קדש) presents another lexical and interpretive link between Psalms 2 and 3.[12] Generally in biblical literature,[13] the phrase "his holy mountain" constitutes a designation of Mt. Zion in Jerusalem, and more specifically the Temple standing on the site, the place where God himself dwells. Immediately after God declares the installation of his anointed one on his holy hill (Ps 2:6), God permits his anointed to request anything of him, even to the ends of the earth (2:8). The promise in Psalm 2 is realized in Ps 3:4 [5], where the psalmist—King David, God's anointed—cries out to the Lord, and subsequently receives an answer from God's holy hill, where God has installed his chosen one. In isolating this idea between the two compositions, the reader is faced with a promise-fulfillment relationship between them. God first promises anything to his king, and later his word proves sure and tested when he answers the call of David.

---

12. The Psalter reflects seven attestations: Pss 2:6; 3:5[4]; 15:1; 43:3; 48:1; 87:1; 99:9. Of these occurrences, the only juxtaposed appearance surfaces here, between Psalms 2 and 3.

13. See, for example, Obad 1:16 and Ps 48:1.

Psalm 4

A DIFFERENT TYPE OF title appears at the opening of Psalm 4. Unlike the incipit connecting the contents of the song to an instance in David's life, as in Psalm 3, Psalm 4's title focusses on the instrument that should accompany the psalm's recital למנצח בנגינות מזמור לדוד ("For the choir director; on stringed instruments. A Psalm of David"). Overall, Psalm 4 is an individual lament that deviates from the battle and war imagery depicted in the preceding composition. Primarily, it contains the cry of one who has been falsely accused, together with the confidence[1] he expresses in God to deliver him from his distress. The song begins in v. 1 with a plea for mercy directed at God, with the psalmist recalling past instances of divine deliverance. Verses 2–3 [3–4] shine a spotlight on the psalmist's enemies, though it is not possible to decipher conclusively either the precise identity of the enemy, or the nature of the assault. In these verses, the psalmist reminds his adversaries—and comforts himself no doubt—that God hears the pious man and sets him apart for deliverance. The following verses, vv. 4–5 [5–6], further address the unidentified adversaries, warning them against inflicting their evil inclinations upon the psalmist. They are advised to turn to God, offer sacrifices to him, and trust him, becoming more like the psalmist. The closing verses, 6–8 [7–9], express a degree of confidence, as the psalmist takes solace in recalling the comfort God has previously afforded him. Remembrance of God's past benevolence generates security and comfort that allows the psalmist to both lie down and sleep, for he knows God resides with him.

---

1. Craigie and Tate, *Psalms 1–50*, 79, primarily understand the composition as a song of confidence.

Directly linking Psalm 4 to its predecessor are the words, רבים
אמרים, ("many are saying," v. 6 [7]). Notably, except for Psalms 3 and 4,
the Psalter fails to attest further instances of the expression. In 4:6 [7], the
words depict those in despair and suffering from similar verbal attacks;
their cry is "Many are saying, 'Who will show us *any* good?'" In this instance, the "many" represent similar victims of slander. Contrasting this
is Ps 3:2 [3], where the offenders speak out, taunting the psalmist, leading
him to declare, *"Many are saying* of my soul, / 'There is no deliverance
for him in God'" (italics added). Having the same phrase appearing in
two consecutive texts recalls a similar phenomenon mentioned in the
Introduction, where unique words or phrases apparently influenced
the editors of biblical literature to juxtapose texts. That said, however,
it is difficult to ascertain whether an instance of literary borrowing occurs here,[2] or whether the compositions were independently composed,
and the arranger aligned them into this configuration due to the shared
phrase.[3]

Further lexical and thematic connections arise between Psalms 3 and
4. Both psalms reflect the actions of lying down and sleeping in peace with
the security of knowing that God watches and protects the psalmist while
he rests. Psalm 3:5 [6] proclaims, "I lay down and slept [שכבתי ואישנה];
/ I awoke, for the LORD sustains me." Similarly, at the end of Psalm 4, v.
8 [9] the psalmist announces, "In peace I will both lie down and sleep
[אשכבה ואישן], / For You alone, O LORD, make me to dwell in safety." In
both psalms, the statement expresses unshakable confidence in the Lord,
accentuating the level of comfort and safety he provides. Although the
psalmists dwell under the threat of their enemies, knowledge of God's
ability to protect allows them to sleep soundly at night, unafraid of all
potential dangers.[4] Furthermore, the aforementioned wording supports

2. Though personally, I suspect an instance of literary borrowing, proving it cur-
rently remains difficult.

3. Words such as קרא ("to call") and כבוד ("honor") further connect Psalms 3 and
4, but they frequently appear in the Psalter (see Pss 22:2 [3] and 28:1; and Pss 7:5
[6], 8:5 [6], 16:9, and 19:1, respectively). Laments frequently involve individuals and
communities crying out, קרא, to God; therefore, its appearance in both laments is
not surprising. Though McCann, "Psalms," 696, identifies both words as connecting
markers, their presence may simply reflect the genre.

4. Because the diachronic relationship between Psalms 3 and 4 remains unclear,
three possibilities exist for explaining their similarities. First, the author of Psalm
3 appropriated material from Psalm 4; second, Psalm 4's author borrowed images
of "sleeping" and "waking" from Psalm 3; third, a single author composed both

the notion that these two psalms were originally designated for recital at specific times in the day: Psalm 3 in the morning, expressing gratitude for protection during the night; and Psalm 4 in the evening, requesting protection during sleep.[5] This continuity reflects a further motive for their juxtaposition: liturgical considerations, prayers sequenced according to specific situations or events. The pairing of the compositions may not have reflected the centerpiece of an elaborate ceremony but may still have functioned together as part of a specific prayer routine for priests at night.

A consecutive reading of Psalms 3 and 4 further provides an interpretive nuance to Psalm 4. Psalm 4:2 [3] refers to בני איש ("sons of men"), who speak vain words against the psalmist, tormenting him. As expected with laments, the specific identity of the wicked remains hidden from the reader. Moving from Psalm 3 to Psalm 4, however, creates a connection between the oppressors in both contexts. From such a reading, the anonymous enemies in Psalm 4 find identity in the company of Absalom, who gathered an army in pursuit of David.[6] Thus, the psalm's sequencing helps to fill a lacuna in Psalm 4.

Focusing on v. 6 in the present psalm, another lucid intertextual association arises: an allusion reaching back to the Aaronic blessing.[7] In v. 6 [7] the psalmist appeals to God to lift the light of his countenance upon him (נסה עלינו אור פניך יהוה), and others who similarly suffer through the torments of slanderers. Furthermore, because of the gladness that God has placed on the psalmist's heart, he can lie down and sleep in peace, or שלום. Resonating with these sentiments is the blessing in Num 6:26, where Moses instructs Aaron on how to bless the Israelites. Aaron must recite the words, "The LORD lift His countenance on you, And give you peace [ישא יהוה פניו אליך וישם לך שלום]." From the repetition of the common words, a degree of influence undoubtedly arises. Even though the date of Psalm 4 remains indeterminable, the direction of borrowing most

---

compositions, reusing similar imagery. Overall, the thematic and lexical connections between these psalms, though difficult to explain comprehensively, suggest a degree of literary borrowing.

5. See, for example, Cohen, *The Psalms*, 6; Waltke, "Psalm 3," 2; VanGemeren, *Psalms*, 107; Ross, *Psalms*, 231.

6. Supporting this notion, Berlin, "Psalms," 1287, notes that Radak, in addition to some other early commentators, identify "them"—the enemy in Psalm 4—as those who allied themselves with Absalom when he rebelled against David.

7. Robertson, *The Flow*, 43, argues for at least ten appearances of the priestly benediction in the Psalter, citing Pss 4:6; 31:16; 37:6; 67:1; 80:1, 3, 7, 19; 94:1; 104:15; 118:27; 119:135; 139:12.

certainly originates from Numbers 6, which was recognizable by many in ancient Israel, and undoubtedly to the psalmist too.[8]

With the link and direction of borrowing between the two texts established, our attention shifts to the two contexts in which the common material appears, beginning with the book of Numbers. Numbers 6 recalls God speaking the words of the blessing to Moses, instructing him to convey them to Aaron for blessing the Israelites. Within the confines of Numbers 6, the context supplies no specific situation in which the blessing is invoked. Should the blessing be recited before wars, or at the end of feasts, or was it part of a daily prayer for the nation? The author fails to indicate the specific context, and nothing immediately arises from the content.[9] In contrast, the author of Psalm 4 situates the blessing directly in the face of threatening behavior, when the psalmist (and others similarly suffering) desperately seeks solace. Even in the face of despair, the psalmist breathes hope into his situation by exclaiming, "Lift up the light of Your countenance upon us, O LORD!" (v. 6 [7]). In the psalm's context, the words of the Aaronic blessing represent an invocation to God to assist those who suffer under a threat. Thus, the psalmist blends Moses' words in Numbers 6 with the context of divine protection against a slightly more specific threat.[10]

8. Here, it is worth noting that the Aaronic blessing's exact form was fluid in transmission. The seventh-century silver amulet found at Ketef Hinnom bears witness to a form differing from MT. Furthermore, the scroll's function at Ketef Hinnom indicates a context of protection and security (see Levine, *Numbers 1–20*, 242), like the psalm.

9. Levine, *Numbers 1–20*, 244, states, "In conclusion, we are warranted in regarding the priestly benediction as multifunctional, surely in the exilic and postexilic periods," implying the benediction was not limited to a single ceremony or occasion.

10. Use of the Aaronic blessing in the context of protection occurs elsewhere in interpretive texts. Targum Pseudo-Jonathan evidently reframes the blessing into an apotropaic context, "The Lord bless thee and keep thee. The Lord make His face to shine upon thee and be gracious unto thee. The Lord lift up His countenance upon thee, and grant thee peace. The Lord bless thee in all thy business, and keep thee from demons of the night, and things that cause terror, and from demons of the noon and of the morning, and from malignant spirits and phantoms" (Tg. Ps.-J, Num 6:24; see Etheridge, *Targums of Onkelos*, 538).

Psalm 5

SIMILAR TO PSALM 4, Psalm 5 mentions an instrument in the incipit, but the present psalm recalls a different one, הנחילות, which the NASB translates, "for flute accompaniment." Like its two predecessors, Psalm 5 constitutes another relatively short individual lament.[1] Slightly differentiating this work from the previous compositions, however, is the detailed window into God's character, particularly regarding his disdain for evil. The psalm begins with a cry by the psalmist to God, to respond to his prayers and his groaning (vv. 1–3 [1–4]). From the psalmist's plea, attention shifts to God's character, especially his abhorrence of the wicked: He hates all evildoers and destroys those who speak lies (vv. 4–6 [5–7]). Switching from descriptions of God's character, the psalmist strikes a more personal tone in vv. 7–8 [8–9] as he lauds his own pious attitudes and behavior in contrast to the evildoers who the Lord hates. The author experiences God's steadfast love, and fearfully worships his Lord, and as a result, he benefits from the privilege of seeking divine guidance for navigating dangers posed by his enemies. Verses 9–10 [10–11] return to the behavior of evil men, furthering calls for God to judge them, urging him to perform his retribution among them. Finally, the composition adopts a positive tone, encouraging all who trust in God to be glad and rejoice in him because he is faithful to protect and bless them.[2]

---

1. For this designation, see VanGemeren, *Psalms*, 114; Craigie and Tate, *Psalms 1–50*, 85. The latter further defines it as a psalm of innocence; however, such a specific designation does not affect the present discussion.

2. Likely, the psalm was written during the monarchy, due to v. 7 [8], "At your holy temple I will bow in reverence for You," which implies active worship in an extant temple. Unfortunately, locating the psalm within this time frame still proves futile when defining the psalm's relationship to other compositions.

Psalm 5's genre instantly associates the composition with Psalms 3–4, and from a lexical perspective it connects via the incipit, ... למנצח מזמור לדוד ("For the choir director ... A Psalm of David"), which appears in the two preceding works.[3] Although markers such as these may explain why Psalms 4 and 5 are juxtaposed, they do not reveal why this particular order was chosen and not a reversed sequence. To begin to understand the present arrangement, it is worth considering the temporal continuity between Psalms 4 and 5. In the closing words of Psalm 4, the psalmist speaks of the peace he experiences when he lies down to sleep, "In peace I will both lie down and sleep, / For You alone, O LORD, make me dwell in safety." Almost as a direct response, Ps 5:3 [4] continues by depicting the morning after, when the psalmist wakes up. The Lord has watched over him, but he continues to call out to God for help, "In the morning, O LORD, You will hear my voice; / In the morning I will order *my prayer* to You and *eagerly* watch." Juxtaposition of these two works in this specific order aptly expresses the continuity of the psalmist's plea; it extends beyond a single day, even though the Lord grants him safety. The persistent threats continue to assail the psalmist into a new day, and he still depends upon divine aid for relief and deliverance.[4]

3. The phrase איש דמים ומרמה ("men of bloodshed and deceit," v. 6 [7]) appears again in only one other Old Testament verse, Ps 55:24. Regarding their relative dates, it is impossible to say who borrowed from whom (if borrowing occurs at all). Psalm 55 bears little in the way of dating indicators, though it reflects slight signs of literary influence. Tate, *Psalms 51–100*, 55, suggests a palpable connection to Jer 29:5–6. Countering his position, Hossfeld and Zenger, *Psalms 2*, 56, intimate connections to Ezekiel. Psalm 5 presents similar difficulties regarding its date, and further reflects weak but detectable associations to other biblical works. VanGemeren, *Psalms*, 113–14, summarizes the wide range of scholarly views, and Botha, "Psalm 5" posits a connection between Psalm 5 and Psalm 1. Not only are the relative dates indeterminable, but the nature of the expression, "men of bloodshed and deceit," further suggests an echo as opposed to a purposeful allusion. Additionally, the expression "for you" (כי אתה), appears at the close of Psalms 4 and 5, which possibly contributed to their present sequence.

4. Liturgical considerations may have influenced the juxtaposition of psalms here. Psalms 3–5 reflect a sequence of morning-evening-morning, possibly reflecting the order of prayers recited by a particular community.

Psalm 6

EXPERIENCES OF SUFFERING AND distress immediately surface in the opening of Psalm 6, as the psalmist directs his plea to the ultimate source of his affliction: the Lord. Verses 1–3 [1–4] indicate that the author suffers from a nondescript physical ailment stemming from divine chastisement, "O Lord, do not rebuke me in Your anger" (v. 1 [2]). The theme of personal sickness introduces a new element into the Psalter at this point. Previously, threats to the psalmist originated from intimidating individuals and nations. Following his cry, in vv. 4–7 [5–8], as typically found in laments, the psalmist lists various reasons why it is incumbent upon God to deliver him—God's lovingkindness, the psalmist's inability to praise him from the grave, and his deep unbearable distress. The psalm's closing verses, vv. 8–10 [9–11], expressing hope and confidence, further align the composition to the lament genre.[1] Here, the psalmist addresses his enemies, warning them that God has heard his prayers, and they will be shamed and turned back. As with the previous psalm, and laments in general, the precise identity of the psalmist's enemies remain hidden.

Almost as a corrective to Psalms 3–5, Psalm 6 introduces the idea of sin into the psalmist's (or Israel's) life, it plays a role in his suffering. Because of the psalmist's sin, God expresses displeasure with him, and permits his suffering. Hinting at the psalmist's wrongdoing, though subtle, raises a topic thus far unseen in the Psalter: accountability for punishment. A similarly new element manifests itself in the form of God as the "enemy" who assaults the speaker through an undefined physical sickness.

1. Generally, scholars consider this psalm a lament in the literature, but some further qualify the definition. Craigie and Tate, *Psalms 1–50*, 91, define it as a "psalm of sickness." Ross, *Psalms*, 258, calls it "a penitential psalm." See Brueggemann and Bellinger, *Psalms*, 46, for more detail regarding this type of psalm ending.

The present psalm connects to the previous work via references to the time of day. Psalm 5 constitutes a morning prayer, as evident from the phrase "In the morning, O LORD, You will hear my voice" (v. 3a). Following this in Psalm 6, the psalmist reflects on a restless and weary night, in which sleep escapes him, "Every night I make my bed swim, / I dissolve my couch with my tears" (Ps 6:6 [7]). These words represent a logical connection between the two compositions, depicting an image of constant suffering, day and night. Furthermore, the word combination, שמע קול (hearing a sound/voice), further generates a close association with the previous psalm, bearing in mind its next occurrence is not until Psalm 18. Though the likelihood of direct literary borrowing between the compositions is slight, the common words between the psalms apparently influenced their juxtaposition.[2] Additionally, the way in which the phrase is utilized by the psalmists creates a logical sequence. From an unanswered cry in Ps 5:3 [4], "In the morning, O LORD, you will hear my voice," to confidence that the cry has been heard, "The LORD has heard my supplication" (Ps 6:9 [10]). Also regarding juxtaposition, the phrase כל פעלי און ("all workers of iniquity"), which additionally appears in the previous psalm (5:5 [6]), warrants attention because it is relatively rare in the remainder of the Psalter.[3] Psalm 5 employs the phrase to depict the object of God's disdain and hatred for evildoers, "The boastful shall not stand before Your eyes; / You hate all who do iniquity" (5:5 [6]); consequently, they cannot stand before him. In Ps 6:8 [9], the author calls directly on the workers of iniquity to depart from him, because God has heard his cry, and will come to his rescue.[4] Though both usages are simi-

2. Psalm 5 uses the phrase in a slightly different context than Deuteronomy and Psalm 6. In Psalm 5, the phrase forms part of a personal statement of confidence, not aimed towards an enemy, "In the morning, O Lord, You will hear my voice" (Ps 5:3 [4]).

3. See Pss 9 [10]; 14:4; 92:7 [8]; 94:4; 101:8.

4. Miller, "Trouble and Woe," deserves attention at this point, though it falls outside the present author's definition of intertextuality and allusion. He associates certain laments with biblical narrative contexts from which they may have arisen. Regarding Psalm 6, Miller connects it to 1 Samuel 1, recounting Hannah's contention with her rival Peninnah. Among the parallels between the texts, Miller recognizes the word כעס that connects the provocation caused by the rival and the psalmist's suffering (1 Sam 1:6; Ps 6:8). Via this connection, the unnamed enemy in the psalm finds a concrete representation in Peninnah. Although it is unlikely the author intended this specific allusion, the association provides a tool for identifying the elusive enemy mentioned in the lament. Miller continues with further potential contexts for the psalm, such as Jeremiah's complaints against God in Jeremiah 12. Avishur, "Chapter 6," 41–42, connects the psalm with passages from Isaiah.

lar, not enough evidence exists to argue for a purposeful and conscious allusion. As a result, these words most likely reflect common poetic vocabulary employed by psalmists, but they may further have influenced an editor or arranger to juxtapose the two compositions.

Outside of Psalm 6's immediate neighbors, v. 7 [8] generates an intertextual link with Psalm 31, via the expression עששה מכעס עיני ("My eye is wasted away from grief"). Besides its appearance in Psalm 6, the phrase, denoting this deep inexpressible sorrow, only appears in one other location, Ps 31:9 [10]. At this point, however, it is impractical to define further the relationship between the two compositions. Evidently, they both use the phrase in similar contexts: Denoting an individual's suffering caused by his enemies. However, the only hint suggesting a direction of borrowing stems from the literary character of Psalm 31. Because Psalm 31's author appears more reliant on other biblical texts, Psalm 6 probably represents the source if literary borrowing plays a part in the relationship.[5]

---

5. Remarkably this psalm contains two similar instances of the psalmist utilizing a phrase appearing in only one other place in biblical literature. The phrase, יגעתי באנחתי ("to be weary with sighing") is also found in Jer 45:3; similarly, יבשו ויבהלו ("to be shamed and dismayed") only resurfaces in Ps 83:17.

Psalm 7

ALTHOUGH PSALM 7 FOLLOWS on the heels of a chain of individual laments,[1] it distinguishes itself by including an emphatic protestation of innocence, which appears almost in response to the psalmist's implied guilt in the previous work. Verses 1–3 [1–4] open with the expected plea by the author for divine deliverance from unnamed pursuers. As part of his supplication, the psalmist projects the outcome of his predicament should he fail to receive divine intervention: He will be mercilessly devoured. Following the initial plea, he requests vindication from God in vv. 4–6 [5–7]. Assured of his own righteousness, the psalmist declares a willingness to accept any divine punishment performed by the hand of an enemy, if he is indeed guilty of a transgression. The ensuing stanza, vv. 7–10 [8–11], sees the psalmist entreating God as a judge to arise, vindicate the psalmist, and silence his adversaries. Because of the psalmist's perceived personal righteousness, he feels empowered to call for God's judgment, which he is sure will be favorable. The psalm's final stanza, vv. 12–17 [13–18], details the generic behavior of the wicked as they plot to overthrow the righteous. Yet, through God's judgment, their plans to inflict evil turns against them. These two themes—the characterization of evil behavior, and the wicked ultimately falling into their own snares—frequently recur in Wisdom literature, but nevertheless function well

1. Like the previous psalm, a few scholars prefer to extend the simple categorization of lament. Kraus, *Psalms 1–59*, 168–69, for example, calls it a "prayer song." Craigie and Tate, *Psalms 1–50*, 99, refer to it as "an innocent man's prayer for protection in the face of the false accusations of enemies." The chain of laments from Psalms 3–7, in the view of VanGemeren, *Psalms*, 100, originally formed a smaller complete collection of Psalms that "move from mild lament to lament, from orientation to disorientation to thanksgiving (reorientation)."

here as part of a lament. Finally, in v. 17 [18], the psalmist offers words of thanksgiving to God, knowing that his request has been heard, even if he still awaits divine intervention.

Like many laments, the precise identity[2] of the enemies assaulting and threatening the psalmist remains unknown within the body of the composition. Unlike many other laments, however, Psalm 7's incipit provides information specifying an enemy. As part of the subtitle,[3] the psalm mentions that David wrote the song regarding an individual named Cush,[4] a Benjaminite. Unfortunately, even though the psalmist or an editor names the oppressor, the Bible provides little or no concrete evidence concerning his identity, and when he threatened David. Despite a paucity of concrete evidence, the ancient translations and a few modern commentators present a few possibilities.[5] It is possible to read the word "Cush" as a personal name, as the Septuagint does (Χουσι), and though it reflects a valid biblical name,[6] it remains absent from the Davidic narratives in Samuel. Alternatively, certain scholars associate this individual with Shimei, who curses David as he flees Jerusalem, being driven out by his son.[7] Another view, raised by Berger, posits a potential connection

2. Brueggemann and Bellinger, *Psalms*, 53, agreeing with Gunkel, recognize, "The enemies are described in rather general ways and thus are difficult to identify with any specificity."

3. Note the subtitle syntactic variation. Other psalms, when adding historical contextual data use the formula: infinitive construct + בְ (see, e.g., Pss 3; 34; 51; 56; 60). Departing from this pattern, Psalms 7 and 18 use the pattern: finite verb + אֲשֶׁר. Hutton, "Cush the Benjaminite," suggests the deviated pattern indicates a different function of the subtitle. The word שִׁגָּיוֹן appearing in the incipit also presents an anomaly. For the most part, English translations simply transfer the difficult word to English via transliteration, producing the word "shiggaion." The NET goes a step further, understanding it as "a musical composition." Although the likelihood is that the word reflects a musical reference of some description, its precise interpretation remains obscure.

4. Concerning his identity, Keil and Delitzsch, *Psalms*, 1:138, suggest he was a servant of Saul and his kinsman, like Doeg the Edomite.

5. Berger, "The David-Benjaminite Conflict," 282–83, lists a full range of possibilities.

6. See, for example, Gen 10:7.

7. See Hutton, "Cush the Benjaminite," 133–38, who further mentions "dust" as a potential marker. Psalm 7:5 [6] reads, "Let the enemy pursue my soul and overtake *it*; / And let him trample my life to the ground / And lay my glory in the dust," which reminds the reader of Shimei's actions in 2 Sam 16:13, "So David and his men went on the way; and Shimei went along on the hillside parallel with him and as he went he cursed and cast stones and threw dust at him." Ross, *Psalms*, 277, links him to one of

between Cush and the Cushite runner who brings news to David of Absalom's death (2 Sam 18:21).[8] The Targum of Psalms asserts a bold and direct link between the name Cush and Saul himself, a son of Kish, "*A loud song of thanksgiving* of David, which he sang before the LORD, because *he uttered the song about the misfortune of Saul the son of Kish, who was from the tribe of Benjamin*" (Tg. Psalms 7:1).[9]

Concerning the psalm's title, the more important feature to isolate is not the name Cush, but the designation of a Benjaminite. The recollection of Benjamin coupled with the psalm's content, a composition highlighting false accusations and divine recompense, point to the overall conflict between the house of Saul and the house of David.[10] Specifically, this relates to 1 Samuel 24–26, though other texts detailing the conflict between the two houses spring to mind. First Samuel 24–26 recalls three instances where David is wronged but refuses to claim vengeance for himself, preferring to leave room for divine vindication. In 1 Sam 24 and 26, Saul follows the advice of those falsely accusing David of wrongdoing and pursues him in order to kill him. First Samuel 24:9 reads, "David said to Saul, 'Why do you listen to the words of men, saying, "Behold, David seeks to harm you"?'", recalling a false accusation leveled against David. And later, 1 Sam 26:19 says, "Now therefore, please let my lord the king listen to the words of his servant. If the LORD has stirred you up against me, let Him accept an offering; but if it is men, cursed are they before the LORD, for they have driven me out today." A slightly different case is presented in 1 Sam 25, where David is wronged by Nabal, but Abigail prevents David from exacting judgment with his own hands against her husband.

Saul's men who falsely accused David.

8. Note the compelling literary connections. Seeking recompense against his enemy, the psalmist desires that they are struck with darts (7:13 [14]) and thrown into a pit (7:15 [16]). Such a death corresponds with Absalom's demise. He was impaled by Joab with javelins and then thrown into a pit (2 Sam 18:14, 17).

9. Stec, *Targum of Psalms*, 35. It is difficult to know how the Targum author came to this conclusion, whether it was via a tradition known to him, or whether he associated the words "Cush" and "Kish," blending them with the texts from Samuel. Alternatively, textual corruption may have played a part in his interpretation. The title may also be dismissed as a nonhistorical rubric, and ignored; see Hutton, "Cush the Benjaminite," 127. Ultimately, one must concede that the tradition alludes to individuals no longer known to present-day readers.

10. Many, but not all, of my suggestions here align with Berger, "The David-Benjaminite Conflict," esp. 290.

An intriguing phrase in Ps 7:14 [15] echoes in at least two other places in the Old Testament. As part of the psalmist's depiction of the wicked and their plots against the righteous, he declares, "He conceives mischief and brings forth [הרה עמל וילד] falsehood." This relatively rare phrase in the Bible only occurs in two other places, Job 15:35 and a similar version in Isa 59:4b. In Job, Eliphaz employs the expression in his depiction of the wicked, including Job, "They conceive mischief and bring forth iniquity, / And their mind prepares deception." Reversing the taunt, the psalmist, an innocent man, recalls the actions of the wicked in these terms, as they scheme against him. For Isaiah, the expression originates from the mouth of God via the prophet. Responding to Israel's denial of God's ability to fulfill his promised restoration, God informs them that his unwillingness results from their sins. As part of God's depiction of their disobedience, he declares, "They trust in confusion and speak lies; / They conceive mischief and bring forth iniquity." Presently, it is impossible to ascertain whether literary borrowing occurred at all among these three texts. Yet all of them employ the phrase as a depiction of wicked behavior, even if the speaker and the object of the phrase vary from text to text. The likelihood remains that the expression constitutes a standard portrayal of the wicked that formed part of a poet's repertoire.

Another notable, but equally unsolvable intertextual association unifies Ps 7:5 [6] with Ps 143:3. Though the vector of allusion is virtually impossible to prove, the connection between the compositions is nevertheless hard to ignore. The phrase, "For the enemy has persecuted my soul . . . crushed my life to the ground" (ירדף אויב נפשי . . . וירמס לארץ חיי, Ps 7:5 [6]) uniquely appears in these two biblical locations, though they differ marginally in their representation of trampling and crushing. Psalm 7 uses the Hebrew רמס, whereas Psalm 143 uses דכא. Because both psalms are individual laments ascribed to David, and the phrases appear in remarkably similar contexts, the likelihood remains that the psalmist employs a stock phrase here, part of the lexical repertoire employed by lament composers.[11]

---

11. VanGemeren, *Psalms*, 100, detects an escalation in each lament's intensity as the reader progresses from Psalms 3–7. He argues, "The psalmist of Psalms 3–5 is quiet and confident, is not overcome by the reality of evil, and is confident of Yahweh's protection. Psalm 6 finds the psalmist overcome by his circumstances. He is weak, but he renews himself in the vision of God's victory. In Psalm 7, David comes home. He finds refuge with Yahweh and reorients himself by seeking Yahweh as the righteous king who will deal with the wicked."

Psalm 8

CREATING A BREAK FROM the previous slew of laments, Psalm 8 boldly stands as the first hymn in the Psalter.[1] Although the reader experiences a dramatic shift in genre, one still detects a degree of familiarity through the psalm's incipit, which, like the previous works, attributes the composition to David.[2] Opening the psalm, in v. 1 [2], the psalmist poses a rhetorical question, "How majestic is Your name in all the earth" and attempts to comprehend through his limited human reasoning a suitable answer. In short, the psalmist wrestles with the question of God's omnipotence compared to human frailty. In v. 2 [3], attention shifts to an example of God's greatness, his ability to generate unimaginable power and might from small and insignificant elements.[3] Thematically, the second verse of this composition stands out with respect to the overall tenor of the psalm,[4]

1. Though Craigie and Tate, *Psalms 1–50*, 106, initially define the psalm as a hymn of praise, it nevertheless defies the classic definition, leading them to refine the category as a creation hymn. See also Avishur, "Chapter 8," 47. Kraus, *Psalms 1–59*, 179, calls it a "hymn of an individual." VanGemeren, *Psalms*, 137, additionally observes that the psalm's contents, together with Psalm 1, create an inclusion, defining the portrayal of the ideal human as one who meditates on the Torah daily, is made a little lower than God himself, and is crowned with glory and splendor.

2. The title of the psalm remains partially mysterious because of its reference to the Gittith, an unknown musical designation or instrument. Despite this, the title recalls the town of Gath, the giant Goliath's birthplace.

3. Here I propose reading עז as "strength," and not "praise," for improved resonance with the immediate context; doing so generates a lucid oxymoron conveying the notion of drawing dynamic power from a weak vessel. Furthermore, the translation of "strength" supports the idea of driving God's enemies away from the psalmist.

4. Mentioning the moon and stars, and not the sun, leads certain scholars to assume the psalm was composed at night, with a dark sky in view. The backdrop of the night sky recalls the earlier theme of day and night. In Ps 4:8, the psalmist lies down

which contrasts God's unfathomable potency with man's diminished status in the grand scheme of created entities. Within this broader context comes v. 2b, which declares that God establishes strength to overcome his enemies and to defeat the revengeful. Ostensibly, the notions of revenge and fighting against an enemy fly in the face of the remaining text. What place does the enemy have in the grand scheme of praising God for his work in creation?[5] They are momentarily introduced in the verse, and never mentioned again. After briefly recalling the enigmatic enemy, the psalmist's difficulty in comprehension surfaces in vv. 3–5 [4–6]. Here, he wrestles with the question of why God, who wields power to shape the cosmos and everything in it, notices and even exalts the lowly status of humanity, even to the point of honoring mankind's level of majesty to being just a little less than God himself.[6] Developing the theme, vv. 6–9 [7–10] enumerate elements of creation placed under man's authority, all that swims in the sea, flies in the air, and walks on land. Closing the psalm, v. 9 returns the reader to where the psalmist begins, asking the same question that initially triggers his inquiry. Despite his meditation on the cosmos, God's omnipotence, and man's insignificant place in creation, the psalmist finds no satisfactory answer to his profound question. All he can do is return to ponder the unfathomable majesty of an incomprehensible God.

Notably, in praise, the psalmist frames a rhetorical question magnifying God's unfathomable reputation, מה אדיר שמך ("How majestic is your name"). At the start of the psalm, the psalmist seemingly responds to the ending of the previous composition (7:17b [18b]), where the author promises to sing a hymn honoring the name of the Lord Most high: אזמרה שם יהוה ("And will sing praise to the name of the Lord"). Linking the two psalms, therefore, via the word שם ("name"), an editor shapes a promise-fulfillment relationship between the works, generating a sequencing association. As a result of God delivering the psalmist from distress in Psalm 7, he promises to praise the name of the Lord. Then

---

and sleeps, presumably at night. Then in Ps 5:3 [4], the psalmist says, "In the morning, O Lord, you will hear my voice." Following this, Ps 6:6 reads, "Every night I make my bed swim, I flood my couch with my tears." Then finally, after skipping Psalm 7, one reads of the night sky reflecting the glory of God.

5. Recollection of "infants and babes," from which God generates strength, alludes to the creation of humanity in the Genesis narrative, as posited by Briggs, *Psalms*, 63.

6. Here I affirm the NASB's translation of אלהים as "God," as opposed to the Septuagint's rendition of "angels," (αγγελος) which the ESV follows, translating the word as "heavenly beings."

in Psalm 8, because words of praise leap out of the psalmist's mouth, it
appears he has been delivered, and now fulfills his vow.

After reading the psalm, little doubt arises that the psalmist is, at least
to some degree, inspired by the creation story in Genesis. Surprisingly,
however, lexical markers between the two accounts present a rather obscure picture. Words such as שמים ("heaven"), ארץ ("earth"), אדם ("man"),
כוכבים ("stars"), and ים ("sea"), unfortunately appear relatively frequently
throughout Genesis, and the rest of the Bible. Perhaps the most conclusive
lexical marker is the expression "fish of the sea," rendered as דגי הים in
Ps 8:8 [9] and דגת הים in Gen 1:26, 18. Similar occurrences elsewhere in
biblical literature attest to the phrase; however, only Psalm 8 and Genesis
recall a context of God entrusting man with authority and responsibility over the fish of the sea. Notwithstanding the relative paucity of lexical
markers, thematic elements demonstrate the psalmist's knowledge of creation events recorded in Genesis 1,[7] even if his source does not represent
an exact replica of MT's rendition. The table below highlights the thematic
connections between the Genesis account and the psalmist's rendition.

Genesis	Psalm 8
Light (Day 1)	
Firmament separating waters (Day 2)	
Sea, dry land, vegetation (Day 3)	
Luminaries: greater and lesser lights (Day 4)	Moon and stars (v. 3 [4])
Water and skies populated: Fish and birds (Day 5)	Birds of the heaven and the fish of the sea, whatever passes through the paths of the sea (8:8 [9])
Cattle, beasts	Creation of Man (4–5 [5–6])
Creation of man	Man's authority to rule fish and sea creatures (6–8 [7–9])
Man given authority to rule all (Day 6)	
God rests (Day 7)	

7. Scholars generally identify this as the priestly creation account in Genesis; however, matters concerning the Pentateuch's sources do not affect the present study.

Genesis 1's creation account reflects two distinct stages in the creation process, both following the sequence of heavens, sea, and land. The first stage, days 1–3, depicts the formation of a firmament separating the upper and lower waters, followed by the separation of seas from land. After setting what could be described as a cosmic stage, God returns to populate each region. First, he forms the heavenly bodies;[8] then he populates the sea with life, fish, and water mammals; and then he fills the dry land with the beasts of the earth. Finally, the author of Genesis records God creating mankind, the high point of creation and pinnacle of his creative activity, after which he rests.

Regarding the relative dates of the two texts, it is safe to assume that Genesis reflects the older of the two traditions, and the psalmist reshapes his knowledge of this tradition, or one similar, into his poetic composition. Contemporary scholarship agrees with this hypothesis;[9] furthermore, to imagine that Psalm 8 served as a source for Genesis remains an unlikely proposition.

In assessing the psalmist's reworking of Genesis, the first noticeable change concerns the selection process from the creation account. Whereas Genesis 1 centers on God as sole creator of the universe, all physical matter in heaven and on earth, the psalmist concentrates primarily on day six, God's creation of mankind and his relationship with him. In doing so, he marginalizes the emphasis on God as the universe's sole creator. Instead, he focuses on a single facet of the six-day creation process.

Though the psalmist recalls some of the same creation events, he noticeably reorders them in his work. Undoubtedly, he understands mankind as creation's apotheosis, but reverses his position in the creation order, from last place in Genesis, to first place in the psalm. Additionally, because the psalmist's concern primarily relates to humanity's dominion, the first phase of creation—when the stage was initially set with creation of the heavenly bodies and the separation of water and land—is omitted from his account. In reordering the creation narrative, the psalmist emphasizes man's relationship to the animals under his charge. Another aspect of interpretation relates to the psalmist's portrayal of humans being created מעט מאלהים ("a little less than God"). Psalm 8's author adopts

---

8. The sun, moon, and stars, although Genesis fails to mention them explicitly.

9. See, for example, Brueggemann and Bellinger, *Psalms*, 59; Kraus, *Psalms 1–59*, 180, "There should be no doubt that Psalm 8 has reference to Gen 1:26ff."; Keener, *The Eighth Psalm*, 99–108. The only other viable alternative is that the psalm drew from a source common to Genesis 1.

the phrase to express the creation of humans in Gen 1:26, stating that humanity was fashioned in the image of God and with his form (בצלמנו כדמותנו). Therefore, to maximize the important and exalted status of mankind, the psalmist directly associates humans with the highest authority and power in creation.[10]

In rendering the creation of luminaries, the psalmist prefers a more explicit reference than the Genesis account offers. Instead of simply mentioning the greater and lesser lights, the psalmist unequivocally names the moon and stars in v. 3 [4]. Such a change reflects his freedom from any negative associations attached to heavenly luminaries. Genesis was written at a time when the sun, moon, and stars were worshipped as deities; for that reason, their specific names are avoided.[11] Furthermore, the omission of the sun's formation from the psalmist's rendition of creation events reflects—as various commentators speculate—nighttime as the temporal context of the psalmist's observation. Noticeable too is that the function of the moon and stars differs subtly from their role in Genesis. In Genesis, they primarily serve as boundary markers for time and seasons; whereas Psalms 8 adopts them as props to set the divine stage for the creation and exaltation of humankind.

The phrase, מה אנוש כי ("what is man that . . ." Ps 8:4 [5]), further generates an intertextual link with the book of Job. Apart from these two books, biblical literature fails to attest the phrase, a fact further solidifying the probability of literary borrowing. Regarding the dates of Psalm 8 and Job, one cannot say with certainty which text is later, and therefore who borrowed from whom. Scholarly consensus, however, leans towards the probability of Job borrowing from the psalmist's words.[12]

Though Job utilizes the word combination in at least three places,[13] only the phrase's appearance in Job 7:17 resonates with the appearance in

10. The psalmist adds the phrase "crowned him with splendor and majesty" in v. 5 [6], which is absent from Genesis. This is best understood as a poetic addition to the text, further exalting the status of man, and associating him with the majesty ascribed to God in v. 2 [3].

11. See Milgrom, "The Alleged 'Hidden Light.'"

12. See Pope, *Job*, 75; Clines, *Job 1–20*, 192; Fishbane, *Biblical Interpretation*, 286; Keener, "Canonical Exegesis," 117.

13. The same words appear in Job 9:2b, "But how can a person be in the right before God?" but not as part of the expression witnessed in Psalm 8. Similarly, Job 15:14, says, "What is man, that he would be pure? / Or he who is born of a woman, that he would be righteous," which equates to similar wording with a different context. Fishbane, *Biblical Interpretation*, 286, reads Eliphaz's words in Job 15:14 as an adaptation

Psalm 8. In both contexts, Psalm 8 and Job, the speaker adopts the phrase to question God; neither of them can quite fathom out how God—who is so mighty, lofty, and exalted—devotes time to noticing the insignificance of humanity. Job, however, views God's gaze upon humanity generally, and himself specifically, within a wholly negative framework. He contends that God not only notices him but is vindictive enough to recall his sin and torment him, punishing him for all his shortcomings. Why, in the mind of Job, should a God so exalted even care about the life and actions of a single man?

The psalmist, like Job, expresses unbridled amazement at God's desire to notice mankind, using the same words, "What is man that you take thought of him" (Ps 8:4 [5]). Unlike Job, however, the psalmist limits the scope of God's attention to humanity in general, as opposed to a specific individual, Job. Moreover, the psalmist frames these within a positive context. For him, the real wonder is that God focuses on humanity not to punish individuals for sin, but to exalt them and grant them a place of honor. For Job, God's attention to detail represents a divine characteristic that causes discomfort, pain, and misery, but for the psalmist, it represents a source for joy and a reason to break forth in praise.

---

of the phrase in 7:17–18, where both expressions play on ambiguity in the psalmist's question. Another relevant passage is Ps 144:3, "O Lord, what is man, that You take knowledge of him? Or the son of man, that You think of him?", which adopts a variant form, מה אדם. Likely, Psalm 144 represents the later composition. Booij, "Psalm 144," 173–74, argues for a late (postexilic) date for Psalm 144, adducing the use of the particle שֶׁ (the relative pronoun). Kraus, *Psalms 60–150*, 542, similarly dates Psalm 144 to a relatively late period.

Psalm 9/10

THE FOLLOWING TWO COMPOSITIONS in the Hebrew and English Bibles
will be treated as a single work, Psalm 9/10, for various reasons. Together
they form an acrostic that apparently employs successive letters of the
Hebrew alphabet,[1] which strongly suggests the two units originally constituted a unified composition. Certain early translations of the Hebrew
Bible, such as the Septuagint and Vulgate, additionally support the unification of the two works. Furthermore, Psalm 10's lack of a title suggests,
with specific reference to Book I, that it never existed as an independent
composition. Except for Psalms 1, 2, and 33, all psalms in Book I bear
titles linking them to David. This tacitly suggests that Psalm 10 originally
formed part of Psalm 9 and the songs were mistakenly divided in MT.[2]
Moreover, certain phrases reveal an undeniable unity between the two
parts.[3] Perhaps the most important is עתות בצרה ("times of trouble"). As

1. The acrostic pattern is not perfectly maintained due to levels of textual
corruption.

2. Other scholars similarly treat the two compositions as one; see, for example,
Clifford, *Psalms 1–72*, 71. Kraus further notes that the position of the term *selah*, at
the end of Psalm 9 in v. 20 [21], indicates that the psalm does not end there. *Selah*
never appears at the end of psalms, but, as a musical term, it is reserved for locations other than the beginning and end of compositions (see Kraus, *Psalms 1–59*, 191).
More importantly, within the wealth of medieval manuscripts a great deal of variation
exists regarding psalm's divisions within the Psalter. See Yarchin, "Psalms Collections,"
781–87.

3. In addition to עתות בצרה, "times of distress" (9:9 [10]; 10:1), note also the root
עני, "afflicted," "poor," or "oppressed," and אנוש, "man" or "humanity" (9:19 [20];
10:18). Additionally, note the use of זו as a relative pronoun, which appears in 9:15
[16] and 10:2, and the adjective עני, "afflicted," which frequently appears throughout
both sections of the psalm (9:13 [14], 18 [19]; 10:12, 17). Other keywords unify the
composition, such as דך, for "oppressed" or "crushed," which appears only three times

59

an expression in the Psalter, it only appears in Ps 9:9 [10], "The Lord also will be a stronghold for the oppressed, / A stronghold in times of trouble" and Ps 10:1b, "Why do You hide *Yourself* in times of trouble?" The exclusive use of the expression in Psalm 9/10 further reduces the notion of two entirely independent compositions.

Thematically, the idea of forgetting further unifies the two sections of the composition. Psalm 9:12 [13] introduces the theme, stating that God does not forget the cry of the afflicted. And an inversion follows in v. 17 [18], where the nations who forget God are destined for *sheol*. When the psalmist then states in v. 19 [20] that the needy will not always be forgotten, the reader is reminded of 9:12 [13], which explicates the agent, God, who does not forget the afflicted one's cry. In Ps 10:11 the psalm returns to the wicked, who behave as though God has forgotten his acts, failing to see his evil deeds, his oppression of the afflicted. Responding to this attitude of the oppressor, v. 12 turns again to the declaration of 9:14, and calls upon God not to forget the oppressed.[4]

Structurally, Psalm 9/10 is difficult to navigate and, likely, suffered significant corruption,[5] redaction, and correction throughout its lifetime. Despite such challenges, four themes dominate the composition. First are

---

in the Psalter, twice in this composition (9:9 [10]; 10:18).

4. Some evidence exists supporting the possibility of Psalm 9/10 as two independent entities. Thematically, Psalm 9 resembles a hymn, whereas Psalm 10 reflects a lament; moreover, both psalms could represent two separate partial acrostics, which are known from other sources such as Qumran (see 11QPs, 155). Keil and Delitzsch, *Psalms*, 1:175, uphold this stance, arguing, "It is impossible that the two psalms should be one," further maintaining that David composed both psalms, and Psalm 10 was later appended to Psalm 9. More recently, VanGemeren, *Psalms*, 143, leans towards separate compositions as defined by MT. However, the probability of two independent psalms coincidently forming an acrostic—with shared rare phrases between them—though possible, seems highly unlikely. Furthermore, the preponderant weight of scholarship supports the unity of the two works. See Leslie, *Psalms*, 218; McCann, "Psalms," 716–17; Craigie and Tate, *Psalms 1–50*, 116; Avishur, "Chapters 9–10," 50; Clifford, *Psalms 1–72*, 71.

5. Various commentators mention aspects of Psalm 9/10's corruption during transmission, which is evident from reading the text. See, for example, Berlin, "Psalms," 1293; Brueggemann and Bellinger, *Psalms*, 63. Craigie and Tate, *Psalms 1–50*, 116–17, propose the most sophisticated theory concerning the psalm's transmission, positing an early corruption of the text before it entered the Psalter; then, an editor, attempting to restore it, rendered it into two distinct units, Psalm 9/10. Among the more notable corruptions concern the acrostic pattern, where the letters *dālet* and *nūn* are absent. Furthermore, a possibility exists that the sequence of *ayin* and *peh* was inverted, but this may simply reflect an alternate version of the alphabet ordering.

the poor, who are oppressed, and the needy, those forgotten by God, and those with whom the psalmist identifies himself. Second are the wicked who constantly plot against the righteous, ignoring God and ostensibly escaping judgment. Third are the pleas for deliverance voiced by the psalmist on behalf of the poor and the needy. Fourth is the enemy, whose identity remains elusive—in the first half of Psalm 9/10, other nations adopt the role, but in the second half, their identity becomes more obscure. Together with lucid depictions of deeds performed by the wicked, the psalmist adds frequent statements of hope, trust, and confidence, indicating that God hears his cry and will ultimately arise to vindicate the cause of the needy.

The Psalm opens with a declaration of praise as the psalmist rejoices, proclaiming what God has done (vv. 1 [1–2]).[6] Following this, in vv. 3–6 [4–7], colors are added to the sketch as the psalmist details his reasons for praise: God vanquishes the enemy and maintains their cause. Details of God's character follow in the next four verses (vv. 7–10 [8–11]), portraying him as a righteous judge who rules the nations, and serves as a stronghold for the oppressed, a place where they seek refuge. After a further declaration of praise, in vv. 11–14 [12–15], the psalmist develops his previous depiction of God as a refuge for the oppressed and applies it to his personal situation. He identifies himself as one who suffers and calls on God for vindication. Verses 15–18 [16–19] continue by expressing the psalmist's hope and confidence, as he recalls the nations who were snared in their own scheming, a result of God executing his judgment upon them. Evidence of the psalmist's aroused confidence surfaces as he declares that those perishing will not be forgotten forever; their cry ultimately will be heard. Then addressing his plea directly to God, the psalmist implores him in vv. 19–20 [20–21] to arise and judge the nations.

In Ps 10:1–2, the psalmist's patience seemingly ends as he cries in apparent despair for God to judge the wicked.[7] In his eyes, God has ap-

6. Structurally, little, if any, consensus exists among scholars, or event translators, concerning the psalm's stanza divisions. The psalm's acrostic structure no doubt contributes to the problem.

7. This part of the psalm is generally recognized as a lament; see Craigie and Tate, *Psalms 1–50*, 116; Ross, *Psalms*, 302. The juxtaposition of two distinct genres within a single composition is not surprising. Psalm 19, for example, displays evidence of both a wisdom (or Torah) psalm and a hymn of praise. Gordis, "Psalm 9–10," 108, further cites a Talmudic viewpoint from b. Ber 32a arguing that a man should always set forth his praise of the Holy One blessed be he, and then offer his prayer.

parently ignored all their actions, and they remain unpunished. Details of the oppressor's boasting, plotting, and scheming ensue in the following nine verses: He does not seek God and is proud (v. 4), he curses (v. 7), and lies in wait for the helpless (v. 10). Thoughts of such behavior once again spur the psalmist to cry to God (vv. 12–15), appealing for him to pity the oppressed and act, even as he has done in the past. Finally, the psalmist closes with expressions of hope and confidence. He recognizes that God has heard the petitions of the humble and exclaims in faith that he will rescue them, vindicating the orphans and oppressed.

Praising God's name (שם), his reputation and magnificent deeds, thematically generates a smooth transition between Psalms 8 and 9/10. At the end of Psalm 8, the psalmist, as he does at the start of the psalm, declares, "How majestic is Your name [שם] in all the earth." The attitude of praise and exaltation continues in Ps 9:2 [3] with the declaration, "I will sing praise to Your name [שם], O Most High." Though God's name and reputation are both lauded in the juxtaposed words, each psalm portrays distinct aspects. Psalm 8, as discussed above, centers on God's works in creation, the establishment of the created order, and the placement of humanity at the apex of the hierarchy. Focus shifts in the subsequent psalm(s) to reflect God's superiority over mankind, specifically his role as a judge for the wicked and source of refuge for the needy and afflicted. Following Psalm 8, which praises and exalts the status of man as ruler over everything created on earth, Psalm 9/10 presents a reminder that man still answers to God.

The Hebrew אנוש ("man") provides the reader with another linking keyword between the psalms, and its appearance in the compositions generates a comprehensive view of humanity. As a relatively rare word in the Psalter, it fails to appear again until Ps 55:13 [14]. Its emergence in juxtaposed compositions lends itself to Delitzsch's principle of as-sociation.[8] Psalm 8 employs the word in a positive context, depicting humanity's exalted and honored role in the created order. The psalmist wonders, "What is man [מה אנוש] that You take thought of him, / And the son of man that You care for him?" (Ps 8:4 [5]). In this context, the psalmist stands in amazement at humanity's exalted status: God considers man more important than other created life forms, to the point of being just a little lower than God himself. Psalm 9/10, however, tempers this perspective somewhat, as the juxtaposed texts remind the reader that man

8. See Keil and Delitzsch, *Psalms*, 1:21–22.

still, despite his exaltation, remains subordinate to God. In v. 9:19 [20] the psalmist appeals to God as a higher authority to limit the deeds and intentions of wicked men: "Do not let mankind prevail"; further in v. 20 [21], he pleads that God would, "Let the nations know that they are but men [אנוש]," which is to say, mortal. They may exhibit dominance over others less capable of defending themselves, but ultimately they fall under the authority and judgment of God. The two uses of אנוש together highlight two extreme sides to humanity. On one hand, humanity was created just below the Godhead, and bestowed the huge responsibility of caring and nurturing creation as God's ambassadors. On the other hand, within the same species lurks a desire to oppress others and abuse the divine authority vested into their care; consequently, humanity remains in need of a judge.

Psalm 11

PSALM 11 FALLS BETWEEN the related genres of lament and song of confidence.[1] The opening words betray the psalmist's vulnerability as he proclaims his intention to seek refuge in God, regardless of what might befall him. After the initial statement of hope, the psalm recalls the words of an accuser against the psalmist and his responding statements of hope in the Lord. Verses 1b–3 depict an enemy poised to attack and defeat a righteous man. They taunt him asking, "What can the righteous do?" In response, the psalmist restores his confidence in the second half of the psalm, vv. 4–7, by focusing on God as the source of his potential deliverance. The psalmist reminds himself of God's character and capabilities: The Lord sees everything from his dwelling place, he judges the righteous, and most importantly, punishes the wicked according to their actions. Verse 6 is particularly noteworthy because words of imprecation fill the psalmist's mouth as he wishes for fire and sulfur to burn against his enemy. Like the psalm's opening, the composition ends with a more tranquil statement of trust, returning the reader's attention to God's righteous character and deeds.

The search for lexical and semantic associations between the present psalm and its predecessor, Psalm 9/10, ends with precious little in the way of meaningful results. Connecting words, רשע ("wicked"), נפש ("soul"), עין ("eye"), and כסא ("throne") commonly appear between the compositions, but also appear numerous times throughout the Psalter,

---

1. Scholars consistently fail to agree upon the psalm's genre, despite the close relationship between the two categories. Clifford, *Psalms 1–72*, 76, interprets it as a song of trust, or confidence, as do Craigie and Tate, *Psalms 1–50*, 132. McCann, "Psalms," 721, however, asserts that the psalm's uniqueness obscures its categorization, and he understands it as an individual complaint or prayer.

especially with regards to laments and songs of confidence. Of the above words, only כסא ("throne") bears any potential as a juxtaposition-inspiring keyword. Although it appears nineteen times in the Psalter, the only three appearances of the word in Book I are in Pss 9:4 [5], 7 [8], and Ps 11:4. In Ps 9:4–7 [5–8], the throne symbolizes the place where God judges the earth, "You have sat on the throne judging righteously" and "established His throne for judgment." Following this, Psalm 11 provides the reader with the location of this throne: Verse 4 declares that "the LORD's throne is in heaven." If the idea of God's throne influenced the juxtaposition of the two units, the reason for their present sequencing—why Psalm 11 appears after Psalm 9/10, and not vice versa—needs addressing. A possible answer to this question lies in the genre of the psalms concerned. Frequently, within the structure of a lament, psalmists close their work with words of comfort and hope, encouraging the reader with statements expressing God's ability to provide deliverance and to respond to their cries. One could extrapolate that editors and arrangers of psalm groups were similarly cognizant of this sequencing and arranged individual psalms under the same consideration. Being guided by this principle, an editor would have thus purposefully placed a song of confidence and trust, Psalm 11, after a lament, Psalm 9/10. Despite this somewhat appealing proposal explaining the sequencing of these psalms, the possibility of coincidental juxtaposition remains.

Another possible literary connection worth mentioning concerns Ps 11:1. Although the psalm contains no midrashic Davidic incipit, v. 1 employs the phrase, "How can you say to my soul, 'Flee as a bird to your mountain'?"[2] This, coupled with the psalm's title ascribing authorship to David, subtly evokes for the reader an incident in David's life that echoes the psalm's sentiment.[3] After David spares Saul's life, repaying him good for evil, he confronts Saul from a safe distance, saying, "For the king of Israel has come out to search for a single flea, just as one hunts a partridge in the mountains" (1 Sam 26:20b). The image of the bird fleeing for safety resonates in both texts. Furthermore, the psalm's context reflects the plight of an innocent man who calls on God to vindicate him and to punish his enemy. In this context, the enemy is described as a wicked person who pursues the righteous psalmist. Because the psalmist rests assured of

2. Although this verse contains no historical superscript, as witnessed in Psalm 3, it serves the same function—connecting a psalm to an incident in David's life.

3. VanGemeren, *Psalms*, 160, notes the connection but fails to elaborate on it further.

his clear conscience before God, he can request a divine examination to prove his innocence (v. 4).

Vindication, however, is not the psalmist's sole desire; he further seeks divine retribution against his enemy, "Upon the wicked He will rain snares; / Fire and brimstone and burning wind will be the portion of their cup" (v. 6). Such sentiments resonate well with David's persecution in 1 Samuel 26, which finds Saul pursuing David, following the counsel of wicked men (1 Sam 26:19). In Samuel, David stands well within his rights to retaliate and kill the man who pursues him without just cause. Instead, he turns to God for vindication and relies on his intervention. When Abishai offers to pin Saul to the ground with one swift stroke, David prevents him saying, "As the LORD lives, the LORD certainly will strike him, or his day will come that he dies, or he will go down in battle and perish" (1 Sam. 26:10), a sentiment resonating well with the psalm.

Reading the psalm in light of 1 Samuel 26 reveals an abstract-to-practical relationship between the two literary units. The psalm's message—imploring the reader to trust God for divine intervention rather than taking matters into their own hands—finds a practical expression in David's life. Reading them together reiterates that waiting for divine retribution is not just a utopian ideal, where the supplicant tenuously grasps the hope of an unlikely vindication, but a proven formula that has worked in the past.

Psalm 12

PSALMS 12'S INCIPIT, למנצח . . . מזמור לדוד, ("for the choir director . . . A psalm of David") associates it with the previous psalm, but the insertion of the phrase על השמינית ("on the *sheminith*"[1]) additionally generates a degree of uniqueness. After the incipit, this individual lament opens with the psalmist's complaint to God, vv. 1–4 [2–5]. His persecution stems from those who speak falsely against him and other oppressed individuals. The oppressors speak soothing words but hold treachery and deceit in their hearts. Emphasizing the surreptitious words directed against the psalmist, the composition repeats verbs and nouns reflecting speech: דבר ("to speak") twice in v. 2 [3]; שפה ("lips") in vv. 2, 3, 4 [3, 4, 5]; and לשון ("tongue,") in vv. 3, 4 [4, 5]. Repetition of these words almost anticipates the ensuing divine speech later in the psalm. The psalmist's primary distress stems from the ever-decreasing number of faithful men left in his community (strangely, he seems less concerned with insults aimed against himself). Closing the section, the psalmist expresses his wish for divine intervention, for God to cease the boasting chatter. Following the complaint is the pivotal fifth verse, which contains God's verbal response, a vow to protect those oppressed and troubled by deceitful speech. This first-person divine utterance distinguishes Psalm 12 from the previous laments discussed thus far. Ordinarily, laments express a community's or an individual's desire for divine intervention without an explicit response

---

1. The Septuagint renders the phrase ὑπὲρ τῆς ὀγδόης, "for the eighth," whereas the Targums prefer, על כינורא דתמניא נימי, "On the lute with eight strings." Various English translations interpret it differently. The ESV, for example, transliterates the Hebrew, rendering "The Sheminith," whereas the NASB reads "upon an eight-stringed lyre," probably under the influence of the word שמונה, meaning "eight." The NET understands the term as a style of music, reading, "according to the *sheminith* style."

from the deity. In the closing verses, vv. 6–7 [7–8], the psalm records words of affirmation and trust by the psalmist, asserting that God will indeed guard the victims of malicious speech. Contrasting the malicious and slanderous words of the oppressors, the psalmist asserts the purity of God's words. Closing the psalm in v. 8 [9], somewhat strangely,[2] is a negative reminder of the psalmist's present reality in which wickedness still exists on every side and worthlessness abounds among the sons of men.[3]

The present psalm bears little in the way of intertextual associations[4] either to its predecessor in the Psalter, or other locations in biblical literature.[5] That said, however, one phrase warrants some discussion. In Ps 12:5 [6], as part of a critical juncture in the composition, God himself begins speaking, opening with the words עתה אקום יאמר יהוה, ("'Now I will arise,' says the LORD"). The specific combination and sequencing of words here appears in one other location in biblical literature, Isa 33:10. Furthermore, the contexts in both passages resonate to a degree because like the psalm, Isaiah deploys the phrase at a pivotal stage in its context. Isaiah 33:1 denounces an unnamed[6] ravaging enemy, and then in vv. 2–9 the author petitions God on behalf of the people, detailing the dire situation of those suffering and the devastation of the land. At this point in the chapter are the words, "'Now I will arise,' says the LORD," which appear as a prelude to the divine response.

The selection of words and their order unquestionably link the two pericopae together. Unfortunately, however, defining a potential vector of allusion, if indeed one exists, remains elusive; the relative dates of the two intertexts cannot be determined with any degree of certainty. Although

---

2. Usually, words of confidence and trust appear at the close of a lament, but here the composition thematically ends where the psalm began, expressing the psalmist's fears.

3. In its present form, Berlin, "Psalms," 1295, suggests the final verse experienced a degree of corruption, which explains such a negative ending.

4. Words such as רשעים ("wicked"), אדם ("man"), and לב ("heart") connect Psalms 11 and 12, but they are also distributed widely throughout the Psalter.

5. A paucity of evidence supporting purposeful juxtaposition of psalms reflects a positive phenomenon in the present context. If the compositions in the Psalter were randomly thrown together without any forethought, then many more instances of juxtaposed psalms lacking any logical association would be prevalent. As it stands, the relatively few cases that appear lend weight to the idea that most psalms in the Hebrew Psalter were organized with relational or interpretational strategies.

6. Although Isaiah fails to mention a specific name, Assyria is most likely intended because they frequently posed a threat to Israel during the days of Isaiah Ben Amoz; see Berlin, "Psalms," 848.

Isaiah prophesied and wrote during the monarchy, the psalm possesses few clues to its date, if any. Further obfuscating the issue is the fact that both compositions are laments, suggesting each author may have independently adopted a known literary form—introducing God's verbal response against the slander of an enemy to create a specific effect.

Psalm 13

UNLIKE THE PREVIOUS PSALM, no recommended instrumental accompaniment appears as part of the incipit, which simply reads, "For the choir director. A psalm of David." These same words connect Psalm 13 with both Psalms 12 and 14. As a lament, Psalm 13 is comprised of three stanzas, each one containing two verses. The Hebrew phrase עד אנה ("how long . . ."), which appears four times, opens the psalmist's rhetorical interrogation of God in the first stanza, vv. 1–2 [2–3]. The anguish of separation from God torments the author, as though he previously pleaded with the Most High, and still awaits deliverance from his plight. In the ensuing stanza, vv. 3–4 [4–5], the psalmist specifies the inevitable outcome of his abandonment: His enemy[1] gains victory over him, which ultimately results in the psalmist's death, and the enemy's continued exaltation over him. Closing the psalm, verses, vv. 5–6 [6–7] reveal a dramatic change as the psalmist declares statements of confidence and trust. Despite his feelings of abandonment and vulnerability, the psalmist discovers a newfound hope in God's faithfulness.

Thematically, the psalmist's repeated plea of "how long" triggers a degree of continuity between Psalms 12 and 13. Psalm 12 recalls an individual complaining to God about the increasing number of treacherous people who speak deceptively. As a response, God answers within the psalm, v. 5 [6], and the psalmist, accepting the divine response, speaks words of confidence and trust in return. The psalm's final verse, however, reflects an unchanged situation in which wickedness still exists on every

1. Although the psalm fails to record any explicit detail of the enemy's identification, a logical assumption is that the psalmist faces an unnamed illness that threatens his life. Consequently, the psalmist's human foes would then find themselves in a position to rejoice over him; see Craigie and Tate, *Psalms 1–50*, 142.

side. Thus, it appears from this final statement that God has not yet arisen as promised. Almost as a response, Psalm 13 opens with the psalmist pleading with God again asking, "How long, LORD? Will you forget me forever?" Through a continuous reading of the two compositions, the psalmist's question creates the illusion that his resolve to wait patiently draws to a close, and he again needs to plea for divine intervention.

Psalm 14

A GLANCE THROUGH SCHOLARLY literature quickly reveals that Psalm 14 represents one of the more challenging psalms to navigate in the Psalter, a characteristic that in all probability points to a complex history of alterations and additions. Overall, the literary character of Psalm 14 differs significantly from the laments experienced thus far in the Psalter. Rather than addressing God in the vocative, or second person, the psalm addresses the deity in the third person.[1] Psalm 14 begins with the definition of a fool as one who does not believe in God, or, more accurately, as one who behaves as though God ignores his actions. Later in the psalm, the psalmist links this character type with the "wicked," all evildoers. Verses 2–3 reflect a shift in scene, depicting God searching for men who seek after him, but ultimately no righteous individuals exist: All have turned away and become corrupt. The two main themes of the psalm established thus far in the composition, the wicked and God, intersect in vv. 4–6. Here, the psalmist condemns the actions of the wicked. They prey on God's people and refuse to call upon him; for that reason, their lives are filled with great terror. Despite the evil intentions of the godless, however, the Lord remains a refuge for the righteous,[2] and protects them. Verse 7,

1. Technically, the psalm represents a mixed type, where elements of both a lament and a wisdom psalm appear. Dahood, *Psalms I*, 80, recognizes both elements within it. Craigie and Tate, *Psalms 1–50*, 146, identify both genres, but maintain that the composition's origins lie in Israel's wisdom tradition. For the most part, scholars freely confess the difficulty in defining the genre, but wisdom and lament are commonly noted (e.g., VanGemeren, *Psalms*, 173; Ross, *Psalms*, 373). Certain commentaries additionally acknowledge a prophetic element in the psalm (see Clifford, *Psalms 1–72*, 88; McCann, "Psalms," 729).

2. The appearance of the "righteous generation" is surprising here because previously the Lord was unable to find any who sought after him. Issues like this are

the psalm's close, veers unexpectedly from the themes established in the previous section. As notions of individual protection fade, the psalmist completes his work with a plea for Israel's restoration and joy.

The relationship between Psalms 14 and 53 warrants attention at this point because the two texts reflect an unusually high number of shared words. Of the two psalms, scholarly consensus,[3] for the most part, understands Psalm 14 as the earlier of the two compositions, primarily due to the psalm's appearance in an earlier collection of Davidic psalms. The relationship between them, however, is not one of literary borrowing; rather, they represent variants of the same psalm. It appears as though an original work was copied, and at least two versions were inserted into independent collections. Through the passage of time, one or more editorial hands combined both collections as part of the Psalter reflected today in MT.

With regards to biblical interpretation, the final verse of Psalm 14 deserves some attention. Many scholars view it as an addition to the original work because,[4] as mentioned earlier, the surprise mention of Israel as a nation, and their need for deliverance, appears foreign to the psalm's main body.[5] If so, a later hand apparently altered the context and meaning of the original composition. Through this change, the fool and the evildoers mentioned in the psalm, though previously abstract, now specifically refer to the Babylonians, those keeping Israel captive.[6] Naturally, within this new context, the "righteous generation" (v. 5), and those to whom the Lord provides refuge (v. 6), relates specifically to Israelites living in captivity in Babylon.

---

indicative of the psalm's complex literary development.

3. See, for example, Keil and Delitzsch, *Psalms*, 1:202; Craigie and Tate, *Psalms 1–50*, 146–47, who additionally note Psalm 53's adoption into the musical director's collection as a further sign of lateness.

4. With respect to an editorial alteration, a psalm's ending is most vulnerable to change, usually by adding one or more verses. Berlin, "Psalms," 1296, states, "In antiquity, it was easiest to make additions at the end of a composition."

5. McCann, "Psalms," 730, discusses the notion, noting the possibility of a postexilic addition, adducing the phrase "restore the fortunes" as evidence. In biblical literature, this expression frequently suggests a context of restoration from major setbacks such as exile. He further quotes Jer 29:14; 30:3; Ps 85:2.

6. Both medieval and modern commentators recognize the final verse's specific association with the exile and Babylonian captivity. See, for example, Berlin, "Psalms," 1296; McCann, "Psalms," 730.

Whether or not the author intended to trigger recollections of events from Genesis 18 in his readers' minds cannot be determined with certainty. However, the connection still merits a closer look. Lexically, the word השקיף ("to look down") creates an ostensible link between the works. In both texts, a divine presence looks down upon a sea of unruly and malicious people, searching for signs of righteous individuals within humanity. Genesis 18:16 recalls the angels who Abraham had entertained. As they leave Abraham, they turn and look down (וישקיפו) on the city of Sodom before personally visiting the inhabitants to confirm the veracity of their reported disreputable behavior. In Psalm 14, the Lord looks down (השקיף) from heaven on the "sons of men" (v. 2) to see if any seek God. Reinforcing the link between the compositions is the root שחת, which depicts the corruptness of all mankind in the sight of the Lord in Psalm 14. In Genesis 18–19, even though it appears in the same stem, *hip'il*, it adopts the meaning of "destroy," which differs from the meaning expressed from the psalm. Notable in Genesis, however, is that the idea of destruction, reflected in the word השחית, serves as a leitmotif echoing throughout the account of Sodom and Gomorrah.[7]

Through this connection, the psalmist performs two noticeable transformations (assuming he was influenced by Genesis). The first one concerns the reapplication of the object of God's divine search. Instead of the inhabitants of a local area, Sodom and Gomorrah, the divine gaze falls upon all humanity. The detestable depravity performed by the inhabitants of Sodom and Gomorrah is implicitly transferred to all the inhabitants of the earth via the presumed intertextual link. Second, an implicit amplification occurs in the urgency of God aiding the poor and destitute. In the psalm, God is their refuge, where they seek and find shelter and protection (v. 6). Intensifying this notion, the image of God in Genesis is not one of protector, but of destroyer. God's defense of the poor extends beyond simply protecting the defenseless from their enemies, he also bears the capability and willingness to destroy them.

---

7. See Gen 18:28, 31, 32; 19:13, 14, 29.

Psalm 15

THE SOMBER TONE OF lament is again interrupted by Psalm 15, in the same way Psalm 8's praise disturbed a sequence of laments. Instead of dwelling on the malicious thoughts and intentions of the wicked and those oppressed by them, Psalm 15 turns towards the righteous and their deeds. The psalm represents a minor genre that scholars recognize as an entrance liturgy,[1] a genre that tethers the present psalm to Psalm 24. The opening verse of Psalm 15 poses a question that is answered in vv. 2–5a. Verse 1b asks, "O Lord, who may abide in your tent?",[2] constituting an inquiry as to who is fit, deserving, or able to live in God's presence, or what characteristics must an individual possess to dwell with God. Answering this question first comes a series of positive qualifications, behavioral characteristics a candidate must possess to gain access to the Lord's presence. Following the positive injunctions in v. 2, v. 3 presents a series of negative injunctions, behavior a candidate must avoid. These commands focus on an individual's relationship with his neighbor, and the way he speaks and interacts with them. The fourth verse alternates a negative characteristic with a positive injunction—specifying that the candidates must hate vile people but honor and fear the Lord. Verse 5a returns to the neighbor's treatment, introduced in v. 3, specifying that the

1. See McCann, "Psalms," 372; Ross, *Psalms*, 368; and Kraus, *Psalms 1–59*, 227, who adds the label of Torah liturgy. Theoretically, requirements did exist for entering a holy place in the ANE (Deut 23:1–8 [2–9]; 2 Chr 23:19). The present composition, however, fails to fit exactly in that mold, but could still be related. Other scholars recognize the wisdom qualities of the psalm, understanding it as a wisdom poem (see Craigie and Tate, *Psalms 1–50*, 150; VanGemeren, *Psalms*, 179).

2. If the psalm is indeed referring to the tent of meeting here, then it would reflect one of the oldest compositions in the Psalter.

righteous individual must not take advantage of others financially. Here, though, there is no mention of whether the psalmist concerns himself with Israelites or non-Israelites. The final portion of v. 5, and probably the most significant one with respect to the context of the Psalter, shifts to enumerate the benefits to those bearing the moral character stipulated within the psalm. In short, they are afforded the protection of the Lord, and are never shaken.

An instantly notable characteristic revealed here by the juxta-position of Psalms 14 and 15 concerns the contrast between the fool mentioned previously, and the righteous. For the most part, Psalm 14 dedicates itself to detailing the thoughts and behavior of the fool: They fail to consider God, turn aside from godly ways, act corruptly, consume the Lord's people, and do not call upon the Lord. Immediately following, Psalm 15 contrasts Psalm 14 by depicting the behavior of the righteous: They do not slander with their tongue, are not malicious towards their neighbor, do not lend money for profit, or take a bribe against the inno-cent. Together, the two compositions reflect a stark comparison between the wicked and the righteous, as found in Psalm 1[3] and other Israelite Wisdom literature.[4] Thus, the arranger, in this instance, may have had de-tailed familiarity with psalm composition together with Israel's wisdom traditions, and as a result, he juxtaposed contrasting behavioral patterns in contiguous psalms as a psalmist would for contiguous stanzas.

The overall structure of Psalm 15 highlights ten instructional state-ments, three positive, three negative, two positive, and then two negative; hence, readers are drawn to compare the psalm with the similar collec-tion of ten injunctions found in the Torah, specifically the Decalogue in Exodus and Deuteronomy.[5] A further examination of the relationships between the two, however, fails to solidify any real notion of literary bor-rowing between them. It is difficult to formulate a convincing argument

3. Biblical wisdom literature often contrasts good and evil behavior.

4. With an eye on preceding psalms, McCann, "Psalms," 732, argues that Psalm 15, "serves to portray the shape of the loves of those who have been mentioned fre-quently in preceding Psalms." Thus, the poor, afflicted, and oppressed mentioned in Pss 2:12; 5:11 [12]; 7:1; 9:9; and 10:2, for example, all exhibit qualities listed in Psalm 15. Furthermore, McCann detects a progressive relationship among Psalms 13–15, noting movement from the threat of being "shaken" (13:4), to the affirmation of God's presence among the righteous (14:5), to the portrayal of the righteous dwelling with God. Overall, the result is that they "shall never be shaken" (15:5).

5. Brueggemann and Bellinger, *Psalms*, 82, explicitly connect the psalm to the Decalogue tradition in the Pentateuch.

that the psalmist was specifically influenced by the Decalogue and sought to modify its contents for his own purposes. More realistically, the connection between the two simply stems from the choice of the number ten. This number widely represents notions of completion and wholeness in the Bible;[6] therefore, rather than specifically suggesting a connection to the Decalogue, the psalmist, presumably borrowed a known rubric for formulating injunctions and stipulations.[7]

Another literary connection deserving further attention concerns the relationship between Psalm 15 and Isa 33:14–16. The table below aligns the texts, comparing their common vocabulary:

Psalm 15	Isa 33:14–16
A Psalm of David. O LORD, who may abide [מי יגור] in Your tent? / Who may dwell [מי ישכן] on Your holy hill? / He who walks [הולך] with integrity, and works righteousness [צדק], / And speaks [דבר] truth in his heart. / He does not slander with his tongue, / Nor does evil to his neighbor, / Nor takes up a reproach against his friend; / In whose eyes [בעיניו] a reprobate is despised [נמאס], / But who honors those who fear the LORD; / He swears to his own hurt and does not change; / He does not put [נתן] out his money at interest, / Nor does he take a bribe against the innocent. / He who does these things will never be shaken.	Sinners in Zion are terrified; / Trembling has seized the godless. / "Who among us can live [מי יגור] with the consuming fire? / Who among us can live [מי יגור] with continual burning?" / He who walks righteously [הלך צדקות] and speaks [דבר] with sincerity, / He who rejects [מאס] unjust gain / And shakes his hands so that they hold no bribe; / He who stops his ears from hearing about bloodshed / And shuts his eyes [עיניו] from looking upon evil; / He will dwell on the heights, / His refuge will be the impregnable rock; / His bread will be given [נתן] *him*, / His water will be sure.

The combination of Hebrew words shown above is unique to these two contexts in the Hebrew Bible, a fact suggestive of literary borrowing.

6. Exodus utilizes a ten-plague rendition in recounting Israel's emancipation; similarly, Elkanah's expression denoting value and worth in 1 Sam 1:8b adopts the number ten, "Am I not better to you than ten sons?"

7. Regarding further potential connections to the Torah, a degree of priestly influence is discernible. The injunction against slander in v. 3 echoes Lev 19:16a, "You shall not go about as a slanderer among your people." Similarly, the command against usury in v. 5 recalls Lev 25:36–37 and Ezek 18:8, 13, 17; 22:12 (see also Miller, "Psalm 15"). It is difficult to assert direct literary borrowing between Leviticus and the psalm due to the broad range of the injunctions; for that reason, a designation of echo seems more prudent.

Further strengthening the case for literary borrowing is the context in which the common words and phrases appear. The opening phrase, מי יגור ("who may dwell"), establishes the qualifications of an individual to approach sacred space, a feature echoed in both texts. Similarly, the word הלך ("walks") in the context of behavior and דבר ("speaking") uprightly connect the compositions. Not all of the shared vocabulary, however, is similarly used; for example, the root מאס appears in *nipʿal* in Ps 15:4, "is despised," but its counterpart in Isaiah is a *qal*, "he rejects." Nevertheless, the similarity of the contexts in which the common words are found sparks interest.

Similarities between the two texts' structure also deserve mention. Both consist of three sections, even though their precise length varies. They open with statements questioning who is qualified for a certain privilege, with the same phrase appearing in both contexts, מי יגור ("who may dwell"). Following this are the regulatory conditions the person seeking the privilege must seek. Both texts demand behavioral requirements, which are formulated with negative and positive injunctions. So, for example, Isa 33:15 demands that candidates walk righteously (positive), speak with sincerity (positive), reject unjust gain (negative), shake their hands so they hold no bribe (negative), refuse to hear about bloodshed (negative), and refuse to look upon evil (negative). Similarly, amid Psalm 15's requirements, are the need to walk with integrity (positive); to practice righteousness (positive); to speak truth in one's heart (positive); not to slander with one's tongue, do evil to one's neighbor, or take up reproach against a friend (all negative). Finally, both pericopae close with a blessing or reward offered to the one who meets the required criteria. Psalm 15 offers protection: The one who complies will never be shaken; but Isaiah, in addition to protection, adds provisions of food and water (v. 16).

Naturally, along with the similarities between the texts, a few differences deserve mention. The blessing at the end of Isaiah's text appears noticeably longer than that of the psalm. Furthermore, the number of injunctions varies. Psalm 15, as noted earlier, contains ten in total, with six positive and four negative statements. Isaiah, on the other hand adopts six injunctions; moreover, the larger context in which the pericope appears contrasts with the psalm. Isaiah is framed within a context reflecting greater fear and trepidation, entering the Lord's presence poses a life-and-death situation. Leading up to the question-and-answer section, Isaiah states that sinners tremble in fear. Although Psalm 15 similarly echoes the notion of entering God's presence, i.e., to abide in his tent, the notions of fear and terror remain noticeably absent.

With respect to the relationship between the two texts, much uncertainty still exists concerning the vector of allusion, or whether the texts are related at all. Structurally one cannot deny the similarities, but this may simply arise from two authors utilizing a common structural or poetic format. The number of shared words and the common theme of entering the Lord's presence, however, continues to affirm a noticeably strong literary connection between them. With that said, two firm conclusions are possible. First, Psalm 15 bears more commonality with Isa 33:14–16 than with either of the two renditions of the Decalogue recounted in the Torah. Second, though the direction of borrowing remains uncertain, a degree of literary borrowing between these two works remains likely. The concrete dating of the psalm, as in numerous other instances, prevents us from drawing further conclusions. Both Psalm 15 and Isaiah 33 reflect products of the preexilic era, and though not conclusive, scholarly opinion leans slightly more towards the psalm predating Isaiah.[8]

Despite the views in favor of reading Psalm 15 as the source, one can construct an argument supporting the psalmist borrowing from Isaiah and adapting the prophet's words. The Isaiah pericope, which addresses the topic of eligibility regarding entering the Lord's presence, may have initially drawn the psalmist's attention. Yet it appears the original context clashed with his requirements. Consequently, he adapted it into a liturgical setting, transforming the notion of entering God's all-consuming presence into the context of coming into his presence in the temple precincts. Support for this literary restructuring stems from the refined presentation of the questions. The psalmist adopts a ten-condition entry formula, with six positive and four negative injunctions, whereas Isaiah uses only six conditions. It therefore seems more logical for an author to add to the six injunctions another four to create a more acceptable whole number, rather than subtracting four prerequisites to create a six-stipulation formula.

---

8. Avishur, "Chapter 15," 67, suggests Isaiah formed the source text, as does Kraus, *Psalms 1–59*, 266. Ultimately, no consensus arises, and Craigie and Tate, *Psalms 1–50*, 151, cautiously, lean towards the psalm representing the source.

Psalm 16

PSALM 16'S TITLE BREAKS the chain of similar titles preceding it. Instead of the simple specification, מזמור לדוד, ("a psalm of David") the psalm is called a מכתם ("mikhtam").[1] To the modern reader, the meaning of this term remains obscure, but the word, nevertheless, forges a connection with Psalms 56–60, which bear the same title. Several questions arise from this observation: Was Psalm 16 separated from the other psalms with the same title? Are there other common features within the whole group of psalms? Does the title imply that the psalms were intended to be read as a group?

Overall, Psalm 16's genre is difficult to determine with certainty, but one can recognize a few hallmarks of a song of confidence.[2] After an initial cry by the psalmist for divine protection, v. 1, he then proceeds to declare God's goodness and his sole dependence on the Lord in v. 2. Verse 3 introduces a stark change in direction, with the psalmist declaring his delight in the saints of the land. They contrast those who run after another god in v. 4; it is from individuals such as these that the psalmist seeks to separate himself and refuses even to mention them.[3] Verses 5–6

1. Obviously, much speculation arises concerning this expression's meaning. Some of the more commonly mentioned possibilities are: an inscriptional poem, a golden psalm, a silent prayer, or an atonement psalm. See Craigie and Tate, *Psalms 1–50*, 154, for a complete list.

2. The broad range of scholarly opinion reflects the difficulty in genre determination. Brueggemann and Bellinger, *Psalms*, 85, for example, refer to it as "a confession of trust in God." Craigie and Tate, *Psalms 1–50*, 156, on the other hand, call it a psalm of confidence, or a prayer of protection. Certain scholars believe the psalm functioned as a prayer recited after conversion to the religion of Israel; see, for example, Clifford, *Psalms 1–72*, 1; and Avishur, "Chapter 16," 70.

3. Overall, the psalm's disjunctive nature resists a seamless division into stanzas, a

adopt the metaphor of physical land inheritance; the psalmist declares the Lord himself as the righteous one's inherited portion, reflecting God's intrinsic value to the psalmist. Switching themes, vv. 7–9 concentrate on the psalmist's deeds that demonstrate his faith in God. Changing direction once again in vv. 10–11, the psalmist declares words of confidence and trust. This focus thematically brings us to the opening words of the psalm, but the psalmist shifts from his plea for protection to confidence in God's ability to protect him. All notions of fear and anxiety dissolve in the final verse as the psalmist ruminates on the pleasures afforded by God's right hand.

Despite an alternative form of the particle of negation, the psalmist's declaration in 16:8, בל אמוט ("I shall not be shaken") resonates with the declaration in the preceding psalm, "He who does these things [keeps the required ordinances] will never be shaken [לא ימוט]" (Ps 15:5b). Through this overlap, it is possible to associate the righteous behavior of Psalm 16's author with the righteous behavior stipulated by the author of Psalm 15 for those desiring to enter the Lord's presence: One who is blameless, speaks the truth, etc. Reading the two works together, therefore, it is possible to deduce that the author of Psalm 16 views himself as fulfilling the previous conditions; consequently, he is eligible to receive the benefit of being unshakable because, as Ps 15:5c states, "One who does these things will never be shaken." As a result, the juxtaposition of the two psalms reveals a transformation from an impersonal and general list of qualifications, as declared in Psalm 15, to a specific and practical example of an individual fulfilling the requirements in Psalm 16.

From a lexical viewpoint, a few additional words deserve some attention. In Ps 15:1b, the psalmist opens with the rhetorical question, "Who may dwell [ישכן] on Your holy hill?" Psalm 16:9, on the other hand, uses the verb to describe dwelling in safety and security, "My flesh also will dwell [ישכן] securely." Although the Hebrew verb שכן connects the two compositions and fortifies their association, doubts arise concerning the word's influence over an editor regarding their juxtaposition because the word frequently appears in the Psalter (twenty-nine times). However, a possibility that the same verb motivated the psalm's juxtaposition exists because the appearance of the root in consecutive

---

fact witnessed by the wide variation among the English translations. Despite the relatively simplistic summary of the psalm here, it reflects a variety of textual difficulties. Note particularly vv. 3–4 (see Berlin, "Psalms," 1297, for example).

psalms is rare. Before Psalms 15 and 16, the root appears in Ps 7:5 [6] and after this, in Ps 31:11 [12].[4]

---

4. The semantic idea of being in the presence of the Lord, unsupported by explicit linguistic evidence, creates a contact point between Psalms 15 and 16. Psalm 15 poses the question, "Who may abide in Your [the Lord's] tent," which implies dwelling in God's presence, abiding in the place where he lives, thus being near him. Psalm 16's final verse (v. 11) reflects the same theme as the psalmist proclaims the fullness of joy experienced in the presence of the Lord.

Psalm 17

PSALM 17 SEES ANOTHER break in psalm type according to the incipit. The opening line of the composition informs the reader that it is a תפלה לדוד, "a prayer of David." Although the title differs from the previous psalm, a similar title appears in Psalm 142:1, "Maskil of David [לדוד], when he was in the cave. A Prayer [תפלה]."[1]

In essence, Psalm 17 reflects the overall characteristics of an individual lament; however, in addition to interceding for himself, the petitioner pleads for his community.[2] After an initial appeal to gain God's attention, the psalmist emphasizes his own innocence in vv. 1–5, even to the point of inviting God to examine and test him. Verses 6–15, the psalm's main body, contain the cry for deliverance, an essential feature of the genre.[3] Within this section, vv. 12–13 distinguish themselves with an intriguing change regarding the identification of the enemy. Verse 11 suggests a multitude of people, stating, "They have now surrounded us in our steps," and this plurality is reflected earlier in the plea for assistance.

---

1. At this point, not much can be determined from the connection because the words repeated in Psalm 142 do not describe the type of psalm, but a petitioner's generic cry to God.

2. This designation is not widely disputed among scholars, though some prefer to detail the simple description. Craigie and Tate, *Psalms 1–50*, 161, specifically designate it as an innocent person's prayer for protection. Clifford, *Psalms 1–72*, 100, qualifies it as the lament of a petitioner hounded by merciless enemies. Some, however, like Ross, *Psalms*, 424, refrain from the specific designation of lament, and settle instead for describing it as a prayer song marked by petitions.

3. Note the word combination, נטה ("to incline"), אזן ("ear"), קרא ("to call"), and ענה ("to answer"), which associate Ps 17:6 with Ps 102:3 [4]; however, any connection between them purely exists through the vocabulary of lament, as opposed to specific biblical allusion.

On the other hand, vv. 12 and 13a suggest a singular foe, "He is like a lion . . . bring him low." Although a shift in the number of enemies seems somewhat strange, laments, in various other ways, are known for obscuring the identity of the persecutors. The final verse, a statement of confidence and hope, is also expected within the genre, where the psalmist expresses satisfaction in the hope of divine deliverance as though it has already transpired.

Regarding Psalm 17's relationship to the previous psalm, a number of lexical and thematic associations are apparent. The table below highlights some of the more prominent lexical connections:

Psalm 16	Psalm 17
I will bless the LORD who has counseled me; / Indeed, my mind instructs me in the night [לילות] (v. 7)	You have tried my heart; / You have visited *me* by night [לילה]; (v. 3a)
The LORD is the portion of my inheritance and my cup; / You support [תומיך] my lot (v. 5)	My steps have held [תמך] to Your paths (v. 5a)
Preserve me [שמרני], O God [אל], for I take refuge in you (v. 1)	I have called upon You, for You will answer me, O God [אל] . . . Keep me [שמרני] as the apple of the eye (vv. 6–8)
In Your presence is fulness [שׂבע] of joy (v. 11a)	From men of the world whose portion is in *this* life . . . They are satisfied [ישׂבעו] with children . . . I will be satisfied [אשׂבעה] with Your likeness when I awake. (vv. 14–15)

Beginning with the word תמך ("support"), and its distribution within the Psalter, one could construct a robust argument that it influenced an arranger to juxtapose these two compositions. Apart from Psalms 16 and 17, the word only appears in two places, Pss 41:12 [13] and 63:8 [9]; thus, lending weight to an instance of the principle of association, where the editor juxtaposes psalms together on the basis of a common word. Further strengthening the association between the psalms is the idea of comfort during the night (לילה) hours.[4] On one hand, the repetition of

4. See also Psalms 4 and 5.

words noted above may simply stem from a pool of stock words common to the genre; on the other hand, if this were true, one would expect the same words to be repeated in other psalms of the same genre. Such repetition, however, is absent, thus necessitating an alternative explanation.[5]

At least three options for the relationship between the two compositions exist. First, the connection reflects an instance of inner-biblical allusion: One author purposefully sought to connect his readers to the other author's work via repetition of certain key words. This proposition, though possible, seems unlikely because no obvious coherent logic exists for connecting the two compositions. With an instance of allusion, one expects to find a clear prayer-answer type relationship between the psalms, where the words in one composition appear in the form of a request, and then the same words resurface in the second composition in the form of a response. Instead, both psalms constitute requests or pleas for divine assistance. Second, and more plausible, a single author composed both works. Though he may not have been conscious of reusing the same words, they remained part of his active vocabulary as he penned the matching psalm. Third, along similar lines, two separate authors may have composed the psalms, where one knew of the other's work, and without specific intent to generate new meaning in his own work, borrowed words and phrases for his own composition. In any event, it is unlikely that the two compositions were written independently by separate authors in different eras without one knowing the work of the other. Furthermore, it seems obvious that the arranger of the two psalms recognized their similarities and juxtaposed them accordingly.

Regarding inner-biblical allusions, little can be said with surety. One connection deserving a mention, however, appears in 17:8, where the psalmist pleads with God for protection as though he were the "apple of his eye," and that God would hide him in the shadow of his wings (כנף).

---

5. Association between the two psalms has not escaped the attention of other commentators. Ross, *Psalms*, 418, notes the similarity, but focuses on the differences, arguing that Psalm 17 increases in urgency. Cohen, *Psalms*, 40, apparently reflects the same sentiment, but describes the dissonance as agitation.

Psalm 17	Deuteronomy 32
Keep me as the apple of the eye [כאישׁון . . . עין]; / Hide me in the shadow of Your wings [כנפיך] (v. 8)	He found him in a desert land, / And in the howling waste of a wilderness; / He encircled him, He cared for him, / He guarded him as the pupil of His eye [כאישׁון עינו]. / Like an eagle that stirs up its nest, / That hovers over its young, / He spread His wings [כנפיו] and caught them, / He carried them on His pinions. (vv. 10–11)

The expression אישׁון עין ("pupil of the eye") appears five times in the Bible, including Psalm 17. Three of those instances are in Proverbs (7:2, 9; 20:20), but their appearance there fails to reflect divine protection. Deuteronomy 32:10 represents the only other occurrence echoing God watching over and guarding a person or people. The author of Deuteronomy 32 depicts God caring for Israel at an early stage in their development as a nation; he devotes meticulous care in protecting them continually like the pupil of his eye. Further in v. 11, the author compares God to an eagle that carefully spreads his wings (כנפיו) over its young as an act of protection. Both expressions in the two locations, together with the similarity in the way they are used, suggest an active inner-biblical allusion. Though it is hard to establish an absolute date for the psalm, logic points to a composition date after Deuteronomy. Therefore, it appears the psalmist appropriated an image depicting divine protection of the nation and reapplied it to his personal situation. God's ability to defend the nation of Israel remains constant in the psalmist's mind; the same capability exists and is available in his day to protect those who seek him.

Similarly, it appears the psalmist borrowed words from another ancient song depicting divine national protection: Exodus 15, the song of Moses. Consider the following comparisons:

Psalm 17	**Exodus 15**
Wondrously [הפלה] show Your lovingkindness [חסדיך], / O Savior of those who take refuge at Your right hand [בימינך] / From those who rise up *against them.* (v. 7)	Who is like You among the gods, O LORD? / Who is like You, majestic in holiness, / Awesome in praises, working wonders [פלא]? / You stretched out Your right hand [ימינך], / The earth swallowed them. / In Your lovingkindness [בחסדך] You have led the people whom You have redeemed; / In Your strength You have guided them to Your holy habitation. (vv. 11–13)

The literary connection to Exodus, as shown above, reflects another biblical allusion. Three words and expressions—lovingkindness, right hand, and wonders—found in both texts only appear in three other biblical locations: Psalm 17, Exodus 15, and Psalm 98. Of the two potential sources, Exodus 15 and Psalm 98, the former presents itself as a more likely candidate because, as previously witnessed, a separate allusion exists to a Torah text. Additionally, the overall context of protection, further associates Psalm 17 with Exodus more than Psalm 98.[6]

Primarily, the Torah allusions above strengthen the psalmist's plea for protection from his enemies. Both texts to which he alludes are poetic recitations of God's intervention to protect his people, Israel, from their enemies. Exodus specifically recalls God's protection at the Sea of Reeds, when he split the sea enabling Israel to pass though on dry land, and subsequently closed the sea over Israel's enemies, the Egyptians. Deuteronomy presents a less specific recollection of Israel's humble beginnings in the desert, and God's role in watching over them and protecting them as they grew into a large nation.

In addition to protection, the notion of implied innocence transfers from the source texts to the psalm. Exodus 15 reflects an early stage of Israel's development as a nation and their relationship with God. Consequently, they had not yet accumulated their catalog of sin that began in earnest during the desert wandering period. Similarly, Deuteronomy 32 depicts the nation of Israel still in a young and innocent developmental phase. The idea of presumed innocence, and the divine protection it

---

6. A few commentators notice the Torah allusions but fail to discuss further their relationships. See Craigie and Tate, *Psalms 1–50*, 163; Cohen, *Psalms*, 40; McCann, "Psalms," 740.

warrants, plays an important role in the psalmist's composition. He too, like Israel, stands innocent before God, and declares it in v. 1b, "Give ear to my prayer, which is not from deceitful lips." From this place of innocence, the psalmist pleads for the protection it affords.

Despite the elements transferred from the source to uphold the psalmist's theme, an important act of interpretation deserves mention. Both contexts to which the psalmist alludes reflect corporate or national interests, but the psalmist reframes his sources into a personal and individual request for protection. In Ps 17:6 he says, "I have called upon You, for You will answer me, O God." For the psalmist, because God in the past actively protected his people during the exodus from Egypt, he can again act to protect an individual, a descendant of the desert generation.[7]

---

7. Two comments from scholars deserve mention at this point. Clifford, *Psalms 1–72*, 100, argues for a thematic connection among Psalms 15–17, generated through their concern with the temple. Psalm 15 concerns itself with examining one's conscience before entering the temple, then the delights of being in the temple find expression in Psalm 16. Finally, in Psalm 17 the psalmist describes being in God's presence, which reflects the possibility of a physical location in the proximity of the temple compound (see also VanGemeren, *Psalms*, 180, who notes that Psalm 15 anticipates themes—affirmations of integrity, dwelling in God's presence, and not being shaken—in the proceeding psalms). Even though the connection, once enumerated, is evident, it seems unlikely that an editor or arranger of the Psalter was influenced by these specific connections when aligning the works.

Psalm 18

PSALM 18 IS A royal psalm of thanksgiving[1] whose incipit, like Psalm 17, mentions David. However, as an interpretive key to understanding the whole composition, the title temporally locates the psalm at a specific juncture in Israel's literary history: Towards the end of David's life, when God had delivered him from all his enemies. Since the psalmist employs a rich variety of seemingly abstract metaphoric descriptions throughout the composition, linking specific acts of deliverance in the psalm to events in David's life presents the reader with a challenge.

Basically, the psalm divides into five sections.[2] Opening the song, vv. 2–6 [3–7] declare and establish God as a constant source of shelter and deliverance. Numerous times in this relatively brief section the reader stumbles across words and expressions depicting God as one who protects: "a rock," "a fortress," "a shield," "a stronghold" (v. 2 [3]), "saved from my enemies" (v. 3 [4]). Another notable feature of the section is its persistent adoption of the first-person pronoun and pronominal suffix, emphasizing a deeply personal and intimate expression of thanksgiving. The closing verse, v. 6 [7], of the opening stanza summarizes its contents, reiterating God's response to the psalmist's request.

Details of the divine response to the psalmist's plight appear in the second section, vv. 7–15 [8–16]. Here, the psalm employs theophany imagery to convey God stirring in heaven at the sound of the psalmist's plea. God's anger is aroused at the thought of his servant's distress. Smoke

---

1. Most commentators share this designation of the genre. See, for example, Clifford, *Psalms 1–72*, 105; Ross, *Psalms*, 437; Kraus, *Psalms 1–59*, 257.

2. In this proposed division, the present author prefers to overlook the commonly discussed division in the psalm between vv. 1–30 [1–31] and 31–50 [32–51].

emanates from his nostrils (v. 8 [9]), and he rides swiftly on the wings of the wind (v. 10 [11]). Theophany imagery like this resonates with poetic compositions such as Habakkuk 3 and Psalm 29. Although literary borrowing is not implied through these associations, the psalmist has chosen to adopt a common pattern for conveying God appearing in the fullness of his divine power and glory.

After God stirs in his anger and appears in section two, the following stanza, vv. 16–24 [17–25] recalls his actions. Two themes are prominent in this section. First, the divine rescue is re-emphasized with various expressions: "He drew me out of many waters" (v. 16b [17b]);[3] "He delivered me from my strong enemy" (v. 17a [18a]), "He rescued me" (v. 19b [20b]), etc. Although various acts of deliverance are stated, the reader remains in the dark concerning the specific instances in David's life to which the psalmist refers. Second, the psalmist labors to emphasize the reason for God responding to his plight: God acts because the psalmist walks blamelessly before him, or as v. 20a [21a] states, "The LORD has rewarded me according to my righteousness." Because of his innocence and upright behavior, the psalmist qualifies for divine protection and deliverance.

Moving on from the psalmist's deliverance, focus gradually shifts in vv. 25–34 [26–35], detailing further aspects of God's character and abilities, especially how he empowers the psalmist for battle. God enables the psalmist to perform almost like a comic-book hero in battle. With divine assistance the psalmist can "leap over a wall," (v. 29 [30]), run securely on high places (v. 33 [34]), and "bend a bow of bronze" (v. 34 [35]). In this description, the author resists portraying God as one stirring from heaven to fight his battles, rather the depiction demonstrates God providing strength, courage, and power to the psalmist so he can fight for himself against his enemies.

Then vv. 35–45 [36–46] detail the battle, and the psalmist's defeat of those who rose against him: He pursues his enemies, (v. 37 [38]), thrusts them through so they could not rise (v. 38 [39]), beating them as fine as dust (v. 42 [43]). Throughout the conflict, however, the psalmist remains steadfast in recognizing his divine aid: "Your right hand upholds me" (v. 35b [36b]); "You enlarge my steps under me" (v. 36a [37a]); "You have delivered me from the contentions of the people" (v. 43a [44a]).

---

3. Taking this literally, one would assume a deliverance at sea (see Clifford, *Psalms 1–72*, 105), even if sailing were not an activity naturally associated with David, with whom the psalm's incipit connects the contents.

The final section veers towards a general theme of praise, and the words in vv. 46–50 [47–51] resonate with the incipit. Setting the context for the psalm, the title places the composition in David's mouth towards the end of this life as he reflects on all God has done for him.[4] In the final verses, expressions such as "subdues peoples under me" (v. 47b [48b]) and "You lift me above those who rise up against me" (v. 48b [49b]), resonate with the context of a king reflecting on a lifetime of divine assistance. Furthermore, the final verse specifically mentions the name David, which creates an inclusion for the whole composition and relates the events recorded within the composition to King David himself.

The relationship between Psalm 18 and 2 Samuel 22 is not one of allusion, so to speak, where a single author appropriated words, phrases, or ideas from an earlier work, reshaping and perhaps reinterpreting them into his new context.[5] Due to the remarkably high number of lexical similarities between the compositions and their precision, the two songs reflect two versions of the same composition. Despite this conclusion, the differences between the works warrant an explanation. While certain variations between the versions are easily explained—such as the presence and absence of *matres lectionis*—other alterations, such as alternative and additional vocabulary items, resist a simplistic explanation. Three reasonable possibilities can explain the relationship between the works. [6] One, the psalm represents the original composition, and the author of Samuel altered it directly before blending the psalmist's song into

4. A questionable element speaks against Davidic authorship. Verse 6 [7] recalls God hearing the cry of the psalmist from the temple (היכל), but this structure was not erected during David's lifetime.

5. Similarly, connections are noticeable between the psalm and other poetic texts embedded within narrative. Compare, for example, Psalm 18 with Exodus 15, Deuteronomy 32, Judg 5:4–6, Isa 30:27–28, and Habakkuk 3. Such similarities are not allusions, but a reflection of various authors reusing common theophany motifs depicting God's supernatural intervention to deliver. A perceptible adaptation in Psalm 18's and 2 Samuel's renditions concerns the target of divine intervention: an individual, as opposed to the nation of Israel.

6. Regarding the composition's date, scholars, for the most part, agree that the psalm bears the hallmarks of an ancient poem, possibly originating as far back as the ninth or tenth century BCE. Klaus, "Chapter 18," 76, leans towards an early date for the composition. Berlin, "Psalms," 1299, even suggests that it is one of the oldest psalms in the Psalter. Kraus, *Psalms 1–59*, 258, similarly opts for a preexilic date, and additionally mentions the possibility of a long redactional history. Because the psalm is old, the differences between it and 2 Samuel's version may result from independent oral transmission developments.

the narrative of David's life. Two, the composition in 2 Samuel reflects the original, and the psalmist or an arranger adapted it before juxtaposing it with Psalms 17 and 19. Three, an original composition, in either oral or written form, sourced both the version on display in 2 Samuel and in the Psalter. Before insertion into their final literary homes, both arrangers had the option to alter the source. Of these three possibilities, the present author tentatively leans towards the third option, simply because 2 Samuel 22, as a poetic text, is not entirely organic to its surrounding narrative. Were the song composed by the author of the surrounding narration, one would expect more decisive and detailed literary connections between the song and the events in David's life. Thus, before the reader lies the result: a single composition reflecting minor stylistic, linguistic, and poetic variations appearing in two separate literary contexts.[7]

To be sure, as one reads through the psalm, numerous thematic elements and echoes accord well with its presumed historical context, the life of David. Beginning with Ps 18:2 [3], the psalmist declares that God is his סלע ("rock") and his fortress. Notwithstanding the frequency with which this metaphor appears in the Psalter,[8] added significance arises with respect to David's life. In 1 Sam 23:25–28, Saul pursues David in the desert of Maon, where it is said that David came down to הסלע ("the rock") to seek refuge. Later, when Saul receives word of an attack by the Philistines against another Israelite territory, he is forced to turn away from pursuing David, thus allowing David to escape. For that reason, the name of the place where Saul abandoned his search for David becomes known as the Rock of Escape or separation (1 Sam 23:28). Because Psalm 18 adopts a divine perspective of the incident, its metaphorical representation of God as a rock additionally reflects a practical reality: Through the physical rock, God provided David with a figurative rock of deliverance. Furthermore, Psalm 18's specific recollection of Saul in the title substantiates the connection between the psalm and David's deliverance at Maon.

Further reflections of David's and Saul's conflict appear in Ps 18:17 [18], with the words, "He delivered me from my strong enemy, / And

7. Scholarly consensus on the matter varies. Craigie and Tate, *Psalms 1–50*, 172, suggest that Samuel reflects the earlier version, as does Cohen, *Psalms*, 43. Kraus, *Psalms 1–59*, 256, on the other hand, leans towards Psalm 18 being older, and "closer to the prototype." A cursory analysis of the linguistic alterations fails to yield any conclusive evidence of LBH used in either composition.

8. See, for example, Pss 32:4; 42:10.

from those who hated me [מִשֹּׂנְאַי], for they were too mighty for me."
From the account in 1 Sam 19:10, Saul's jealousy of David increases as
the latter begins his ascent to kingship. Although it is not explicitly stated
with the Hebrew שׂנא ("to hate"), this verb undoubtedly reflects their relationship. The book of Samuel recalls that Saul kept a jealous eye upon
David (1 Sam 18:9); moreover, on at least two occasions he tried to kill
David by thrusting him with a spear (1 Sam 18:10–11; 19:10). Notably,
at this stage in their relationship, Saul represented the dominant force,
and if David wrote the psalm, he would aptly describe Saul as "my strong
enemy" (Ps 18:17).

Events relating to Saul again echo in v. 41 [42], which recalls God
destroying David's enemies, those who cried to God for help, but he did
not answer. This verse reflects Saul's final battle against the Philistines; 1
Sam 28:6 recalls Saul's desperation as he sought God for advice on how
to proceed with the battle, but the Lord ignored him. Consequently,
through desperation he consults a medium to raise the spirit of Samuel.
Saul's actions in 1 Samuel 28 specifically recall an enemy of David who
calls to God but receives no answer; furthermore, Saul's subsequent death
allows David to surpass his enemy and ascend to the throne. Reflecting
David's ascension to the throne, Ps 18:43 [44] depicts God elevating the
psalmist's status, appointing him head of the nations. In this context, the
designation "head of the nations" surely implies an elevation to a ruling
status of kingship or above.

In addition to the alternate version of the song in 2 Samuel 22,
Ps 18:1 connects to 2 Samuel 8, with a surprising number of parallels.
Psalm 18's incipit provides a temporal framework for the psalm's context, locating the events at a time when the Lord had defeated David's
enemies. Later in the composition, the scope of divinely aided victories
broadens as the psalmist recalls subduing many nations, "A people who I
have not known serve me" (v. 43c [44c]), and "Foreigners submit to me"
(v. 44b [45b]). Such references echo events in 2 Samuel 8, which mentions David's defeat and subjugation of various nations. In addition to the
Philistines (v. 1), it mentions Moab (v. 2); Hadadezer, the king of Zobah
(v. 3); and David's placement of garrisons in Edom and their subjection
to him (v. 14). Amid the description of God defeating the psalmist's
enemies in v. 41 [42], stands the somewhat peculiar phrase stating that
some of these enemies even cried out unto God himself for help against
the psalmist. Naturally, one would think in the immediate context that
foreign enemies of the psalmist were compelled to call upon the name of

their own gods for assistance, but that is not the case here. If, however, Saul is included among these foreign adversaries, then he would fit the description presented by the psalmist. As an Israelite, from the tribe of Benjamin, he would have called on God for help. Framing Saul as an enemy of David constitutes a significant part of the psalm's theme, as previously mentioned, so the reference to enemies calling out to God for mercy further solidifies the connection to Saul.

David's conflict with his own people echoes in v. 43a [44a], "You have delivered me from the contentions of the people." Here, in contrast to the second part of the verse, the danger emanates not from other nations, but from those who David led. By intimating strife from within, the psalmist recalls incidents such as 1 Sam 30:6, where, after the Amalekites raid David's camp, his own men band together with the intention of stoning him. After David seeks God's advice (1 Sam 30:8), however, he is delivered from the threat of his own men. Similarly, the verse recalls the civil war that erupted in his kingdom when his son, Absalom, revolted against him seeking to overthrow and kill him (2 Samuel 15–18). Yet despite these things, the psalmist declares that the Lord delivered David and elevated him to the position of king.

Verse 50 [51] triggers a final thematic connection between Psalm 18 and events in David's life, recalling God's steadfast love for his anointed (למשיחו), one specially chosen to rule as king over his people. Here, the declaration of David as God's anointed recalls 1 Sam 16:13a, "Then Samuel took the horn of oil and anointed him [וימשח אתו] in the midst of his brothers." Supplementing this echo, other locations in the book of Samuel refer to David specifically as his anointed (2 Sam 19:21; 23:1).[9]

With all the similarities and literary echoes between the current psalm and the life of David, one apparent contradiction deserves mention. Psalm 18:21–24 [22–25] flies in the face of David's life as recorded in the book of Samuel. Psalm 18 suggests David led a blameless and guilt-free life. Verse 20 [21], for example claims, "The LORD has rewarded me according to my righteousness; / According to the cleanness of my hands He has repaid me." Statements like these overlook and gloss over the premeditated murder of Uriah the Hittite, the mismanagement of his own family, and his ill-advised decision to count the number of fighting men in Israel. In this regard, Psalm 18's author reflects compositional

---

9. Second Samuel 2:4; 5:17.

tendencies of the Chronicler, who similarly glosses over negative incidents occurring within the life of David.

At this juncture, it is important to note that without the explicit reference in the incipit to David's reign, and the corresponding reference to David at the end, the events within the psalm itself remain vague enough to apply to various Israelite kings. The inclusion of these references, however, compels readers to generate thematic literary connections between the images presented in the psalm and events in the life of King David.

Overall, the psalm, reflected in 2 Samuel 22, appears after a portrayal of David's final battles with the Philistines and the acts of his mighty men. Reading the psalm after these events illuminates the incipit, recalling David's words when the last of his battles, or those of Israel during his rule, ended. In this context, the psalm guides the reader, leading one to understand that despite the magnificent and heroic deeds of David's mighty men, God ultimately bears primary responsibility for David's victories in war.

With respect to juxtaposition, a notable thematic link appears between Psalms 18 and 17 that deserves mention. Psalm 17 dwells upon and develops ideas of the psalmist's individual righteousness before God. The psalmist in this composition, as part of the lament genre, persistently declares his innocence before God, as well as his determination to turn from sinful men and ungodly behavior. Verse 4b states, "I have kept from the paths of the violent" and v. 5a reads, "My steps have held fast to your paths." At the beginning of the psalm, these declarations underpin the ensuing request for deliverance. Because of the psalmist's ardent dedication to walking uprightly in the ways of the Lord, God—adhering to an assumed principle of retribution—is somehow obliged to honor the psalmist's behavior by protecting and delivering him. Echoes of the principle of retribution surface again in the third stanza, vv. 16–24 [17–25] of Psalm 18. This section presents a lucid statement of God's relationship with the righteous and just individual. For the psalmist, God provides protection in the day of disaster (v. 18 [19]), bringing him forth into an open place (v. 19 [20]). Moving beyond simply recounting God's actions on behalf of the psalmist, the psalm provides a rationale for divine intervention. For the author, God acts because of the psalmist's innocence, or "cleanness of . . . hands" (v. 20 [21]). The notion that God delivers him because of his righteousness ultimately finds expression in 18:24 [25], "Therefore the LORD has recompensed me according to my righteousness, / According to the cleanness of my hands in his eyes." Verse 24 [25] emphasizes God's desire to reward righteousness with deliverance, a blessing the psalmist enjoys due to his persistence in avoiding iniquity.[10]

In the Psalter's context, Psalm 18 provides a degree of completion for the preceding composition. Psalm 17, an individual lament, lacks any sense of response to the psalmist's pleas for divine protection. Specifically, the psalmist calls for God to wondrously show his steadfast love (v. 7), and further pleads for God to arise and confront his enemy (vv. 13). Building on this request, Psalm 18 demonstrates exactly what the previous psalm requested. Although the same linguistic markers remain absent, God is portrayed as rising up to the psalmist's aid, and doing so in magnificent and awe-inspiring fashion via a physical appearance that causes all creation to quake.

10. Klaus, "Chapter 18," 76, suggests that the psalms were juxtaposed according to a common theme, the declaration of the psalmist's own righteousness, which appears in both Psalms 17 and 18.

Psalm 19

PSALM 19'S TITLE CREATES a rudimentary link with its predecessor via the incipit, למנצח מזמור לדוד ("For the choir director. A psalm of David"). All three words appear in Psalm 18's title, though additional words link Psalm 18 to specific events in David's life. The precise wording in Psalm 19's title opens a brief collection of psalms with the same incipit, Psalms 19–21.[1]

Presenting readers with a somewhat enigmatic composition, Psalm 19 appears blatantly divided with respect to its theme.[2] Verses 1–6 [2–7] proclaim how creation itself, especially the heavenly bodies, persistently declares God's greatness and splendor. Unlike the expected pattern found in biblical songs of praise, creation, as opposed to Israel, raises its voice in praise and adoration. Nothing, according to the psalmist's perspective, remains concealed from exposure to the greatness of God, and nothing hides from his splendor. Within the first section, God's revealed glory extends, reaching to the ends of the world, "Their line has gone out through all the earth, and their utterance to the end of the world" (v. 4a [5a]).

Contrasting the theme of creation expressing God's magnificence, the second part of the psalm focuses on the benefits and intrinsic value of divine instruction; thus, a composition praising God's law follows a

---

1. An interesting question arises concerning the psalms' titles. If they are indeed secondary, then why do these specific compositions have a title different from the surrounding works?

2. The psalm relates both to the creation motif, as discussed in Psalm 8, and the Torah theme reflected in Psalm 1. Kraus, *Psalms 1–59*, 269–72, treats the composition as a unity, but suspects that two songs merged: a preexilic song together with a postexilic addition. Moreover, he notes a degree of interpretation involved, where the psalmist adapts ancient Near East sun worship traditions into the monotheistic belief of the sun as a created entity subservient to and praising YHWH.

hymn of praise. Verses 7–10 [8–11] contain a formula that first lauds a quality to God's instruction (e.g., "The law of the LORD is perfect") and continues with a resulting benefit (e.g., "restoring the soul"). Because of the deliberate structure, synonyms for divine instruction, such as תורה ("law"), משפט ("judgments"), and עדות ("testimonies"), litter the entire section.[3] As a climax to the unit, v. 10 [11] contains two cola focused on reemphasizing the precious value of the law: It is more desirable than gold and sweeter than honey. The final four verses develop this idea by personalizing the values of the Torah,[4] moving from abstract statements proclaiming the law's goodness, to concrete and practical expressions of its benefits to the psalmist. For the author, God's Torah represents a manifestation of the divine will; accordingly, through his obedience to it, the psalmist remains under divine guidance, purification, and protection. The psalmist's expression of gratitude appears in the closing verse, as he recognizes the benefits of divine instruction and offers words of thanksgiving in appreciation.

Despite the stark topical contrast between the psalm's two halves, one theme, divine wisdom, undoubtedly unifies the otherwise disparate sections. In the first half of the composition, divine wisdom orders creation along its set path, a theme Proverbs explicates well, "The LORD by wisdom founded the earth, / By understanding He established the heavens" (Prov 3:19). Similarly, divine wisdom reveals itself in God's law, his Torah, the theme of the second part of the psalm.

While the first half of Psalm 19 resonates with other creation psalms, such as Psalms 8, 104, and 148, the claim of literary borrowing remains only a distant possibility. Psalm 19 focuses on present and everyday aspects of creation—specifically the sun as it rises and sets each day—elaborating on God's involvement in maintaining the created order. More specifically, the psalm almost detaches the elements of creation from operating under God's control and portrays them instead as separate entities responding to God in acts of praise and worship.[5] More-

---

3. A Torah psalm amid a group of royal psalms—Psalms 18, 20, and 21—reflects Deut 17:14–20, where the idea of kingship mingles with the laws and instruction of God.

4. VanGemeren, *Psalms*, 218–19, collects these verses into a third section of the psalm, forming a prayerful reflection.

5. Craigie and Tate, *Psalms 1–50*, 182, suggest the possibility of Psalm 19 functioning as a subtle elaboration of Genesis 1–3, and extrapolate comparisons between the Torah and the tree of knowledge, with the former proving superior to the latter.

over, the psalm's primary emphasis on the sun, its portrayal as a hero and its movements across the sky, are unique among the creation psalms.

The notion of creation reacting to God's presence represents an important theme that possibly influenced an arranger in organizing Psalms 18–19. Although elements of the creation motif appear in Psalm 18, God's relationship and interaction with creation elements undoubtedly generates a nexus between these textual units. Psalm 18 recalls the earth's fear as it reels and rocks at his appearance (v. 7 [8]), and the foundations of the world are laid bare (v. 15 [16]). Before him lightning flashes and hail descends from the sky, preparing a way for his intrusion into the affairs of men, intervening to rescue the psalmist. Resonating with Psalm 18's depiction, though adapting the severity and violent jarring nature of the response, Psalm 19 presents creation responding to God's presence in praise and vocal adoration as opposed to fear. The heavens and the sky proclaim his praise in a wholly positive context.[6]

---

6. Certain words repeat between the compositions, but for the most part they reflect ubiquitous vocabulary throughout the Psalter, e.g., עין ("eye"), מי ("who"), and צור ("rock"). The single occurrence of a rare word between the two psalms is תבל ("world"), a poetic term for earth. Even in this instance, however, it is difficult to argue that its appearance influenced an editor. In addition to the thematic connection mentioned above, however, one could argue that a "declaration of innocence" theme unites the two compositions. Psalm 18:20–24 [21–25] reflects the psalmist's declaration of his own innocence; because of his blamelessness, God proved himself faithful by dramatically delivering him from his distress. On the other hand, Ps 19:12–13 [13–14] adopts a slightly less self-righteous reflection of innocence. Here, though the psalmist still proclaims his own innocence, he achieves it through God's intervention, and not purely via his own efforts (v. 13).

Psalm 20

PSALM 20, A SONG of confidence, opens with a series of jussives invoking the Lord to visit, strengthen, and support the psalmist and his community. The combination of sequential jussive forms, so far unseen in the Psalter, creates delimiting markers for the first section of the composition, vv. 1–5 [2–6]. From this attitude of petition, an unforeseen change in circumstances diverts the tenor of the psalm in v. 6 [7], spurring the psalmist to declare, "Now I know that the LORD saves His anointed," words that open the second stanza (vv. 6–9 [7–10]). This transformation to a more personal statement of confidence that the psalmist's petition has been heard suggests a tangible experience of God's ability to save. Employing antithetical parallelism, the psalmist proceeds in the following two verses to contrast the hope rooted in divine deliverance with that found in military might. His conclusion, which encourages him, is that only God's power is sufficient for protection. The final verse turns again to petition, as the psalmist offers supplication for the king, in addition to the community that recites the prayer.[1] The specific mention of the king together with the reference to the Lord's anointed (v. 6 [7]) generates a consensus among commentators that the composition is a royal psalm.[2]

Although the word סוס ("horse") appears in four other locations in the Psalter, it is only in Ps 33:17 where the image specifically represents

---

1. Craigie and Tate, *Psalms 1–50*, 185, suggest the psalm was recited before a king went out to battle, thus constituting a prayer for success in war and a safe return. Their presumed context aptly unites the two sections of the psalm.

2. See, for example, McCann, "Psalms," 755. Kraus, *Psalms 1–59*, 278, refers to it as a psalm that relates to the king, citing the appearance of מלך ("king") and משיחו ("his anointed"), and further refers to it as a prayer song and a song of thanksgiving. Avishur, "Chapter 20," 88, understands it as a psalm of the king.

false hope, an apparent source of help that fails to deliver, "A horse is a false hope for victory; / Nor does it rescue anyone by its great strength."[3] Isaiah 31:1 adopts the same metaphor, "Woe to those who go down to Egypt for help / *And* rely on horses, / And trust in chariots because they are many / And in horsemen because they are very strong, / But they do not look to the Holy One of Israel, nor seek the LORD!" Although possible, it remains unlikely that any literary borrowing occurred among these three compositions.[4]

A connection between Psalms 19 and 20 that deserves attention concerns the repetition of the jussive. It surfaces at the end of Psalm 19, where the psalmist opens his request with the words "Let the words of my mouth . . ." The appearance of the modal form here blends with the opening verses of Psalm 20, "May the LORD answer you . . ." With this connection in mind, it is hard to ignore a literary discourse between the two psalms. Psalm 19 ends with a first-person singular request to God for the psalmist's words to be acceptable almost as a verbal sacrifice placed on the altar. Psalm 20 tangibly responds to this request with a third person voice supporting the petition in Psalm 19. Thus, in Ps 20:3 [4], "May He remember all your meal offerings," the psalmist draws alongside the petitioner in Psalm 19, merging his request.[5]

---

3. In Ps 32:9, the horse symbolizes a dumb animal that cannot understand or respond to instruction. Psalm 147:10 presents the horse as a symbol of strength, along with the thighs of man, but contrasts these human symbols of power with the desires of God, he prefers those who fear him and wait on his kindness.

4. It is worth mentioning here that Acts 10:4 appears to echo Psalm 20. In Acts, Cornelius, a righteous Roman officer, is told in a vision that his prayers and offerings have been accepted by God and that he has remembered them, which is to say God responded favorably to them. Responding to petitions in this way reflects the prayer of the psalmist, who asks that God remembers his sacrifices (v. 3 [4]), and consequently fulfills his petitions (v. 5 [6]).

5. The word שמים ("heaven") connects Psalm 20 with the two previous compositions. Outside of these psalms, the word appears earlier in Psalm 14, and then after in Psalm 33. Regarding the theme of heaven, one could argue that it connects Psalms 19–20. In Psalm 19, the heavens declare the glory of God, and these same heavens constitute the source of the psalmist's help in Psalm 20, "He will answer him from His holy heaven" (v. 6). Additionally, the thematic nexus between Psalms 20 and 18 warrants attention. Psalm 20, a royal psalm, resonates with Psalms 18 and 21 through a common genre. This grouping raises questions concerning the placement of Psalm 19, which has no obvious associations with kingship or royalty. The natural, but otherwise unprovable, assumption generated from the present sequencing of psalms is that Psalm 19 reflects a late insertion into an established collection of three psalms featuring kingship as a dominant theme.

Psalm 21

IN A SIMILAR VEIN to Psalm 20, Psalm 21 reveals signs of a composition honoring a king, and consequently it receives the designation of a royal liturgy.[1] An extended chiasmus delineates the psalm's opening section creating an inclusion around the psalm with the sequence "the LORD" and "king," appearing in v. 1, which then reverses in v. 7 [8]. Within this section, the psalmist declares the blessings the Lord has bestowed upon the king, such as, granting all his desires (v. 2 [3]), a crown of gold (v. 3 [4]), and length of days (v. 4 [5]). Then in v. 7, as a possible response to the perceived blessing, the king trusts in the Lord. The following section, vv. 9–13, details acts of divine assistance offered to the king. God will destroy his enemy's offspring (v. 10 [11]) and turn his divine bow against them (v. 12 [13]). Then the composition closes with an exclamation of praise that recalls the opening verse with the words יהוה בעזך ("O LORD, in your strength," v. 13 [14]), creating an inclusion with v. 1 [2], reminding the reader that anything the king accomplishes in his life results from divine assistance.

Reading Psalm 21 immediately after Psalm 20 presents a lucid thematic connection: the intimate relationship between God and king. More specifically, the juxtaposition illuminates God's willingness to grant the king his desires. In Ps 20:4 [5] it is expressed with the words יתן לך כלבבך וכל עצתך ימלא ("May he grant you your heart's desire, / And fulfill all your counsel"). These words correspond with Ps 21:2a [3a]: תאות לבו נתתה לו

---

1. See Craigie and Tate, *Psalms 1–50*, 189, who further recognize themes relating to songs of thanksgiving and confidence; and VanGemeren, *Psalms*, 229. Some have assigned other related genres to the psalm, including McCann, "Psalms," 757, who calls it a royal psalm; and Clifford, *Psalms 1–72*, 118–19, who further specifies a royal psalm of thanksgiving.

("You have given him his heart's desire"), and though the words appearing in each composition differ, the intent remains the same.[2]

Furthering the God-king thematic nexus is a request-response relationship between the same two psalms. Psalm 20 reflects a scene in which a king and his army prepare for battle. In this context, the psalm functions as a petition to the Lord to bless and protect the king on his campaign. As part of the plea, the composition declares the king's and the community's ultimate dependence on the Lord, not on horses and chariots. The final line of the psalm ends with a special request to save the king. Following this, Psalm 21 reports of the king rejoicing in the salvation of the Lord and receiving the desires of his heart, almost a direct response to Psalm 20. The first section of Psalm 21 responds to the requests and petitions in the previous psalm: Victory and success in battle were requested and granted.[3]

Having identified the relationship between these psalms, one can now surmise the rationale behind their sequencing. First, it is difficult to imagine that independent authors separated by time and location wrote the psalms, and by sheer coincidence they reflect such a close thematic and lexical similarity. For that reason, alternative explanations are necessary. One possibility is that Psalm 21's author sought to compose a complement to Psalm 20, a psalm that demonstrates God's faithfulness in responding to the request for the king's protection in Psalm 20. Another realistic possibility is that a single author penned both psalms to complement each other, and purposefully sequenced them in their original arrangement. At a later stage, they were incorporated into the present arrangement of psalms in their preserved order. Of the two options above, the latter presents a more probable scenario.

A series of lexical and thematic associations further connect Psalm 21 with David and his battle against Rabbah in 2 Sam 12:29–30. Second

---

2. The verb חדה ("to make glad," 21:6 [7]), which is rare in the Old Testament, generates a tenuous link to Exod 18:9, where Jethro rejoices over God's deliverance of Israel from Pharaoh's armies. The connection here arises from the notion of a leader rejoicing in God. The only other place the verb occurs is Job 3:6, where Job despises the day of his birth, not wishing any happiness upon it.

3. It is possible to read the psalm's second section in the past tense, even as Dahood (*Psalms I*, 130–34) does. This understanding reflects the king further rejoicing in God for defeating and driving away his enemies. Thus, the request-response relationship between the two compositions remains preserved. Keil and Delitzsch, *Psalms*, 1:291, suggest further similarities between the two psalms: opening with synonymous parallelism, increasing in fervor, closing with an ejaculatory cry to the Lord, the reference to the king as המלך and the use of rare forms of expression.

Samuel recalls David gathering his army together to fight against the
Ammonite city of Rabbah.

Psalm 21:1–3	2 Samuel 12:29–30
O LORD, in Your strength the king [מלך] will be glad, / And in Your salvation how greatly he will rejoice! / You have given him his heart's desire, / And You have not withheld the request of his lips. *Selah*. / For You meet him with the blessings of good things; / You set a crown [עטרה] of fine gold [פז] on his head [ראש].	So David gathered all the people and went to Rabbah, fought against it and captured it. Then he took the crown [עטרה] of their king [מלך] from his head [ראשו]; and its weight *was* a talent of gold, and *in it was* a precious stone; and it was *placed* on David's head [ראש]. And he brought out the spoil of the city in great amounts.

After defeating the city and capturing the king, David acquires the
crown (עטרה) fashioned from gold (זהב)[4] from the king (מלך) and places
it on his own head (ראש). The scenario depicted in David's conquest unquestionably resonates with the psalm, where the king is blessed with salvation and deliverance from the battle, in addition to a crown of fine gold
for his head. Whether or not the acts in 2 Samuel inspired the psalmist is
a moot point, but in any event, a thematic and lexical connection exists.
Furthering these connections by viewing the events of 2 Samuel through
the lens of the psalm generates a degree of interpretation. In the narrative
account of David capturing the Ammonite capital, no mention of God
and his part in the events appears. Through the eyes of the psalmist, however, the same situation highlights God's role: He blesses the king with
victory and bears responsibility for crowning him with the Ammonite
king's crown.

---

4. The word פז in the psalm is a poetic word for gold.

Psalm 22

THE HOPE OF DIVINE deliverance in the second portion of Psalm 21 un-
ceremoniously crashes to the ground with failed expectation expressed
in the opening words of Psalm 22, "My God, my God, why have You
forsaken me?" These words establish a theme of desperation and abandonment that echoes throughout the opening two verses.[1] Tempering
the first two verses, the ensuing section, vv. 3–5 [4–6], recalls God's past
faithfulness, remembering Israel's forefathers who called to God and received his deliverance—the same God the psalmist addresses with his
entreaty. Moving from the remembrance of past deliverance, the psalmist returns to recounting his misery in the following section, vv. 6–18
[7–19], but this time in far more detail. The reader specifically learns of
the enemies who surround the psalmist, taunting him with their words,
even suggesting that God cannot save him. Verses 19–21 [20–22] reflect
a pivotal point in the composition, and the psalmist's tone dramatically
shifts.[2] At this juncture, it appears as though he experiences the help he
so desperately seeks. Within this section, the psalmist transitions from
desperation, with cries of "Do not be far off" and "Deliver my soul from
the sword," to reassurance, stating, "From the horns of the wild oxen You
answer me." From this point onwards in the psalm, vv. 22–31 [23–32],

1. Regarding the genre, Craigie and Tate, *Psalms 1–50*, 197, identify three undeniable possibilities: lament (vv. 2–22), prayer (vv. 12, 20–22), and praise and thanksgiving
(vv. 23–32). As a general description of the psalm, however, many simply recognize it
as a lament (see Brueggemann and Bellinger, *Psalms*, 113; VanGemeren, *Psalms*, 235).

2. Due to the dramatic change in theme at this point in the psalm, some, such as
Kraus, *Psalms 1–59*, 293, assume the composition originated from two independent
works. One needs not accept this conclusion, however, to recognize that the break in
the two distinct sections is notable (see Malul, "Chapter 22," 94).

the psalmist turns to praise, speaking out words and statements of assurance, expressing unreserved confidence in God's character and ability (v.
25 [26]). Notable too is the change from personal complaints, detailing
individual suffering, to a more universal and all-encompassing outlook.
In this section, the psalmist addresses "All the ends of the earth" (v. 27a
[28a]) and "All the prosperous of the earth" (v. 29a [30a]).

No immediately obvious or meaningful lexical connections arise
between Psalms 21 and 22, though they share common words such as
כל ("all"), כי ("for"), יהוה ("the Lᴏʀᴅ"), and ארץ ("land"); these hardly
represent unique or even rare instances across the Psalter. Moreover, one
detects a degree of thematic dissonance between the compositions. Psalm
21 closes with a sense of hope, recounting how God will put the psalmist's
enemies to flight, but the opening words of Psalm 22 dashes this hope to
the ground as the psalmist declares feelings of abandonment by his God.

With regards to intertexts outside of the Psalter, one lexical connection involving the words אדם ("man") and תולעת ("worm") in v. 6 [7],
deserves a closer look. Outside of the psalm, the expression only appears
in Job 25:4–6. When Bildad speaks to Job he depicts the lowly state of
man with the words, "How then can a man be just with God? / Or how
can he be clean who is born of woman? / If even the moon has no bright-
ness / And the stars are not pure in His sight, / How much less man, *that*
maggot, / And the son of man [אדם], *that* worm [תולעה]!" Bildad applies
these words to Job's predicament, emphasizing the lowly state of mankind
before an omnipotent God. The psalmist similarly adopts the expression
to depict his present debasement. He freely confesses that he is a worm
(תולעה) and not a man, a reproach of men (אדם) and a scorn of people.

A case for literary borrowing from this evidence is difficult to prove.
Both contexts employ the metaphor—depicting mankind as a worm or
maggot—to emphasize intense humility; consequently, the repeated expression likely reflects a common image for that specific purpose. The
image of the worm as the most wretched and miserable of creatures
seems a natural choice to reflect the humility brought about through
suffering. Despite the probability of coincidentally shared imagery, two
features raise the possibility of literary borrowing, albeit slightly. The first
concerns the expression's word ordering, which is reversed between the
two compositions. Beentjes' study on inverted quotations, like this one,
indicates a purposeful act of literary borrowing between Job and Psalm

22, even if the direction of borrowing remains a mystery.[3] The second relates to the contexts surrounding the expression. As noted above, Ps 22:6–18 [7–19] not only depicts the humiliated state of the supplicant, but further elaborates on those who surround and hate the psalmist, verbally taunting him. Job finds himself in the same situation, surrounded by friends who have turned against him. Job's three companions begin in a spirit of encouragement, but as their discussion continues, the companions' words transform into more aggressive taunts and accusations against Job. Reading the psalm with Job's situation in mind adds dimension to the psalmist's struggles, recreating a practical instance in which an individual suffers verbal and psychological attacks by those surrounding him.[4] Despite the intriguing nature of this literary connection, concrete evidence proving biblical allusion remains elusive.

The psalm's incipit, למנצח על אילת השחר מזמור לדוד, ("For the choir director; upon Aijeleth Hashshahar.[5] A psalm of David"), deserves further discussion here because it resonates with Psalms 19–21. Each of the three preceding psalms adopts a shorter version of this title, למנצח מזמור לדוד, without the words אילת השחר ("Aijeleth Hashshahar"). The insertion of these words into the incipit may have been influenced by the composition's internal contents. Within the body of the psalm appears the *hapax legomenon* אֱיָלוּתִי ("my help," 22:19 [20]), which bears a notable similarity to the form אַיֶּלֶת in the title. Thus, it appears as though the contents of the psalm may have influenced the lexical construction of the psalm's title.

---

3. Beentjes, "Inverted Quotations," draws our attention to a number of inner-biblical citations in which the word order is reversed, and he recognizes it as an extant literary technique authors use to signify an intertextual relationship.

4. New Testament gospel writers additionally sought to relate the general experience of the psalmist's suffering in Psalm 22 to a real biblical figure, i.e., Jesus. See Matt 27:39, 46; Mark 15:29, 34; Luke 23:35–36.

5. Here, the NASB transliterates the uncertain Hebrew words. Other English translations opt for interpretations such as "to the doe of the dawn" (ESV), or the "deer of the dawn" (CSB).

Psalm 23

PSALM 23 IS PERHAPS the most well-known psalm in the Psalter, and though the title refrains from using the term למנצח, it nevertheless represents a Davidic psalm (מזמור לדוד), like its predecessor. Scholars widely recognize it as a psalm of confidence,[1] and it divides into two relatively distinct sections. Shepherding imagery dominates the first section, vv. 1–4, which depicts God as a shepherd who leads and provides for the psalmist in all circumstances. Verbs of leading and movement—e.g., ינהלני ("he leads me") in v. 2, and ינחני ("he guides me") in v. 3—generate an overall sense of motion in the first section. The adoption of the 3ms verb form to address God further unifies the section.

Imagery in the second section, vv. 5–6, changes from the shepherding motif to that of a feast, and the welcoming of a long-awaited guest. Craigie and Tate see the feast as celebratory, with the psalmist rejoicing at the protection God has provided.[2] Unlike the 3ms verb forms addressing God in the first section, the second stanza switches to the 2ms, generating a more personal and direct reference to him. The psalm's final verse ostensibly abandons both metaphors, and the composition ends with the psalmist expressing his desire to dwell in the presence of Lord always. However, the psalmist's longing for God's presence still unifies the composition because it is only through dwelling in God's presence that he can walk in the shadow of divine protection.[3]

1. See, for example, VanGemeren, *Psalms*, 251, who calls it a song of confidence and trust; or Kraus' designation of a prayer song with an expression of trust (*Psalms 1–59*, 305).

2. See Craigie and Tate, *Psalms 1–50*, 208.

3. Brueggemann and Bellinger, *Psalms*, 122, note, in passing, that the second half of the psalm functions as a continuation of the shepherding motif, but the change in

Thematically, general echoes reverberate between Psalm 23 and the early part of David's shepherding life. The psalm's title specifically connects David with the composition, and the book of Samuel unequivocally identifies David as a shepherd before he ascends in power to hold the position of king in Israel. First Samuel 16:11 and 17:15 recall David working as a shepherd tending sheep. Furthermore, the book of Samuel explicitly recounts instances where God intervened to deliver David, protecting him from wild animals. In 1 Sam 17:34–37, David not only mentions defeating a lion and a bear while shepherding, but additionally attributes the victories over these animals to the Lord, acknowledging, "The LORD who delivered me from the paw of the lion and the paw of the bear, He will deliver me from the hand of this Philistine" (v. 37).

A few scholars have noted an intertextual connection,[4] or perhaps more accurately a biblical allusion, that Psalm 23 bears with Israel's exodus tradition. According to this reading of the composition, the sequence of events recounting Israel's flight from Egypt and journey into the promised land influenced the psalmist's depiction of God's leading.[5] The associations between the two texts are both thematic and lexical in nature. As previously noted, Psalm 23's opening four verses reflect a desert setting emphasizing movement with a divine guide. The Israelite's journey through the desert after their emancipation from Egypt corresponds with the psalmist's experience of divine leading. God provided for Israel in the desert just as he provided for David when he served as shepherd. At the end of the psalm, the final two verses reflect a sense of rest as the psalmist adopts imagery of a journey's end, being welcomed into a feast and further supplied with abundant provision. Paralleling the psalmist's experience, the Israelites ended their journey when they entered the land of Canaan, frequently described in terms of its abundance as a land flowing with milk and honey.

Among the more prominent lexical allusions, the verb חסר ("to lack") particularly stands out. Psalm 23:1 states, "The LORD is my shepherd, / I shall not lack [לֹא אחסר]." In Deut 2:7, as the Israelites reach

---

language negates such an understanding.

4. See Craigie and Tate, *Psalms 1–50*, 205–7, who identify markers between the psalm and the exodus tradition: נוה ("pastures") in Ps 23:2, and נוה ("habitation") in Exod 15:13; נהל ("to guide") in Ps 23:2 and Exod 15:13.

5. In many respects this comes as no surprise because the Exodus tradition is the most influential motif in the Bible, both Old and New Testaments. For more on its prevalence throughout scripture see Zakovitch, *And You Shall Tell*.

the end of their desert sojourn, Moses reminds the people of God's great provision for them, arguing that while they wandered in the wilderness they did not lack (חסר) anything. Additionally, Ps 23:2 depicts God leading (ינהלני) the psalmist by still waters, and Exod 15:13 reflects a similar level of guidance: God leads (נהלת) the Israelites to his holy habitation, the promised land. A degree of irony arises when comparing these two passages, however. For the psalmist, the waters reflect a symbol of preservation, a provision in the desert that keeps the psalmist alive. Contrasting this, Exod 15:13 presents God leading the Israelites though the Reed Sea, which becomes a weapon against the pursuing Egyptians; although it preserves the Israelites, it destroys the Egyptian army.

Additional connections with the Exodus motif appear in literature outside of the Torah. God's undeserved goodness to the psalmist in terms of acting for his own namesake (למען שמו), and not because of the psalmist's earned merit, echoes in Ps 106:8, "Nevertheless He saved them for the sake of His name, / That He might make His power known," which recalls the deliverance at the Sea of Reeds. Likewise, the psalmist's description of walking fearlessly through deep darkness (צלמות) echoes in Jeremiah's recollection of the exodus, "Where is the LORD / Who brought us up out from the land of Egypt, / Who led us through the wilderness, / Through a land of deserts and of pits, / Through a land of drought and of deep darkness [צלמות]?" (2:6).

Finally, Ps 78:19 deserves a mention because it depicts God's provision of food to the Israelites in the wilderness. As part of a persistent pattern of discontent, the Israelites test divine patience by asking, "Can God prepare a table [לערך שלחן] in the wilderness?" With a less provocative tone, the psalm boasts that God prepares a table for the psalmist (תערך שלחן, v. 5) in the presence of his enemies. Further echoes between the two compositions strengthen the connection between them. The same verb נחה appearing in Ps 23:3 depicts God guiding Israel in a pillar of fire and cloud in Ps 78:14, and further in v. 53 as he led them through the Reed Sea. More importantly, however, the same verb describes David as God's chosen shepherd with the responsibility of leading his people, Israel.

Thematically, Psalm 23 resonates with Psalm 78 regarding rest after divine leading. At the close of Psalm 23, the composition depicts the psalmist's journey ending, as he reaches his destination, the presence of the Lord. Psalm 78:55 reflects a similar place of rest as the Israelites arrive at the promised land. Similarly, both compositions reflect scenes of individuals at peace and able to relax in the face of danger. Psalm 78:53

recalls the Israelites standing at the shores of the Reed Sea watching their enemy's destruction, "He led them safely, so that they did not fear; / But the sea engulfed their enemies." The Israelites had no fear of the pursuing Egyptians because God plunged them into the heart of the sea. Reflecting the same notion, Ps 23:5a says, "You prepare a table before me in the presence of my enemies," which almost serves as a poetic depiction of the Israelites' situation.[6]

The relationship between Psalms 22 and 23 deserves further elaboration regarding their genres. Psalm 22, as noted earlier, is a lament, which precedes Psalm 23, a song of confidence. The sequencing of these two themes reflects the combined elements often exhibited in laments. Regularly in the construction of a lament, psalmists close their compositions with words of confidence and trust. With the sequencing of Psalms 22 and 23, though two compositions are involved, they can be read together as an extended lament with Psalm 23 forming, or adding to, the confidence expressed in the previous psalm. McCann hints at a recognition of this potential thematic coupling noting that the depth of trust expressed in Psalm 23 is more fully appreciated after reading Psalm 22.[7]

6. Interestingly, Clifford, *Psalms 1–72*, 130—not entirely detached from the exodus from Egypt—notes a connection to the theme of a new exodus, with a new march through the wilderness, and a new covenant. Supporting the notion, he remarks that during the exile, certain circles understood that the promises of David extended to the whole nation. Hints towards such thinking surface from texts like Psalm 95, where Israel identifies themselves as the "people of His pasture, and the sheep of His hand" (v. 7). Furthering the notion, Avishur, "Chapter 23," 105, raises the question of whether the psalm is communal, with a representative speaking for the congregation. Targum psalms offers support for this possibility, "It is the Lord who fed his people in the desert; they lacked nothing" (Stec, *Targum of Psalms*, 35).

7. See McCann, "Psalms," 769. He further notes that the conclusion of Psalm 22 anticipates the ending of Psalm 23. Thus, the psalmist's presence in the house of the Lord (Ps 22:25) reflects the same presence in God's house in Ps 23:6; additionally, the personal assurance articulated in Psalm 22 is finally experienced in Psalm 23. From the perspective of Psalm 22, VanGemeren, *Psalms*, 236, states that compositionally, Psalm 22 prepares for Psalms 23 and 24. The dramatic turn from distress to praise thematically transits the reader into a psalm lauding God's ability to lead and deliver. Regarding this viewpoint, the question remains as to whether the sequential reading reflects undeniable intent from an author, or whether this connection results from coincidence.

Psalm 24

PSALM 24 BEARS NOTABLE similarities to Psalm 15 with respect to its genre: both compositions are widely recognized as entrance liturgy. Despite the similarity, however, the present psalm additionally contains material reflective of other genres.[1] The psalm divides into three distinct sections with the name of the Lord linking each one. Verses 1–2, the introduction, establish God as creator and owner of the world, "The earth is the LORD's. . . . For he has founded it upon the seas." Discernible, in v. 3, is a clear shift in theme, which marks the opening of the second section (vv. 3–6). In this part of the psalm, attention focuses on those seeking entrance into the temple, and the conditions necessary to enter its sacred precincts. Only those with moral integrity, clean hands, and a pure heart are deemed worthy to enter. Closing this section, the psalmist offers a blessing to those qualified to enter the temple. Then, in the final stanza, vv. 7–10, the psalmist surprisingly addresses the gates of the temple, that they open to permit the Lord to enter. Connecting the final two stanzas is the verb נשא, to lift or carry, appearing twice in the previous stanza and four times in the last section.[2] The gates are lifted, and the fullness of God is revealed;[3] he is the king of glory. God's revelation in the final section receives special emphasis via the repetition of key phrases depicting divine revelation: v. 7 repeats in v. 9, and the expression "who is the King of glory" appears in vv. 8 and 10.

---

1. See Craigie and Tate, *Psalms 1–50*, 211.

2. McCann, "Psalms," 722, further notes the divine warrior theme linking the first and third section.

3. The context here is possibly that of war because the psalmist portrays God as the Lord of hosts in the final verse. See Craigie and Tate, *Psalms 1–50*, 213.

The opening section of Psalm 24 undoubtedly alludes to the creation motif,[4] where the connection reflects an all-encompassing perception of God as creator, as opposed to a specific link to an isolated text. Furthermore, the connection aligns with the poetic traditions in the psalms—such as Pss 33:9; 77:19 [20]—as opposed to the Genesis tradition. The psalm alludes to divinely fashioned elements that reflect physical inanimate aspects of the created world, specifically the sea and dry land. The author avoids mentioning the heavenly bodies, the beasts of the sea, and humanity—elements previously recalled in Psalm 8. A potential reason for the psalmist's focus on the physical space that creation occupies stems from the sacred space mentioned in the following section. In as much as God created and owns the physical space of creation, he further commands a smaller portion of it, separating it as his holy hill (v. 3).

Though a degree of uncertainty exists surrounding two lexical associations from the psalms, they nevertheless deserve a mention. Consider the following:

Ps 24:1–2	Ps 89:11 [12]
The earth [ארץ] is the LORD's and all it contains [מלואה], / The world [תבל] and those who dwell in it, / For He has founded it [יסדה] upon the seas and established it upon the rivers.	The heavens are Yours, the earth [ארץ] also is Yours; / The world [תבל] and all it contains [מלאה], / You have founded them [יסדתם].

From a purely lexical perspective, the combination of Hebrew words indicated above generates a nexus between the verses. Despite the change in person—Psalm 89 addresses God in the second person, whereas Psalm 24 adopts the third person—the similarity in word choice is difficult to ignore. A similar combination of words additionally appears in Ps 98:7, "Let the sea [ים] roar and all it contains [מלאו], / The world [תבל] and those who dwell in it [ישבי בה]." Regarding Psalm 98, one can plausibly argue at least for an echo of Psalm 24. Instead of attributing these words to God in praise of creation, however, Ps 98:7 adopts them to depict a theophany, God appearing in judgment, causing all creation to flee his

---

4. Clifford, *Psalms 1–72*, 134, suggests the psalmist reflects his knowledge of the combat myth known from ANE literature, specifically the theme of acquiring victory in battle to then returning victorious and being crowned by an assembly. Notable, too, is the Septuagint's addition to the title, "for the first day of the week," which further connects the psalm with creation.

presence. Overall, though the combinations of words create unique links between the psalms, confirming instances of allusion between them remains elusive, and so the probability of an echo remains the most probable explanation for the relationship.

Another tangible echo concerns Ps 24:3 and its connection with Deut 17:8. The psalm asks, "Who may ascend [יעלה] into the hill of the Lord [יהוה]? / And who may stand [יקום] in His holy place [מקום]?" These words echo those in Deuteronomy, set in a judicial context, "If any case is too difficult for you to decide . . . then you shall arise [וקמת] and go up [ועלית] to the place [המקום] which the Lord your God chooses." Except for Jer 31:6, the Hebrew words indicated above fail to appear elsewhere, though Jeremiah applies the words to a starkly different context.

With respect to Psalm 24's relationship to Psalm 23, little compelling evidence suggests a logical connection from a lexical viewpoint. Although common words and particles appear—כי ("because"), דוד ("David"), מן ("from"), and לא ("not") for example—it is unlikely that any of them influenced an arranger to juxtapose the two compositions.[5] Thematically, however, a more robust connection appears with references or allusions to the house of the Lord, his dwelling place. The end of Psalm 23 recalls the author desiring to dwell in the house of the Lord forever (v. 6). Following this, after the introduction, Psalm 24 asks the question, "Who can ascend into the hill of the Lord," a presumable reference to Mt. Zion, where the temple stands. With the placement of these references within the same literary proximity—the end of Psalm 23 and the beginning of Psalm 24—it seems natural to place the compositions in this order.[6]

The clearest intertextual connection with Psalm 24 springs from Psalm 15, where the nexus derives from both the literary and lexical evidence. Notwithstanding the probability of similarities due to genre,[7] the lexical connections present a robust case for literary borrowing.

5. Brueggemann and Bellinger, *Psalms*, 127, note the associated themes of hospitality and divine provision. Such thematic connections, in the present author's view, seem somewhat vague and additionally fail to explain the present sequencing of the psalms.

6. This rationale for placement resembles the motivation behind the placement of Joel next to Amos. Clifford, *Psalms 1–72*, 133, pushes further to include the similar themes of God as shepherd and God as king as part of the motivation behind their placement. Although a thematic correlation exists with respect to the notion of leadership, it remains problematic to suggest that this thematic connection constituted a primary influential force guiding the arranger's hand.

7. Craigie and Tate, *Psalms 1–50*, 211, for example, argue that both compositions

Ps 24:3	Ps 15:1
Who [מי] may ascend into the hill [הר] of the LORD? / And who [מי] may stand in His holy place [קדשו]?	O LORD, who [מי] may abide in your tent? / Who [מי] may dwell on Your holy hill? [הר קדשך]

From a literary standpoint, both psalms fundamentally ask the same question: Who can enter God's temple? Moreover, they both designate the temple using the term "holy" ("Your holy hill" and "His holy place") and repeat the notion of oath making. Psalm 15:4 lauds the quality of upholding a vow (נשבע) even to the detriment of the oath maker, an idea corresponding with Ps 24:4 which tests for suitable candidates who avoid swearing (נשבע) deceitfully. Another qualification for the candidate entering God's presence involves the verb נשא ("to lift up"). Psalm 15:3 requests one who avoids taking up (נשא) a reproach against his friend, and Psalm 24 seeks one who has not sworn (נשא לשוא) deceitfully (24:4).[8] Additionally, the desire for purity as a qualifying trait surfaces in both psalms. Psalm 24's author prefers the term בר לבב ("a pure heart," v. 4) whereas Psalm 15's writer opts for הולך תמים, "He who walks with integrity." Despite the differing phrases, the intention remains the same. Finally, both compositions bestow blessings on those meeting the accepted criteria. Psalm 15 blesses the recipient with confidence in divine protection, stating that he will never be shaken; whereas Psalm 24 offers the more generic reward of a blessing from the Lord and righteousness from God. The table below additionally highlights the corresponding thematic sequence between the psalms:

---

are examples of entrance liturgy, a view echoed by other commentators. A pilgrim poses a question, and a priest responds, then an affirmation comes from the priest's representative. Because both compositions reflect common genre-based attributes, one could argue that none of the similarities between the works stem from allusion—direct borrowing between the psalms. However, that is not the only option available. In the same way, for example, even though all prophetic literature belongs to a common genre, it does not necessarily follow that prophets did not borrow material from each other.

8. The verb נשא functions as a leitmotif in the present composition due to its repetition, once in v. 5, twice in v. 7, and twice in v. 9. From a literary standpoint, the word's repetition serves as an important link between the second and third stanzas.

Theme	Psalm 24	Psalm 15
Opening questions	v. 3	v. 1
Response from pilgrim	v. 4	vv. 2–5
Closing promise	vv. 5–6	v. 5

The two compositions are strikingly similar, and consequently, a strong case exists for the probability of an intertextual connection between them. Although the correspondences between compositions may simply result from a shared genre, the repetition of words between them seems abnormally high to attribute them purely to a common type. For example, when comparing either of these psalms with Psalm 95, another entrance liturgy, the repetition of common words and themes is far less apparent than that which appears between Psalms 15 and 24. Thus, the probability remains that one author acquired a familiarity, at least to some extent, with the work of the other. As with many psalms, however, distinguishing who borrowed from whom remains problematic.[9]

At this stage, because of the excessive challenges in establishing a vector of allusion, it is prudent simply to comment on two key differences between the two compositions. First, Psalm 24 addresses God indirectly. Instead of using a second-person pronoun, "your" tent and "your" holy hill, Psalm 24 prefers the third person: Who shall go up to the mountain of "the LORD," and who may stand in "His" holy place. Addressing God in this way, aligns with the psalm's opening two verses depicting his work in creation. Second, Psalm 24 incorporates the shared elements of Psalm 15 into a more extensive literary work, where the entrance questioning does not constitute the composition's main idea. This fact alone, albeit tentatively, suggests Psalm 24 is the later of the two texts.

An intertextual connection worth mentioning concerns Ps 24:4b, which contains a qualification for entering the temple. The verse states, "he Who has not lifted up [נשא] his soul[10] to falsehood [לשוא] / And has

---

9. Adopting the principles established by Carr, "Method in Determination," 10–11, Psalm 24 represents the later text because it is longer than Psalm 15. The general trend in textual development suggests that texts expand as time progresses.

10. With respect to the words "his soul," the MT reads a *yôd* instead of a *wāw*, suggesting "my soul." While this reflects a possible reading (attested by Tg. Psalms), it is probably better to read the *yôd* as a miswriting of the *wāw*. This type of scribal

not sworn deceitfully." Here, the wording directs the reader to Exod 20:7, which records the apodictic injunction "You shall not take [תשא] the name of the LORD your God in vain [לשוא]." Though the Lord's name fails to appear explicitly in the present psalm, it is implied when compared to variations of the expression, such as Ps 139:20, "For they speak against You wickedly, / And Your enemies take *Your name* in vain [נשא לשוא]."[11] Despite the repetition of the phrase in Psalm 139, the probability remains that Psalm 24's author borrowed material directly from the Torah material, either Exodus 20 or Deuteronomy 5. With this connection to one part of the Decalogue, it is possible to assume that the whole Decalogue was intended for recollection. Thus, the psalmist may subtly imply that whosoever seeks to enter God's presence must first abide by all of the principles established in the Decalogue.[12]

---

error appears relatively frequently in MT (see Tov, *Textual Criticism*, 229–23), and the reading of the *waw* additionally appears in many Hebrew manuscripts other than the Leningrad Codex. See Craigie and Tate, *Psalms 1–50*, 210.

11. See also the ESV, for example. The italics in the NASB above are inserted by the translators and the words "*Your name*" are absent from the Hebrew text.

12. The expression בר לבב ("pure heart") only appears in Ps 24:4 and 73:1. Because the context in which the phrase appears in Psalm 73 differs significantly from Psalm 24, it is unlikely that literary borrowing exists.

Psalm 25

THE ABBREVIATED TITLE לדוד ("of David") opens Psalm 25 and continues to appear in the following compositions. Previously, the psalmists
employed the longer version מזמור לדוד ("A *psalm* of David") or added
the phrase למנצח ("for the choir director"). This title change in Psalm 25
generates a degree of separation from the previous compositions. For the
most part, the psalm is dominated by an acrostic structure; though within
this structure, three stanzas are discernible.[1] Unifying the whole composition is the root בוש, ("to be ashamed"): "Do not let me be ashamed," (v.
2b); "None of those who wait for You will be ashamed" (v. 3a); "Do not let
me be ashamed" (v. 20b). The distribution of בוש at the beginning and end
of the psalm creates an inclusion. Furthermore, the psalm's overall use of
repetition is notable, as witnessed from its deployment of the root דרך, in
vv. 5, 8, 9, and 12; and the name of the Lord in vv. 1, 4, 6, 7, 8, 10, 11, 12,
14, and 15.

In vv. 1–7, the psalmist first pleads with God for protection against
his enemy, but these cries for protection soon morph into calls for divine
leading and guidance. He seeks an improved relationship with God, to
walk closer to him, pleading to be led by him. Notably, vv. 4–5 repeat
words expressing guidance: The phrase למדני ("teach me") appears twice,
in addition to הדריכני ("guide me"). Then from guidance, the psalm
progresses to mercy. Conscious of his own transgressions, the psalmist
expresses his desire that they would not count against him.

The second stanza, vv. 8–15, shifts theme and focus from the psalmist and his perceived distance from God, to God's character and nature.

1. Typically, one finds that psalms organized as acrostics in this way, with each
verse equating to a subsequent letter of the alphabet, reluctantly lend themselves to a
lucid division with respect to the stanzas.

The Lord is good and upright (v. 8) and his ways are grace and truth (v. 10). More importantly, the psalmist begins to laud God's relationship with the humble and with repentant sinners. Because the psalmist associates himself with this group of individuals, he is at liberty to plead directly for forgiveness of sin (v. 11).

In the final stanza, vv. 16–22, the psalmist earnestly pleads for help, verbalizing his troubled mind. Despite mentioning various afflictions, he nevertheless fails to supply details concerning the source of his problems. He confesses to being "lonely and afflicted" (v. 16), and in distress (v. 17), and even mentions foes that hate him (v. 19). However, the precise identity of these foes remains obscure: are they family members, an opposing army, corrupt officials, or close friends? Such details remain hidden, and the reader is left simply knowing that severe psychological disturbances afflict the embattled psalmist. The psalm's final verse breaks from an individual's concern and calls for God to remember the nation of Israel. The psalmist prays that the nation will be open to divine mercy in the same measure it was afforded to him.

Looking at the lexical markers between Psalm 25 and its predecessor, the phrase נשא נפש ("lift up the soul") emerges as a notable connection. In total it appears only four times in the Psalter, and two of those appearances are juxtaposed here, in Pss 24:4 and 25:1.[2] In this instance of a common phrase drawing psalms together, the meaning differs in each context. Psalm 24 employs the expression as part of a list of qualifications aimed at determining a candidate's worthiness to enter the presence of the Lord. The individual must not lift up his soul to falsehood (נשא לשוא נפשו).[3] In an apparently unrelated use, the author of Psalm 25 declares that he lifts up his soul to God, as an expression of dedication to his Lord, trusting him with the final outcome of his life. Although the meanings of the expressions differ somewhat, they nevertheless create a nexus between the compositions. A consecutive reading of the psalms, with this lexical replication in mind suggests that Psalm 25's author fulfills the requirements determined in Psalm 24. By qualification through association with the previous psalm, the psalmist can enter confidently into God's presence in Psalm 25, seeking his forgiveness and offering supplications.[4]

2. See also Pss 86:4; 143:8.

3. The Hebrew spelling here reflects the correction of the *yōd*, 1cs ending, to the *wāw*, 3ms ending. See the discussion above.

4. An expression worth mentioning that further consolidates the connection between the psalms is אלהי ישע ("God of salvation"). Unfortunately, however, distribution

Psalm 26

CONTINUING FROM PSALM 25, the simple title לדוד ("of David") opens
the present song. Overall, scholars remain divided on Psalm 26's genre.
Within the composition, signs of a lament are apparent, but no actual
words of lamentation appear. Thus, a definition such as "a prayer song"
must suffice.[1] The psalmist's self-declaration of innocence dominates
Psalm 26. In the opening section, vv. 1–3, he calls for God to examine
him for any signs of hidden sin and iniquity. Verse 2 highlights this theme
through repetition of words exemplifying varying degrees of testing and
trial; בחן ("examine"), נסה ("test"), and צרף ("refine") all bear nuances of
examining for the sake of purification. In the second section, vv. 4–7,
the psalmist turns his attention to his own personal behavior. He credits
himself in these verses with commendable intentions and behavior such
as distancing himself from all evildoers and a persistent desire to dwell in
God's presence. The final section, vv. 8–12, contains a plea to God for divine protection from the judgment assigned to wicked and bloodthirsty
men. The closing two verses correspond to a degree with the opening,
generating an inclusion. With the words אני בתמי אלך ("I shall walk in my
integrity") in v. 11, the psalm closes as it began in v. 1, with a declaration
of innocence, אני בתמי הלכתי ("for I have walked in my integrity").

---

of this phrase is relatively widespread, as it appears in Pss 18:46 [47]; 24:5; 25:5; 62:7
[8]; 65:5 [6]; 79:9, 85:4 [5], in addition to various instances outside the Psalter.

    1. See Kraus, *Psalms 1–59*, 325, for this definition. Clifford, *Psalms 1–72*, 143, iden-
tifies it as a prayer originally for priests, which was also used by lay people for temple
visitations. Along similar lines, Craigie and Tate, *Psalms 1–50*, 224, identifies it as a
ritual prayer for pilgrims at the temple gates.

The combination of words, בחן ("examine"), כליות ("kidneys"), and לב ("heart") connect the current psalm to the book of Jeremiah.[2] Together they express God's capability to penetrate the inward thoughts of a man's heart, uncovering his deepest desires. In addition to Ps 26:2, these words are limited to three appearances in Jer 11:20, 17:10, and 20:12. Jeremiah 11:20a reads, "O LORD of hosts, who judges righteously, / Who tries [בחן] the feelings [כליות] and the heart [לב]." Similarly, Jer 17:10 reads, "I, the LORD, search the heart [לב], / I test the mind [בחן כליות], / Even to give each man according to his ways." Finally, Jer 20:12 frames the expression in a similar vein, "Yet, O LORD of hosts, you who test [בחן] the righteous, / Who see the mind [כליות] and the heart [לב]." Both the psalmist and Jeremiah stand righteous before God, and both also stand in danger of being swept away with the wicked when God judges those around them. The psalmist expresses this sentiment earlier in vv. 9–10. And Jeremiah the prophet experienced a similar danger because he knew the Babylonians served as instruments of judgement against the inhabitants of Judah and Jerusalem. Because the prophet himself was captive in Jerusalem, he too risked being swept away when judgment came to the wicked—a predicament parallel to the psalmist.[3]

Within the Psalter, an apparent allusion exists between Psalms 26 and 1—a literary connection albeit difficult to conclusively prove, but worth mentioning. Creating the link are the words רשע ("wicked") and ישב ("to sit/dwell") reflecting the contexts of dwelling and participating in the company of evildoers. In Ps 26:4, the psalmist declares that he does not sit (ישב) with men of falsehood, then later in v. 5 he reaffirms the sentiment, stating his avoidance of sitting with the wicked (רשעים לא אשב). Psalm 1 echoes the same qualities; there the psalmist declares a blessing for those avoiding the company of evildoers, those who do not walk in

2. It is difficult to say with any degree of certainty the precise relationship between these two texts. On one hand, the replication of common words may simply reflect standard phrasing for conveying thoughts of examination and close inspection. On the other hand, a noticeable thematic correlation exists between the psalmist and Jeremiah. Psalm 7:9 [10] employs the same phrase in a similar manner to Jeremiah, "For the righteous God puts hearts and minds to the test [בחן לבות וכליות]." If literary borrowing exists with respect to Psalm 26, the likelihood remains that Jeremiah was the psalmist's source because prophetic writings came to prominence earlier.

3. Two more texts deserve mention at this point, even if their connection to Psalm 26 remains uncertain. Psalm 26:4 utilizes the phrase מתי שוא ("deceitful people"), which only appears again in Job 11:11. Similarly, the expression רחץ בנקיון כפי ("wash my hands in innocence"), which only appears in Ps 26:6; 73:13.

the counsel of the wicked (רשׁעים), stand in the way of sinners, nor sit (ישׁב) in the seat of scoffers (v. 1). In Psalm 1, one of the blessings for those keeping themselves from such licentious company relates to fruitfulness and productivity in all their endeavors. More importantly, however, is that the righteous in Psalm 1 ultimately find vindication on the day of judgment because God knows their ways. He separates the righteous from the wicked and delivers the righteous from punishment. In Psalm 26, the psalmist desires the same divine response when he pleads, "Do not take my soul away with sinners" (v. 9). Within this discourse, Psalm 26's author calls upon Psalm 1 as a promise of protection, and because Psalm 26's author has kept himself from evil, God will remember that, and keep him from judgment with the wicked.[4]

A similar discourse is detectable between Psalms 24 and 26, this time connected with the word שׁוא ("vanity" or "a falsehood").[5] Psalm 24:3 poses the question, "Who may ascend into the hill of the LORD? / And who may stand in His holy place?" Following this, it lists several qualifications for those seeking to enter his presence. Among those qualifications is one "who has not lifted up his soul to falsehood [שׁוא]." Within the context of this psalm, none arise claiming this level of innocence and the question remains hypothetical. Almost as a response to the question, Psalm 26's author declares in v. 4 that he does not sit with deceitful (שׁוא) people. Reading these works sequentially creates an implicit interpretation for the term "lifting up one's soul to what is false." For the psalmist in Psalm 26, it is achieved by avoiding the company of men who practice falsehood.

In both instances discussed above, it is uncertain and possibly unlikely that either psalmist purposely shaped their composition with knowledge of another's work. The need to mention the associations presently stems from the relative scarcity of the common expressions specifically in the Psalter and generally in biblical literature.

Regarding Psalm 26's lexical connection to the previous composition, several words appear in both works, חנן ("to be gracious," 25:16; 26:11), עין ("eye," 25:15; 26:3), חטא ("sin," 25:8; 26:9), חסד ("lovingkindness,"

---

4. Although the root הלך frequently describes metaphoric behavior in the Psalter, its presence here lends further weight to the connection between these works. Psalm 26:1a says, "I have *walked* in my integrity" (italics added), a sentiment repeated in v. 11, forming an inclusion. The root appears again in v. 3, "And I have *walked* in your truth" (italics added). The opening of Psalm 1 reads, "How blessed is the man who does not *walk* in the counsel of the wicked" (italics added).

5. This word is relatively rare in the Psalter, occurring about eighteen times.

25:6, 7, 10; 26:3), אמת ("truth," 25:5, 10; 26:3), נפשׁ ("soul," 25:1, 13, 20; 26:9), and בטח ("to trust," 25:2; 26:1). Individually, many of these words appear frequently in the Psalter, but their concentration between two juxtaposed compositions is remarkable. Similar high volumes of common words have not appeared thus far in the Psalter, so it is hard to imagine that both psalms, with this level of correspondence, were coincidentally juxtaposed. The grouping reflects further evidence of an arranger being influenced in his sequencing of psalms by the vocabulary within the compositions he arranges. Furthermore, it is unwise to rule out the possibility of a single author composing both compositions, thus creating a natural pair that belonged together. In either scenario, however, the final rationale for the specific sequencing of the psalms—Psalm 25 then Psalm 26, and not vice versa—remains unclear.

Psalm 27

IN ESSENCE, PSALM 27 reflects an individual lament where the psalmist sporadically expresses pronounced statements of confidence throughout the composition.[1] In MT, the title לדוד ("of David"), corresponds with the previous two psalms, with no further modification, such as מזמור ("a psalm"). The LXX, on the other hand, reveals a further addition with the words πρὸ τοῦ χρισθῆναι ("before he was anointed").[2]

The psalmist begins in vv. 1–3 proclaiming his hope in the Lord, and God's ability to protect and provide refuge. For the psalmist, he need not fear even when evildoers assail him or when he faces war. Continuing with the themes of confidence and protection, the second section (vv. 4–6) adjusts the nuance slightly as the focus shifts towards finding protection and comfort specifically in the presence of God. Expressions revealing this shift appear in v. 4, where the psalmist declares his desire and longing to dwell in God's house and meditate in his temple. Psalm 27's plea for deliverance begins in earnest with vv. 7–12, where three imperatives

---

1. Craigie and Tate, *Psalms 1–50*, 230–31, understand the psalm as a royal ritual, they recognize two key components: vv. 1–6 constitute a song of confidence; and vv. 7–14 reflect an individual lament. Notwithstanding the two distinct stanzas, they unequivocally affirm the unity of the composition, adducing the common vocabulary between the sections as a unifying factor. Malul, "Chapter 27," 119, likewise recognizes the distinct units, but affirms the composition's overall unity, stressing the unifying theme of closeness to God. Cohen, *Psalms*, 78, also recognizes these divisions. Kraus, *Psalms 1–59*, 332, soundly rejects the presence of an individual lament, preferring to designate the composition as a prayer song.

2. On one hand, the title may simply reflect an extant tradition at the time of the psalm's translation into Greek; on the other hand, levels of interpretation leading to the title's formation cannot be ignored. For the author of the title, something in the psalm, it appears, reflected events in David's life before he was anointed.

pleading for help—"hear," "be gracious," and "answer me"—confront the reader. Further emphasis on the psalmist's desperate plea for divine assistance appears through the repetition of the negative particle אל in v. 9, "Do not [אל] hide Your face . . . do not [אל] turn Your servant away in anger. . . . Do not [אל] abandon me, and do not [אל] forsake me."[3] Also noticeable in this section is the psalmist's change from addressing God in the third person, to a more direct address in the second person. Finally, in the last section, vv. 13–14, our writer once again expresses confidence and hope in God's ability to save. Repetition of the root קוה ("wait/hope") in v. 14 emphasizes the psalmist's resolve to remain patient and hopeful for divine deliverance.

At least one thematic and one lexical element connect Psalm 27 with Psalm 26. Thematically, both songs reflect an individual psalmist's desire to dwell in God's house, and to remain present in his dwelling place, be it the tabernacle or the temple. Psalm 26 contrasts dwelling with evildoers and sinful men with dwelling in the house of the Lord. Verses 4–5 declare, "I do not sit with deceitful men, / Nor will I go with pretenders. / I hate the assembly of evildoers, / And I will not sit with the wicked." With these words, the author shuns and entirely rejects the mere presence of evildoers. Instead, he desires the presence of God, as he proclaims in v. 8, "O LORD, I love the habitation of Your house / And the place where Your glory dwells." In Psalm 27, though the psalmist expresses the same desire, it stems from the need for protection. Being close to God elicits divine protection from the enemy. In Ps 27:4–5, the psalmist states,

> One thing I have asked from the LORD, that I shall seek:
> That I may dwell in the house of the LORD all the days of my life,
> To behold the beauty of the LORD
> And to meditate in His temple.
> For in the day of trouble He will conceal me in His tabernacle;
> In the secret place of His tent He will hide me;
> He will lift me up on a rock.

The place where God dwells, from this viewpoint, reflects the place where his protection is found.[4]

---

3. Author's translation. As with all individual laments, one cannot determine the exact context surrounding the psalm's composition. However, the mention of war (מלחמה) associates the psalm with military conflict.

4. Keil and Delitzsch, *Psalms*, 1:355, recognize the thematic relationship between the compositions, stating, "The same longing after Zion meets us sounding forth from this as from the preceding psalm."

From a lexical perspective, the word מישור ("a level place") additionally creates a point of connection with the previous psalm. Although relatively rare in the Psalter—appearing only in Psalms 26, 27, 45, 67, and 143—its presence between Psalms 26 and 27 reflects the principle of association. For the author of Psalm 26, his foot already stands on level ground (26:12), and as a result, he praises God in the congregation. The author of Psalm 27, on the other hand, lacks the same sure footing, and needs God to lead him to that place of surety.

Lexical connections between Psalms 27 and 23 also deserve a closer look at this point. Both compositions share expressions of the psalmist desiring to dwell in the presence of the Lord for an extended period. The author of Ps 23:6 declares that goodness and mercy will follow him "all the days of [the psalmist's] life" (כל ימי חיי), and that he would "dwell in the house of the Lord [ושבתי בבית יהוה]" forever (Ps 23:6). Here, the author desires always to be near God and his protective power. Paralleling this in Psalm 27, the psalmist requests, "One thing I ask from the Lord, that I shall seek: / That I may dwell in the house of the Lord all the days of my life [שבתי בבית יהוה כל ימי חיי]" (27:4a). The common vocabulary connecting the psalms fails to appear elsewhere in the Hebrew Bible, a fact by itself suggesting literary borrowing. Language reflecting military engagement additionally reinforces the connection between the two works. In Ps 27:3 the psalmist confidently declares, "Though a host encamp against me, / My heart will not fear, / Though war arise against me, / In spite of *this* I shall be confident." This statement about God's ability to deliver paints a picture of one who faces certain and absolute defeat but can stand confidently and without worry because they stand in the shelter of divine protection. Psalm 23 reflects the same image, where God prepares a table for the psalmist in the presence of his enemies. Like Psalm 27, Psalm 23 presents the image of an individual standing without fear or flinching even in the face life-threatening danger. Although both the lexical and thematic connections highlighted here may simply reflect genre—the vocabulary of a song of confidence—, the uniqueness of the word combination in the Old Testament suggests a more intimate connection.[5]

---

5. A connection worth mentioning, though difficult to develop at this stage, concerns the psalm's connection to Jer 50:32. The prophet declares that the arrogant ones will stumble (וכשל) and fall (ונפל), without anybody to raise them, and that the Lord will set fire to their cities, which will devour (אכלה) all around them. The three Hebrew words all appear together in Ps 27:2, but do not cluster anywhere else in the Old Testament.

Along with the considerations discussed above, the position of the common elements within their respective compositions deserves mention. Psalm 27 includes statements of dwelling in God's presence as part of a longer poetic arrangement that develops the idea of pleading and seeking further confidence from God. The psalmist has yet to find God's rest, and further expresses his desire for mercy (v. 7). Psalm 23's author positions the expression at the end of his song. In doing so, the emphasis on comfort becomes more pronounced because in Psalm 23's context, no further words are needed, and he rests assured that God has heard him.

A variety of notable echoes exist between Psalm 27 and a surprising number of biblical texts. In such instances, the case for proving intentional allusions remains difficult to prove, at best, but the literary connections via lexical replication deserve attention. In Jonah 2:2 [3] the prophet, while in the depth of Sheol, cries (קראתי) out in distress to the Lord (יהוה), and the Lord answers him (ויענני), and the Lord hears (שמעת) his voice (קולי) even from such a distant and desperate situation. The psalmist, likewise, echoes these words in his plea, "Hear, O LORD, [שמע יהוה] when I cry with my voice [קולי אקרא], / And be gracious to me and answer me [וענני]" (Ps 27:7). Despite the five common words between these verses, compelling similarities exist between the contexts and genre; consequently, it is more reasonable to assume the echo results from the similarity in genre than direct literary borrowing.

Another notable echo concerns v. 11, which contains five lexical matches with Ps 5:8 [9]. In Ps 27:11, the psalmist asks God (יהוה) to teach him his ways (דרכך) and to lead him (נחני) on a level path because of (למען) his enemies (שוררי). Corresponding with this, a similar plea for direction appears in Ps 5:8 [9], where the author entreats God (יהוה) to lead him (נחני) in righteousness for the sake of his enemies (למען שוררי), and to make the Lord's way (דרכך) straight before him. Despite the five points of lexical contact here, it remains problematic to assert with any degree of certainty that the replication arises from deliberate borrowing. The similarity of genre—both works are laments—further obscures any suggestion for literary borrowing. Psalmists writing within the same genre are naturally expected to draw upon similar words and phrases to complete their work.

Psalm 28

LIKE PSALM 27, PSALM 28 bears the simple title, לְדָוִד ("of David"), de-spite the NASB's insertion of "*A Psalm*." Crossing over from one psalm to the other, the reader thematically transfers from an individual crying out to God for himself, to an individual interceding for God's people. The psalm readily divides into two sections, vv. 1–5, and vv. 6–9.[1] The first section depicts the psalmist pleading and supplicating to God, who seems unresponsive to his cries. Wicked men—those who speak unjustly against the psalmist, who speak peaceably to their friends but conceal wickedness in their hearts (v. 3)—appear to have their way. As a fitting recompense, the psalmist calls for God to turn their own works against them, thus instigating perfect justice via the biblical principle of measure for measure.[2] Lexically, the word יָד ("hand") unites this stanza as a single unit, appearing in vv. 2, 4, and 5. The second stanza progresses past the entreaty and turns to the psalmist expressing praise and confidence in God's ability to rescue, and hope in his willingness to help. It begins with an abrupt change in v. 6, and due to either an external or internal change in the psalmist's disposition, he diverts his attention to thanksgiving, as though the danger that previously beset him in the first stanza has passed. Creating an inclusion for this section is the root בָּרַךְ, which appears in vv. 6 and 9, capturing the more positive tone of divine favor. God as a

1. From the content, many commentators recognize aspects of prayer (or lament) and thanksgiving. Malul, "Chapter 28," 124, argues that the psalm is a prayer song and a song of thanksgiving; Craigie and Tate, *Psalms 1–50*, 236–37, note the classic description of the lament in the first part, but ultimately understand the psalm as a liturgy of supplication.

2. Jacobs devotes his whole volume to investigating this phenomonon in *Measure for Measure*.

fortress and a place of refuge arises as a prominent theme in the stanza. Repetition of synonyms expressing this idea are prominent, God is the psalmist's strength (עֹז), shield (מָגֵן), and saving defense (יְשׁוּעוֹת). Noticeable, too, in this second stanza is the prominence of a national theme. God represents more than just the psalmist's defender; he is recognized and celebrated as the protector of his people. In v. 8, the psalm addresses God as "their strength" and in v. 9, he calls upon God to save his people and bless his inheritance.[3]

Apparent literary connections exist between Psalm 28 and two other poetic texts. The expression נמשלתי עם יורדי בור ("I will become like those who go down to the pit," v. 1) repeats itself in one other place, Ps 143:7, where the context of lament is admittedly similar. Despite the similar genre, the repetition's precision suggests a possibility of literary borrowing.

Psalm 28:1	Psalm 143:7
To You, O LORD, I call; / My rock, do not be deaf to me, / For if You are silent to me, / I will become like those who go down to the pit. [נמשלתי עם יורדי בור]	Answer me quickly, O LORD, my spirit fails; / Do not hide Your face from me, / Or I will become like those who go down to the pit. [נמשלתי עם יורדי בור]

Regarding the direction of borrowing at this stage, a lack of substantial evidence prevents a firm conclusion. The only potential hint concerns Psalm 143's slight but noticeable tendency to rely on additional biblical texts in its formulation, a fact suggesting that Psalm 28 represents the source text.

The other connection concerns Ps 28:4 and its affiliation with Lam 3:64, as seen from the table below:

---

3. Three primary words connect Psalms 27 and 28, קרא ("call"), רעה ("evil"), and מעוז ("stronghold"), but they are of little consequence. Each word appears frequently in the Psalter, and because both compositions exemplify laments, one naturally expects to see them. Clifford, *Psalms 1–72*, 149, recognizes that Psalm 28 is a lament, but also acknowledges the peculiarity of v. 9, which expands to include the people, as an addition that does not fit the genre. For the most part, scholars fail to mention any notion of association between Psalms 27 and 28. McCann, "Psalms," and Clifford, *Psalms 1–72*, who are usually most attentive to the connections between psalms, remain silent on the matter.

Psalm 28:4	Lamentations 3:64
Requite them according to their work and according to the evil of their practices. / Requite them according to the deeds of their hands; / Repay them their recompense [כמעשה ידיהם תן להם השב גמולם להם]	You will recompense them, O LORD, / According to the work of their hands. [תשיב להם גמול יהוה כמעשה ידיהם]

The connection to Lamentations above presents further challenges with regards to identifying signs of borrowing. On one hand, it appears as though the psalmist simply reuses a common literary expression. Solidifying this position is the sentiment of measure for measure reflected in v. 4, which reflects a widely known and utilized expression of justice. On the other hand, the concentration of replication is difficult to ignore. Once again, however, without a firm grasp of the psalm's date, the direction of borrowing remains uncertain. For the most part, however, the existing scant evidence suggests a composition formed during the monarchy,[4] which ultimately points to Lamentations as the borrowing text.

---

4. Within the psalm, no evidence of late language arises. Furthermore, mention of the Lord's anointed in v. 8 implies an Israelite king on the throne. Moreover, most scholars view the psalm as a product of the monarchy; see, for example, Kraus, *Psalms 1–59*, 340; Craigie and Tate, *Psalms 1–50*, 237.

Psalm 29

BREAKING AWAY FROM THE negative cloud of laments in the previous compositions, Psalm 29 establishes a theme of powerful majestic praise and adoration of God. All creation fearfully responds to his earth-shattering presence. The composition divides into three sections, based on the repetition in the opening words of each line: the introduction (vv. 1–2); the body (vv. 3–9); and the conclusion (vv. 10–11). The opening stanza exhorts the listeners to ascribe honor and might to God. Unlike any psalm discussed thus far, the audience in this work is comprised of the hosts of heaven, divine beings (v. 1).[1] Distinguishing itself from the introduction, the psalm's main body, apart from v. 6, begins with the phrase קול יהוה ("the voice of the LORD"). Emphasis in these verses falls upon the supremacy and authority of God's omnipotent and majestic voice over creation. Within this section, no human enemies are mentioned; instead, God's voice reaches out and stirs various locations: many waters (v. 3), Sirion (v. 6), and deserts (v. 8). In addition to earthly geographic regions, created elements respond to the sound of his voice, including trees, the cedars of Lebanon (v. 5), and deer (v. 9). Overall, the section paints a picture of devastation, panic, and fear at the sound of the Lord's voice. In the final section, vv. 10–11, the psalmist no longer relies on "the voice of the LORD . . ." to open each verse. The focus shifts from the desolation caused by the sound of his voice to the Lord himself and his victory over the flood, and then to his people. In contrast to the devastation God brought to creation in the body of the psalm, God provides strength for his people, and blesses them with peace. The notion of strength noticeably echoed in the composition's main body is reinforced with the word

1. For more on this notion of heavenly praise, see Sommer, "A Little Higher."

עז, which creates an inclusion for the whole psalm, appearing in vv. 1 and 11.

Regarding the placement of Psalm 29 relative to the psalms preceding it, at least one element attracts attention. The word קול appears frequently in the Psalter—fifty-nine times—so its presence here, on one hand, is not particularly remarkable. On the other hand, one cannot ignore that the cluster of psalms leading up to Psalm 29 adopt this word to depict an individual crying out to God. Psalm 27:7a says, "Hear, O LORD, when I cry with my voice [קולי]," which is followed by Psalm 28 that twice references the voice of a supplicant, "Hear the voice [קול] of my supplication" (v. 2a), which is similar to Ps 27:7. Then further in Ps 28:6, the psalmist acknowledges that God has heard him, "Blessed be the LORD / Because he has heard the voice [קול] of my supplication." This leads to Ps 29:3 that repeats the phrase "the voice [קול] of the LORD" on numerous occasions. His voice in Psalm 29 constitutes the medium by which God causes the whole of creation to tremble, and it is reflective of his almighty power. Reading the three psalms in sequence guides the reader to the conclusion that the power from God's voice (קול) was the source behind the previous psalmists' deliverance.[2]

Psalm 29 is frequently mentioned in the same breath as the oft-cited kingship psalms (Psalms 93, 95–99). Each psalm in this collection bears at least one instance of the root מלך, as a verb or noun, with respect to divine rule and reign. Within the present psalm, v. 10 corresponds with the remainder of the collection where it reads, יהוה מלך לעולם ("the LORD reigns forever"). Despite this general association with kingship psalms, the connection between Psalms 29 and 96 demonstrates further striking similarities. The table below highlights the common verbiage between the two works:

2. Undoubtedly, Psalm 29 bears more than a casual relationship with ancient Canaanite imagery and texts, and numerous commentators discuss the various literary associations. Avishur, "Chapter 29," 127–29, highlights a plethora of linguistic connections with Canaanite literature. Furthering this, VanGemeren, *Psalms*, 292, not only suggests that Psalm 29 potentially depends on a Canaanite hymn, but he further depicts the psalmist's work as displaying a polemical slant against theological ideas presented in the source. To be sure, this level of adaptation comes as no surprise, considering the reality of independent religious communities adopting texts from each other.

Psalm 29	Psalm 96
Ascribe to the LORD [הבו ליהוה], O sons of the mighty, / Ascribe to the LORD glory and strength [הבו ליהוה כבוד ועז] (v. 1)	Ascribe to the LORD [הבו ליהוה], O families of the peoples, / Ascribe to the LORD glory and strength [הבו ליהוה כבוד ועז] (v. 7)
Ascribe to the LORD the glory due to his name [הבו ליהוה כבוד שמו] (v. 2a)	Ascribe to the LORD the glory of His name [הבו ליהוה כבוד שמו] (v. 8a)
Worship the LORD in holy array [השתחוו ליהוה בהדרת קדש] (v. 2b)	Worship the LORD in holy attire [השתחוו ליהוה בהדרת קדש] (v. 9a)

The level of repetition demonstrated above undoubtedly attests to literary borrowing. Logically, and most probably, Psalm 29 represents the source text. By all accounts, Psalm 29 is widely recognized as one of the earliest compositions in the Psalter.[3] Among the evidence attesting to Psalm 29 as the source is v. 1, and the phrase, בני אלים ("the sons of gods"), which refers to the presence of a pantheon, a theological worldview where more than one god exists. Such a notion appears unproblematic for the writer of Psalm 29, especially if the psalmist reworked a Canaanite hymn, as some have proposed. The later author, however, unfamiliar, or unaccepting of this theological worldview apparently revised the troublesome expression בני אלים, into the more acceptable and demythologized משפחות עמים ("families of the peoples," Ps 96:7).[4]

Another clear instance of allusion appears between Psalm 29 and the flood story in Genesis. Except for Psalm 29, the only other occurrence of the word מבול ("flood") appears in connection with the flood account; consequently, it is difficult to read the psalm without recollection of the deluge recorded in Genesis. Similarly, the psalm invokes the creation account into the reader's mind. A lucid correspondence exists between the

3. The direction of borrowing proposed here finds some support in the literature. Avishur, "Chapter 29," 133, for example, notes the diachronic developmental among the three related compositions as Psalm 29→Psalm 96→1 Chronicles 16.

4. Psalm 96:7 repeats in 1 Chr 16:28, which also adopts the translation "families of the peoples." In this instance, no doubt arises about the direction of borrowing because the author of Chronicles weaves significant literary material from other sources into his composition.

created elements responding to the voice of the Lord in Psalm 29, and the order of creation in Genesis 1, as the table below demonstrates.[5]

Creation	Genesis 1	Psalm 29
Water	Then God said, "Let there be an expanse in the midst of the waters, and let it separate the waters from the waters." (v. 6)	The voice of the LORD is upon the waters; / The God of glory thunders, / The LORD is over many waters. (v. 3)
Trees	Then God said, "Let the earth sprout vegetation: plants yielding seed, *and* fruit trees on the earth bearing fruit after their kind with seed in them"; and it was so. (v. 11)	The voice of the LORD breaks the cedars; / Yes, the LORD breaks in pieces the cedars of Lebanon. (v. 5)
Land beasts	God made the animals of the earth according to their kind, and the livestock according to their kind, and everything that crawls on the ground according to its kind; and God saw that it was good. (v. 25)	The voice of the LORD makes the deer to calve / And strips the forests bare; / And in His temple everything says, "Glory!" (v. 9)
Man	Then God said, "Let Us make man in Our image, according to Our likeness; and let them rule over the fish of the sea and over the birds of the sky and over the cattle and over all the earth, and over every creeping thing that creeps on the earth." (v. 26)	The LORD will give strength to His people; / The LORD will bless his people with peace (v. 11)

Although Psalm 29 undoubtedly connects to the creation account in Genesis, a distinction in the way creation elements are reused deserves

---

5. The phrase, וישב יהוה מלך לעולם ("the Lord sits as king forever"), appearing in Ps 29:10 deserves a mention. On one hand, it seems like a simple stock phrase declaring God's eternal reign as it appears in Exod 15:18 (the Song of Moses) and Ps 146:10. However, Psalm 29's connection to the Exodus pericope represents more than just familiar verbiage. Both the song in Exodus and Psalm 29 describe theophanies; both authors use the shared vocabulary towards the end of their composition; both texts reflect a divine assembly (Exod 15:11; Ps 29:1); and both reflect God's victory over water.

mention. Genesis paints a wholly positive image of God harnessing the power of his word to create the known world order. The psalmist's adaptation introduces elements of fear and trepidation as the voice of the Lord threatens to destroy created elements, e.g., breaks the trees of Lebanon and strips forests bare.

Psalm 30

THE TITLE OF PSALM 30 deviates from the simplistic ascription of מזמור
לדוד ("A Psalm of David") witnessed in the previous composition. Here, the
psalmist opts for an extended title that, like Psalm 3, connects the composition to a specific event in David's life—the dedication of the temple—adding, שיר חנכת הבית ("a Song at the Dedication of the House").[1] In essence,
this psalm of thanksgiving divides into two sections:[2] vv. 1–5 [6], and then
6–12 [7–13]. The point of division hinges on a faint, but detectable, change
in temporal perspective: from past experience to present expectation and
hope for the future. In the opening section, the psalmist exalts God for
hearing his cry, and for delivering him from various threats to his well-be-
ing. He specifies three needs: safeguard from his enemies, who are gaining
victory over him; healing; and deliverance from Sheol and the pit (vv. 1–3
[2–4]). Closing the section, v. 4 [5] calls for all God's righteous ones to play
music to him, and then v. 5 [6] articulates God's merciful and benevolent
nature: His anger is temporary, but his favor lasts a lifetime.

The psalmist's declaration of confidence introduces the second section; while he prospers, he feels immovable, and his confidence persists
throughout the remaining verses. Indicative of future hope, the author
employs a concentration of imperfect verbs reflecting a future tense. In

1. This is the first instance of the designation "song" to a psalm title. Overall, the
title is somewhat peculiar because David had died well before Solomon completed the
temple. Therefore, the appearance of the title leads scholars such as Clifford, *Psalms
1–72*, 157, and VanGemeren, *Psalms*, 296, to conclude that the extended psalm titles
are secondary, written after the original psalm was composed.

2. Most scholars agree on the classification of a song of thanksgiving. See, for example, McCann, "Psalms," 795; Kraus, *Psalms 1–59*, 353; Avishur, "Chapter 30," 138;
VanGemeren, *Psalms*, 296.

v. 8 [9] the psalmist "will call" (אקרא) unto God and "will seek his favor," (אתחנן);[3] furthermore in v. 10 [11] he employs two imperatives pleading for God to hear his plea and show mercy. Expressions such as these reflect a desire for, and hope in, an unrealized deliverance. Closing the section, and the psalm, the psalmist leverages his plea, suggesting his future eternal thanksgiving remains contingent upon God's imminent rescue. An inclusion encapsulating the second stanza, appearing in v. 6 [7] and 12 [13], using the word לעולם ("forever") reinforces the notion of eternity.

Ostensibly, Psalm 30 is peculiar because it attempts to associate David with the temple's dedication, assuming the term בית ("house") refers to the temple. Such a claim conflicts with events recorded in 2 Samuel 7 and 1 Kings 8 that lucidly inform us that David was denied permission to build the temple, but his son Solomon completed and dedicated it. Despite this conflict, a discernible link exists between Psalm 30's title and 1 Chr 6:31 [16], "Now these are those whom David appointed over the service of song in the house of the LORD, after the ark rested *there*." Amid the genealogies of Levi's descendants, Chronicles recalls men who David (דוד) commissioned for the service of song (שיר) in the house (בית) of the Lord. Chronicles continues explaining that these men continued to minister with song (שיר) before the tent of meeting until Solomon built the house (בית) of the Lord in Jerusalem. Through this connection it appears David not only commissioned choir members who sang at the ark and then later at the temple, but he also composed songs for these individuals. Furthermore, such compositions may have been written not just for the tabernacle, but also to anticipate the dedication of the temple, even if David never lived to see it. From 2 Samuel 7, it is apparent that despite God denying David the privilege of building his temple, David nevertheless envisioned a day when a permanent structure for the ark would materialize.[4]

Continuous reading of the psalms beginning with Psalm 28 raises a connection between Psalms 28 and 30, where both contain the phrase ירד בור ("going down into the pit"). In Ps 28:1, the author cries out to God for deliverance, pleading with him, and arguing that if God remains silent then his servant would descend into the pit. Although later in the same composition, the psalmist expresses a degree of reassurance that God has heard his plea, no mention appears of him being saved from the pit. In Ps 30:3 [4], however, the psalmist offers specific words of thanksgiving that

3. Author's translation.

4. Alternatively, one could hypothesize that the "house" mentioned in the incipit points to a temporary structure housing the ark when it came to rest in Jerusalem.

declare how God has restored the psalmist's life from among those who go down into the pit (יורדי בור). The phrase linking both works, "going down in the pit," rarely appears in the Psalter, occurring in two other places, Pss 88:4 [5] and 143:7. As a result of the distribution, the attraction between Psalms 28 and 30 intensifies. Thus, the present sequencing of Psalms 28–30—were the principle of association a dominant motivating factor—suggests Psalms 28 and 30 originally formed a pair and Psalm 29 represents a later insertion. Adhering to this proposition further explains why Psalm 29, which bears no connections to the lament genre, appears within a series of laments.[5]

Despite the disconnect, the temple theme tenuously connects Psalms 29 and 30. Psalm 29 recalls activity in the heavenly realms and exhorts those dwelling in heaven to ascribe honor and glory to God on account of his majestic deeds reflected in creation. As a response, the psalm reveals that all in the temple cry "glory" (v. 9). In Psalm 29's context, the temple (היכל) represents a divine dwelling in heaven, where God resides, and where the heavenly beings recalled in v. 1 proclaim his praise. Through the incipit of Psalm 30, the reader can trace a parallel occurrence on earth. In the same way that heavenly beings ascribe glory to God in the heavenly temple, so too David prescribes words exalting God for his acts of deliverance at the inauguration of the earthly temple in Psalm 30.

Delitzsch mentions a potential allusion between Psalm 30 and Hezekiah's prayer in Isaiah 38, and to be sure, intriguing repetitions in vocabulary exist between the two compositions. The literary associations are summarized below:

Psalm 30:3 [4], 9 [10]	Isaiah 38:18
O LORD, you have brought up my soul from Sheol [שאול]; / You have kept me alive, that I would not go down [יורדי] to the pit [בור] . . . "What profit is there in my blood, if I go down [ברדתי] to the pit? / Will the dust praise [יודך] you? Will it declare your faithfulness [אמתך] . . ."	For Sheol [שאול] cannot thank you [תודך], / Death cannot praise you; / Those who go down to the pit [יורדי בור] cannot hope for Your faithfulness [אמתך].

5. Despite the ostensible disconnect, Keil and Delitzsch, *Psalms*, 1:374, suggest the theme of praise joins the three works. In their view, praise directed to heavenly bodies in Psalm 29 redirects to praise from the pious below.

An initial look at the common vocabulary between the two texts suggests a degree of literary borrowing. Furthering the possibility is the content of both works: They respond to an experience of divine deliverance. God intervened with both Hezekiah and the psalmist to save them from a life-threatening illness, and they respond with a song of thanksgiving. Despite the associations between the two, the likelihood remains that the connection simply reflects genre-specific vocabulary. The primary evidence reducing the probability of allusion concerns the frequency of common vocabulary. Much of the shared vocabulary frequently appears in laments and songs of thanksgiving, בור ירדי ("going down to the pit"), as mentioned above, also surfaces in Pss 28:1, 88:4 [5] and 143:7.

Psalm 31

IN COMPARISON TO THE previous composition, Psalm 31 bears a relatively short title למנצח מזמור לדוד ("For the Choir director. A Psalm of David") that simply connects the song to David. The pronounced need for deliverance opening the present psalm creates a degree of thematic dissonance with the previous composition, which closed with a sense of accomplished salvation. Psalm 31 opens in vv. 1–10 with an undeniable plea for help in vv. 1–2 [3], which is followed by a declaration of trust in vv. 3–8 [4–9]. Within this section, the psalmist employs expected metaphors and statements of assurance, such as "You are my rock and my fortress" (v. 3 [4]), that express God's ability to protect and guide. After openly declaring attributes of God's faithfulness, the psalmist entrusts his spirit to the divine deliverer. Verse 7 [8] reveals the speaker's desire to exalt and rejoice in the lovingkindness of God, but this is further tempered by his plea for God to notice his distress and defend him against his enemy.

In the following section, vv. 9–13 [10–14], the psalmist details his personal physical suffering, including images of his strength failing and his eyes wasting in vexation. Changing the tone, vv. 14–22 [15–23] express an increased level of trust and confidence in God's goodness as the psalmist again unreservedly places his fate into the hands of the Almighty. This he accomplishes through further statements of God's ability to deliver and protect. Then, as one often reads in laments, the psalm begins closing with statements of confidence reflecting an unrealized deliverance, with statements such as, "You heard the voice of my supplications" (v. 22). Finally, in vv. 23–24 [24–25] the author's focus turns to those in his community, and he implores them to trust in God, encouraging them to be strong and wait patiently for him.

Overall, Psalm 31 reflects a literary mosaic constructed from other compositions in the Hebrew Bible. The first clear connection is to Psalm 71, and the table below demonstrates the shared vocabulary:

Psalm 31	Psalm 71
בְּךָ יְהוָה חָסִיתִי אַל־אֵבוֹשָׁה לְעוֹלָם בְּצִדְקָתְךָ פַלְּטֵנִי	בְּךָ־יְהוָה חָסִיתִי אַל־אֵבוֹשָׁה לְעוֹלָם
In you, O Lord, I have taken refuge, / let me never be ashamed; / In your righteousness deliver me (v. 1b [2])	In you, O Lord, I have taken refuge; / let me never be ashamed (v. 1)
הַטֵּה אֵלַי אָזְנְךָ מְהֵרָה הַצִּילֵנִי	הַטֵּה־אֵלַי אָזְנְךָ וְהוֹשִׁיעֵנִי
Incline Your ear to me, rescue me quickly (v. 2a [3a])	Incline Your ear to me, and save me (v. 2b)
כִּי־סַלְעִי וּמְצוּדָתִי אָתָּה וּלְמַעַן שִׁמְךָ תַּנְחֵנִי וּתְנַהֲלֵנִי	צַוִּיתָ לְהוֹשִׁיעֵנִי כִּי־סַלְעִי וּמְצוּדָתִי אָתָּה
For You are my rock and my fortress; / For Your name's sake You will lead me and guide me (v. 3 [4])	You have given commandment to save me, / For You are my rock and my fortress (v. 3)

Regarding the repeated words in the table above, it is important to note their failure to appear elsewhere in the Hebrew Bible. As a result, the probability of literary borrowing escalates dramatically. The placement of shared vocabulary within introductory material, in both psalms, further solidifies the connections between them: One author apparently borrowed and modified the opening words of an earlier work. Due to the high volume of repeated elements, it seems unlikely that both authors simply relied on common formulas. Unfortunately, with respect to the vector of allusion one cannot formulate any conclusive solutions. Ordinarily, Psalm 31 would be considered the borrower because of the wide range of vocabulary it shares with other psalms. However, the author of Psalm 71 similarly exhibits a proclivity to reuse other biblical texts. As a result, although biblical allusion remains probable, establishing the direction of borrowing cannot be determined at this time with any certainty.

Psalm 31 further connects with at least one short passage in the book of Jeremiah, as seen below:

Psalm 31:13 [14]	Jeremiah 20:10
כִּי שָׁמַעְתִּי דִּבַּת רַבִּים מָגוֹר מִסָּבִיב בְּהִוָּסְדָם יַחַד עָלַי לָקַחַת נַפְשִׁי זָמָמוּ	כִּי שָׁמַעְתִּי דִּבַּת רַבִּים מָגוֹר מִסָּבִיב הַגִּידוּ וְנַגִּידֶנּוּ כֹּל אֱנוֹשׁ שְׁלוֹמִי שֹׁמְרֵי צַלְעִי
For I have heard the slander of many, / Terror is on every side; / While they took counsel together against me, / They schemed to take away my life.	For I have heard the whispering of many, / "Terror on every side! / Denounce _him_, yes, let us denounce him!" / All my trusted friends Watching for my fall say: / "Perhaps he will be deceived, so that we may prevail against him / And take our revenge on him."

The underlined words in the table above marks the most convincing evidence of scriptural reuse. Replication of the word combination between Ps 31:13 [14] and Jer 20:10 fails to appear elsewhere in Scripture. Regarding this expression, it is possible to detect a rationale for our psalmist to employ and allude to Jeremiah's words. In Jeremiah's complaint to God, he expresses his displeasure at the problems stemming from his obedience in declaring divine oracles against Judah. Consequently, those around him threaten him, and even his friends plot against him, all because he desires to serve God. The constant presence of the voices and whispers all around him generate a sense of deep fear and anxiety for the obedient prophet. These same feelings of fear and anxiety transfer into the psalmist's work. In v. 13 [14], the psalmist describes the slander he hears on every side as part of his complaint to God. By recalling the words of Jeremiah, the level with which the psalmist suffers intensifies. Jeremiah provides a background and a practical example of a known individual who suffers under the same psychological torment. Just as the feelings of suffering transfer between the two literary works, so too the reason for suffering identified in Jeremiah's situation applies to the psalmist. In the same way Jeremiah suffered through his obedience in declaring the word of the Lord, the psalmist suffers because he obeys God and desires to serve him.[1]

1. Although the phrase מִיַּד אוֹיֵב וּמֵרֹדְפַי appears relatively frequently throughout the Hebrew Bible, one could argue that the psalmist borrowed it directly from Jeremiah because of the earlier connection to Jeremiah. On at least four occasions, Jeremiah used the phrase יַד אוֹיֵב וּבְיַד מְבַקֵּשׁ נֶפֶשׁ ("The hand of the enemy and the hand of he who seeks my life"), which reflects a similar construction. The psalmist may have abbreviated the form omitting the second occurrence of יַד, in addition to altering the word depicting the pursuer from מְבַקֵּשׁ נֶפֶשׁ to מֵרֹדְפַי (Hos 2:7 [9] shows that בקש and

Another potential allusion supports the idea of the psalmist's innocence in light of persecution from those around him. Describing his plight, the psalmist complains that all around him conspire against him, בהוסדם יחד עלי (Ps 31:13 [14]). This phrase surfaces in only one other place in the Hebrew Bible, Ps 2:2. In Psalm 2, the Lord's anointed is the object of the aggressive threats. The kings of the earth gather against both the Lord and his anointed one (נוסדו יחד על יהוה ועל משיחו). Thus, the theme of unjust aggressive threats aimed against the innocent unifies both Psalm 31 and Psalm 2.

Finally, the rare phrase שומר הבלי שוא ("those who regard vain idols"), deserves mention because it appears only in Ps 31:6 [7] and Jonah 2:8–9a [9–10a]. Both Jonah and the Psalmist employ the expression as part of an antithetical construction. Jonah declares "Those who regard vain idols / Forsake their faithfulness, / But I will sacrifice to You / With the voice of thanksgiving." Similarly, the psalmist contrasts his faithful behavior with those deficient in moral fiber, "I hate those who regard vain idols, / But I trust in the LORD." The similarity of word choice and parallel construction lends more weight to the probability of literary borrowing.

Although the connection here almost certainly reflects direct influence, determining the vector of allusion remains problematic. However, because the author of Psalm 31 appears influenced by other biblical texts, it is logical to assume he had some knowledge of the book of Jonah, or at least the psalm found in Jonah 2.[2] The psalmist, on one hand, may simply have recalled the common expression from a well-known composition without thinking too much about the original context from which he borrowed the phrase. On the other hand, he may have fully understood the context of Jonah's words, seeking to apply them to his cause. Jonah 2 unequivocally depicts an extreme instance of God's redemptive work in an individual's life. After being thrown from a ship, Jonah falls into the sea and descends into the depths of the ocean. At this point, he should have died. Despite the apparent inevitability of the situation, however, God intervenes to rescue him, redeeming his life and offering him another chance to complete the mission he originally refused. Such an act

---

רדף appear interchangeably). The equivalent phrase in Jeremiah, as mentioned, only appears in three places (21:7; 34:20; 44:30), and except for these locations, the phrase only appears in Psalm 31, hence the suspected case of literary borrowing.

2. Because the psalm in Jonah 2 may not be organic to the composition, Psalm 31's author may have accessed an independent version of Jonah's song of thanksgiving. See Trible, "The Book of Jonah," 464–65.

of personal redemption intensely resonates with the psalmist's work. Just like Jonah, the psalmist experiences divine intervention and deliverance. Notable too in this regard are the psalmist's words in v. 12a, "I am forgotten as a dead man," which undeniably resonates with Jonah's situation.[3]

Casting a shadow of doubt over all the proposed intertextual associations described above is the possibility of a well-read psalmist. Because the number of borrowed phrases discussed fails to reflect the full extent of the psalmist's reuse of poetic phrases and expressions,[4] it remains possible that many of the connections simply reflect instances of biblical echo, where the psalmist reuses expressions from memory without purposefully attempting to import meaning into his composition. Although such a proposition is less likely, it deserves mention.

Regarding the juxtaposition connections between Psalms 30 and 31, precious little arises supporting the notion of purposeful sequencing. Most of the common words between the two texts are additionally ubiquitous across the Psalter. The only tangible evidence of association relates to their genre—both are laments—but this reveals little about an arranger's rationale for their placement, as laments dominant the shape of Book I.

---

3. With respect to God as the subject and man as the object, the phrase, האירה פניך על ("Make your face to shine upon"), warrants attention, though it may simply reflect an echo. The exact phrase only appears in Ps 4:6 [7], but the wording recalls the Aaronic blessing in Num 6:25, יאר יהוה פניו אליך ("The Lord make his face shine on you"). Despite the expression's relative frequency throughout the Bible (Pss 4:6 [7]; 67:1; 80:3 [4]; and Dan 9:17, for example), the possibility of the psalmist reading from Numbers, because it is part of the influential Pentateuch, remains a noteworthy possibility.

4. See Craigie and Tate, Psalms 1–50, 260, for a detailed list of all common expressions used.

Psalm 32

BREAKING FROM THE LAMENT grouping that began with Psalm 30 is a wisdom composition, Psalm 32. For the first time in the Psalter, though the composition is still connected to David, the title Maskil (משׂכיל) appears, associating the song to Israel's wisdom traditions. Verses 1–2 declare the blessedness of those who have been declared righteous by God and who have had their sins and iniquities removed, an experience apparently known to the psalmist, who begins relating to the reader what he has suffered. In vv. 3–4, the writer recounts the time of his unconfessed sin, and the physical turmoil caused by the unbearable weight of his transgressions and guilt. He arrives at a turning point in v. 5, where he confesses his sin and receives forgiveness. From this renewed state of deliverance, the psalmist turns to his audience requesting that they too adopt his course of action when faced with similar circumstances. Now that the psalmist achieves a right relationship with God, he finds himself in a position to receive a divine oracle, which forms the substance of vv. 8–9. Here, God directs the psalmist, and by implication any who seek him and his forgiveness. Furthermore, the divine voice instructs the psalmist against stubborn behavior and resisting the divine will. Closing the psalm, the final two verses exhort the righteous to trust in the Lord and rejoice in him.

The theme of forgiveness unifies Psalm 32's opening verses with the book of Exodus. In Exodus 34, while on Mt. Sinai with Moses, God not only manifests his presence, or his back, to Moses, but also important aspects of his divine character. God reveals himself to be longsuffering, slow to anger, gracious, and compassionate. Furthermore, he is one who forgives (נשׂא) iniquity, transgression (פשע), and sin (חטאת), but does not leave the guilty unpunished (34:6–7). In the opening section of Psalm 32, the psalmist recognizes and lauds the recipients who benefit from these divine qualities. In vv. 1–2, the psalmist declares the blessedness of the one whose transgressions are forgiven (נשׂוי פשע), and whose sins (חטאה) are covered. In addition to the three common words connecting the passages, God further reveals himself to the psalmist in Psalm 32, as he does in Exodus, via the spoken word. In v. 8 God begins freely to offer direct verbal instruction to teach and to guide the psalmist in the way he should go, in a similar way to his interaction with Moses.

Linking these two texts via the lexical and thematic connections above creates an appreciation of both the divine willingness to pardon transgressions and the necessary human response. God's willingness to remit sins only represents one part of the process of forgiveness. In addition to this, the human recipient is required to avoid withholding his sin from God, even as the psalmist tried. To receive what God offers, the psalm suggests that humanity bears the responsibility to confess their sin and acknowledge their wrongdoing.[1]

It is difficult to assert with any conviction that an arranger implemented a concrete juxtaposition strategy between Psalms 31 and 32. The only potential candidate is the exhortation to the godly, which appears towards the end of both compositions. Psalm 31:23 [24] proclaims, "O love the Lord, all you His godly ones [כל חסידיו]," and responding to this, Ps 32:6 echoes, "Therefore, let everyone who is godly [כל חסיד] pray to You in a time when You may be found." Unfortunately, the word חסיד appears relatively frequently in the Psalter, and is therefore difficult to adduce as a rationale for the juxtaposition of the psalms.[2]

---

1. A notable echo appears between Ps 32:11, a wisdom psalm, and Ps 64:10 [11], an individual lament. For its closing words, Psalm 32 declares, "Be glad in the Lord [שמחו ביהוה] and rejoice, you righteous ones [צדיקים]; / And shout for joy, all you who are upright in heart [כל ישרי לב]." The word combinations indicated here appear in one other Old Testament location, Ps 64:10 [11], which exhorts the righteous to rejoice in the Lord [ישמח צדיק ביהוה] and seek refuge in him, and the upright in heart [כל ישרי לב] to praise. The appearance of these word groupings at the end of both works lends towards the possibility of textual borrowing. If the appearance of these words simply reflects a common end formula, one would expect other instances scattered across biblical literature, if not in the Psalter, then in other poetic compositions.

2. Contra to Keil and Delitzsch, *Psalms*, 1:393, who confidently assert that the exhortation to the godly ones constitutes substantial evidence of purposeful juxtaposition, together with the word אמרתי, "I said."

Psalm 33

THE DETOUR FROM LAMENTS continues with Psalm 33, a hymn of praise.[1] Notably, the present composition further breaks with the previous psalms with respect to the incipit: Psalm 33 in MT contains no title and no direct ascription to David.[2] As expected from a hymn, the opening lines, vv. 1–3, exhort the hearers to praise God, playing music to him with a variety of instruments, including the lyre and the harp of ten strings. Following this, in vv. 4–9 the psalmist supplies the reason for praise, beginning with a focus on creation: Praise him because he created the heavens by his word (v. 6), the seas and waters of the deep too (v. 7). Building on his handiwork in creation, the psalm continues to enumerate God's relationship with creation's human inhabitants. Then, in vv. 10–17, the writer draws an acute contrast between God bringing the counsel of the nations to naught, but blessing his nation, the people that he has chosen, a probable reference to Israel. Supplementing the contrast, the psalmist adds a warning against placing hope in that which cannot save (vv. 16–17). Verses 18–19 develop the theme of God's desire and capacity to protect those who fear him, rescuing them from death. The final verses, vv. 20–22, turn from words of praise and the recollection of the mighty deeds of God to pleadings and supplications. Twice in this section the psalmist employs words expressing hope, יחל ("hope") and חכה, ("wait") as he entreats God's assistance on behalf of his community. Because God blesses the nation (v. 12) and watches those who hope (מיחלים) in him (v. 18), the psalmist can trust in him to assist them as they wait (יחלנו) on him (v. 22).

1. See Gruber, "Chapter 33," 152.
2. The Septuagint differs, adding the words τῳ Δαυιδ (To David).

147

Because Psalm 33 lacks an incipit in MT, the psalm automatically connects, from a literary perspective, to the previous composition. A similar phenomenon arises with Psalm 10, where the absence of a title links it with Psalm 9. Concerning Psalm 33, however, no further evidence arises to suggest that it originally formed part of Psalm 32. If anything, the Davidic inscription appearing in the Septuagint unequivocally speaks against any such union between the two compositions.

Despite the evidence supporting Psalms 32 and 33 as independent compositions, a remarkable literary connection appears between them. The closing words of Psalm 32 reappear in the opening of Psalm 33. At the end of Psalm 32, the psalmist closes with an exhortation: "Be glad in the LORD [ביהוה] and rejoice, you righteous ones [צדיקים]; / And shout for joy [הרנינו], all you who are upright in heart [ישרי לב]." The opening words of Psalm 33 unmistakably correspond with Psalm 32's ending: "Sing for joy in the LORD, O you righteous ones rejoice [רננו צדיקים ביהוה]; / Praise is becoming to the upright [לישרים]." Thus, the words and theme of praise generates a smooth continuity from one psalm to the next, creating a sequencing association.[3] In addition to the smooth lexical transition, one can hardly ignore the thematic development, with Psalm 32 requesting that the righteous shout and praise the Lord, and Psalm 33 responding to the request, with the righteous and upright in heart shouting their praises to him. A precedent for the request-response relationship was previously established in the connection between Psalms 7 and 8.

The presence of this word cluster, closing one psalm and opening another, seems more than coincidental. However, tracing the historical development leading to the present configuration of psalms remains slightly elusive. The two compositions possibly represent two entirely separate works that an arranger, noticing the commonalities, placed in this sequence to create a smoother lexical connection. Alternatively, Psalm 33 may have originally existed without v. 1; as part of an invasive editorial process the first verse, modeled on Ps 32:11, was subsequently added to Psalm 33 specifically to improve the transition between the works. Although possible, however, this latter proposal is unlikely, and the probability remains that complying with an editorial norm, an arranger aligned these two psalms in their present arrangement.

Another word that possibly influenced the juxtaposition of these psalms is סוס, ("horse"), which appears in Pss 32:9 and 33:17. Apart from

---

3. Concerning the connection, McCann, "Psalms," 809, suggests Psalm 33 responds to Ps 32:11's invitation to praise.

these appearances, the word only surfaces in the Psalter three times: Pss 20:7 [8]; 76:6 [7]; 147:10. This distribution solidifies the probability of association in the arrangement,[4] where arrangers sequence psalms according to rare words and expressions.[5]

A noticeable allusion generated by Psalm 33 concerns its reuse of the creation story, where the writer apparently recalls aspects of the priestly creation account reflected in Genesis 1. Although the psalmist fails to adopt the exact wording, certain concepts unmistakably point the reader to the Genesis text. He emphasizes that the heavens were formed by the word of the Lord, and all their lights by the breath of his mouth (v. 6). Further in v. 9, he asserts that God "spoke, and it was done; / He commanded, and it stood fast." With these words, the psalm unequivocally alludes to the power of God's spoken word at creation, recalling phrases such as, "Then God said, 'Let there be light'; and there was light" (Gen 1:3). Additionally, in v. 7, the psalmist depicts God gathering the waters into a mound and storing the deep in vaults. Although poetically rearranged, these words echo the separation of the seas in Gen 1:9, "God said, 'Let the waters below the heavens be gathered into one place, and let the dry land appear'; and it was so."

Images of God's power at creation, however, receive a twist by the psalmist in v. 15. Rather than describing the creation of man, with respect to how his flesh was formed from the dust, the psalmist recalls God as one who fashions the hearts of humanity and bears responsibility for creating and monitoring their thoughts.[6] Recollection of God's might in creation therefore serves two purposes in the psalm: his power to deliver in times of war (suggested in v. 16), and his omnipresent attributes: Nothing escapes his gaze, so he sees and delivers all those who fear him (v. 18).

---

4. Keil and Delitzsch, *Psalms*, 1:19–23; Cassuto, "Sequence and Arrangement," 1–6.

5. A distant echo worth mentioning concerns the depiction of God peering down upon the affairs of men from heaven. Thus far in the Psalter, this notion is only reflected in Ps 14:2a, "The Lord has looked down from heaven upon the sons of men." In this context, God gazes from heaven searching for any righteous among the dwellers of earth. Similarly, God looks down from heaven in Ps 33:13, watching the sons of man. In this latter context, however, he is not seeking out the righteous, but protecting them, "Behold, the eye of the Lord is on those who fear him . . . to deliver their soul from death" (Ps 33:18–19a).

6. Concentrating on this aspect of creation draws a notable contrast with Psalm 8, which recalls the beasts of the field and the birds of the air. Noteworthy too is Psalm 8's focus on humanity's vested authority to rule over creation.

Images of the exodus motif clearly resound throughout the composition too. When the psalmist portrays God heaping up the ocean's waters into a mound, (כנס כנד מי הים, 33:7a), it is difficult to ignore the poetic tradition in Exod 15:8a–b, "At the blast of Your nostrils the waters were piled up, / The flowing waters stood up like a heap [נערמו מים נצבו כמו נד]." The depiction of the Reed Sea waters standing like a heap (נד) links the psalm to Exodus 15's rendition of the sea crossing. Moreover, similar wording with respect to the sea appears in Ps 78:13b, "And He made the waters stand up like a heap [כמו נד]." As with Exodus 15 and Psalm 78, Psalm 33 removes intermediaries from the miracle at the sea, and our psalmist restricts his view to God directly operating against the forces of creation.[7]

In addition to the Reed Sea crossing, elements of Joshua parting the Jordan loosely intersect with our psalm. When Joshua led the Israelites into the promised land, God intervened, as he did with Moses, to assist the Israelites in crossing an obstructive body of water. This miracle bears numerous similarities to the Reed Sea crossing and marks the end of Israel's desert wandering period. In Josh 3:15–16, when the feet of the priests who bore the ark of the covenant touched the water of the Jordan, it responded by standing up in a heap ("The waters which were flowing down from above stood *and* rose up in one heap" [ויעמדו המים הירדים מלמעלה קמו נד אחד]). The lexical similarity here, however, connects Joshua to the exodus tradition more so than to Psalm 33.

Drawing upon these images of God at work for the Israelites in their deliverance from the sea—together with his presence with them prior to the conquest of Canaan—sets a concrete stage for the psalmist's abstract claims. The king, who is not saved by a mighty army (v. 16), adopts the persona of Pharaoh, as well as the numerous kings defeated by Joshua and his army during the conquest. Similarly, when the psalmist says, "A horse is a false hope for victory" (v. 17a), the exodus context recalls that Pharaoh's horses, the chariots, and the horsemen were hurled into the sea, never to be seen again. Such mighty acts from Israelite literary history support the psalmist's message, and he can declare with further confidence, "Behold, the eye of the LORD is on those who fear him" (v. 18a).

A few notable echoes deserve mention at this point, despite a low likelihood of shared knowledge existing between the authors. The first concerns Ps 33:18, which proclaims that the eye of the Lord is on those who fear him (יראיו), and on the ones who hope for his lovingkindness

7. One can add the psalmist's reference to God choosing Israel for himself as his chosen possession as an allusion to events at Sinai; see Pss 78:71; 114:1–2.

(למיחלים לחסדו). The combination of Hebrew words, those in parenthe-
ses, only appears again in Ps 147:11, "The Lord favors those who fear
him [יראיו], / Those who wait for His lovingkindness [המיחלים לחסדו]."
Conceivably, the connection here represents an echo, words reflected in
both psalms creating an unintentional literary association.[8] Another
echo relates to the expression of God's grace filling the earth (חסד יהוה
מלא ארץ), which, like the previous example, is restricted to one other
place in the Hebrew Bible, Ps 119:64, "The earth is full [מלאה הארץ] of
Your lovingkindness [הסדך], O Lord; / Teach me Your statutes."

A further echo that appears, but with less significance, is the depiction of God as a help and a strength (עזר ומגן), which is relatively rare,
but functions as a logical word pair. Psalm 33:20 employs it together with
Deut 33:29 and Ps 115:9, 10, 11. The echoes in Psalm 115 fail to ignite
flames of interest, but the connection to Deut 33:29a deserves attention
because it states, "Blessed [אשריך] are you, O Israel; / Who is like you, a
people [עם] saved by the Lord." These words correspond with Ps 33:12a
declaring, "Blessed [אשרי] is the nation [גוי][9] whose God is the Lord." If
one considers this echo as an allusion, it is possible to see the literary connection solidify a vague reference in the psalm. Israel, as a nation, fails to
appear in the psalm, and a need arises to clarify exactly the identity of the
people whose God is the Lord. Via the connection with Deuteronomy, a
presumably known text, the reader specifically identifies this people as
Israel. They are the nation whose God is the Lord, and he is their help
and shield (v. 20).

8. If there is literary borrowing in this instance, then Psalm 33 more likely represents the source text due to the lateness of Psalm 147, which was composed after the
exile. See Kraus, *Psalms*, 556; Schwartz, "Psalm 147," 318.

9. The Hebrew words עם and גוי, ("people" and "nation") are frequently inter-
changeable in Hebrew poetry; see Jer 6:22 and Ps 96:3, for example.

Psalm 34

CONTRASTING THE LACK OF subtitle in Psalm 33, the present composition includes an interpretive incipit linking the contents to a specific event in David's life: When he feigned madness to escape from Abimelech (or Achish), king of the Philistines. This psalm represents the third acrostic in the Psalter, with the first letter of each verse following the sequence of the Hebrew alphabet. At least two alterations, however, disturb this sequence: the omission of *wāw*, expected in v. 6 [7], and the letter *pê* in the last verse (v. 22 [23]) where a *tāw* is expected.[1] Partially as a result of being an acrostic, the psalm resists division into clearly distinguished stanzas.[2] However, as a tool for overall unification, it appears the psalmist inserted the name of the Lord in every verse, with the exception of vv. 12–14 [13–15], and 20–21 [21–22].

Verses 1–3 constitute an open invitation to praise and exalt the name God. Within this section appear both personal expressions of praise, "I will bless the LORD at all times" (v. 1), in addition to corporate

---

1. It is difficult to assert that these unquestionably represent sequencing breaks because they may reflect an alternative ordering of the alphabet. Psalm 25 similarly displays a degree of dissonance in alphabetic sequence with the omission of *wāw* and the addition of the letter *pê* after the *tāw*. McCann, "Psalms," 813, additionally observes that the initial letters in vv. 1, 11, and 22 constitute the Hebrew word אלף.

2. See Craigie and Tate, *Psalms 1–50*, 282, who acknowledge this characteristic of acrostics. Regarding the genre, wisdom obviously surfaces as the dominant theme, as recorded in commentaries such as McCann, "Psalms," 813. Additionally, however, it is hard to ignore the elements of thanksgiving that punctuate the composition as a whole; see VanGemeren, *Psalms*, 323. Recognizing the additional theme of thanksgiving suggests another type of reuse, that of genre, where a psalm originally designed for didactic purposes, guiding and instructing individuals, transforms to serve the purpose of thanksgiving.

exhortations, "O magnify the LORD with me" (v. 3 [4]). A narrative portraying the speaker's divine rescue appears in vv. 4–10 [5–11]; the psalmist describing himself as a poor/humble individual who calls on the Lord. His description here corresponds somewhat with the exhortation in v. 2 [3], where he pleads with the humble, just like himself, to hear his testimony and rejoice, sharing in his personal experience of deliverance. Elements within this section resist a detailed depiction of the psalmist's rescue, and instead constitute a general portrayal of God's ability to save, recalling statements such as "How blessed is the man who takes refuge in Him!" (v. 8b [9b]). The third section, vv. 11–22 [12–23], adopts an instructional tone, with undeniable elements from Israel's wisdom tradition. Here, the psalmist shares his experience of trust in God, and subsequent deliverance, to others who would listen. He has learned wisdom through his direct experiences of God's assistance and desires to disseminate this knowledge to encourage his audience to do the same. Overall, the latter part of this section lingers on the faithfulness of God's character, encouraging the listener to trust in the Lord's ability to hear and deliver (v. 17 [18]). Furthermore, the psalmist encourages the righteous, recognizing that even though they may suffer hardships, God still rescues them from their afflictions. After an individual opening to the composition, where the psalmist emphasizes his perpetual reliance on God, the psalm finishes in v. 22 [23] with a declaration of God's redeeming power for all his servants.

Psalm 34's incipit, לדוד בשנותו את טעמו לפני אבימלך ויגרשהו וילך ("A *Psalm* of David, when he feigned madness before Abimelech, who drove him away and he departed") unequivocally connects the composition to events in 1 Sam 21:10–15 [11–16],[3] recalling David's desperate escape

---

3. To be sure, there exists at least one difficulty with this intertextual connection, and that concerns the king's name. The psalm recalls the Philistine king as Abimelech, whereas 1 Sam 21 recognizes him as Achish. Notwithstanding this difference, the writer of the incipit undoubtedly recalled the events of 1 Sam 21 when writing, even if the king's name differs. The most probable reason for the conflicting names is that the word Abimelech reflects a Philistine monarchic title, like the title Pharaoh is used in Egypt. Consequently, either the name Achish or the title Abimelech may apply to the same individual. Regarding this proposition see Gruber, "Chapter 34," 156; and Craigie and Tate, *Psalms 1–50*, 287, with whom I agree: it is difficult to conceive that a psalmist wrote the name of one individual as a mistake for another. See Seitz, "Psalm 34," for an excellent discussion on the alternative interpretations for the incipit. Far from suggesting an editorial mistake, Seitz further raises the possibility of a purposeful allusion linking David's experiences with those of Abraham and Isaac, who were also endangered by a Philistine king, Abimelech (Seitz, "Psalm 34," 285–86).

to Philistine territory to flee from the threat of Saul. The unique context and wording build the foundation of the allusion, as shown below:

Psalm 34:1 [1–2]	1 Samuel 21:10–13 [11–14)
A *Psalm* of David when he feigned madness [בשנותו את טעמו] before Abimelech, who drove him away and he departed. I will bless the LORD at all times; / His praise shall continually be in my mouth.	Then David arose and fled that day from Saul, and went to Achish king of Gath. But the servants of Achish said to him, "Is this not David the king of the land?" . . . David took these words to heart and greatly feared Achish king of Gath. So he disguised his sanity [וַיְשַׁנּוֹ אֶת־טַעְמוֹ] before them, and acted insanely in their hands, and scribbled on the doors of the gate, and let his saliva run down into his beard.

Adding to the lexical connection between the two texts is the root הלל, describing praise in Ps 34:2 [3], "My soul will make its boast [תִּתְהַלֵּל] in the LORD"; but contributing to a depiction of madness in 1 Sam 21:13 [14], portraying David as behaving insanely (וַיִּתְהֹלָל). Although the meanings differ, repetition of the root in both texts helps to connect them.

When considering the incipit, a notable change occurs in the reader's perception of the psalm's genre. Usually, scholars interpret the composition as a wisdom psalm; however, with the incipit connecting the song to an act of deliverance, the psalm transforms into a song of praise or thanksgiving. The context generated by the connection of the psalm's title to a specific event in David's life, after a miraculous act of deliverance, promotes the profile of thanksgiving within the composition.

Furthermore, the intertextual connection between the pericopae creates a practical-to-abstract relationship:[4] An act of practical deliverance—David suffered persecution, and was exiled from his own land, threatened, and in need of divine assistance—transforms into general principles for God's deliverance. Although David fled to Philistine territory, he remained in full view of God, because "The eyes of the LORD are toward the righteous, / And his ears are *open* to their cry" (v. 15 [16]). The righteous, therefore, have no need to call out because the ever-present God watches them, prepared to intervene. In 1 Samuel, David's arch enemy was not Achish—with whom he developed an amicable

---

4. Similar examples appear in Psalm 3.

relationship—but Saul. However, by the end of 1 Samuel, Saul ultimately meets his demise, allowing David to ascend to the throne. With Saul's death, the practical example in Samuel is theorized by Ps 34:22b [23b], "And none of those who take refuge in him will be condemned." David took refuge in the Lord and was not condemned.

Reading the psalm into the context of David's actions in 1 Samuel generates an important interpretive effect. In Samuel, David's fear for his own life inspired him to concoct a plan to deceive Achish, king of Gath. David solely initiated the plan and implemented it, and God remained absent during the whole affair, a situation reminiscent of Abraham telling Sarah to say that she was his sister (Gen 12:10-13). When reading Samuel, however, with a background knowledge of the psalm, God's role elevates to the forefront of the proceedings. With Psalm 34 in the reader's mind, the idea of feigning insanity was at least partly inspired by God, and ultimately David's deliverance came through divine assistance. Psalm 34:4 [5] attests to divine deliverance, boasting that God answered the psalmist, David, and saved him from all his terrors. Furthermore, v. 6 [7] depicts a man of lowly estate calling to God, and subsequently receiving a divine response (see also v. 17 [18]). Expressions such as these enable the reader to project God's involvement into Samuel's report of David's deliverance even though God's explicit intervention remains absent. Without reading, or having knowledge of the psalm, the Hebrew Bible offers no recognition of David acknowledging the Lord's presence and offering thanksgiving after his narrow escape.[5]

Apart from the incipit in v. 1, Psalm 34 fails to reveal further inner-biblical allusions. The careful reader, however, can detect numerous places in which the psalm echoes words and phrases from Israel's wisdom traditions. Comparisons between the righteous and the wicked in Ps 34:16–17 [17–18], further surface in Prov 13:5, 14:32, 15:28, and 24:16. Similarly, the call for a student's attention בנים שמעו לי ("children listen to me") in Ps 34:11 [12] is also common to Proverbs.[6] Another expression, סור מרע ועשה טוב ("turn from evil and do good"), generally associates

---

5. Directly implying the notion of divine aid in this act of deliverance is the presence of the מלאך יהוה, who appears in the military context of Josh 5:13–15 as the captain of the Lord's armies. His task was to fight for the Israelites in their conquest of Canaan. Clifford, *Psalms 1–72*, 174, refers to him as a military escort for those who do his will.

6. See, for example, Prov 5:7; 7:24; 8:32. One could perhaps add to this the expression אשרי הגבר ("blessed is the man"), which appears in Pss 40:4 [5], 94:12, and 127:5, in addition to Israelite wisdom traditions.

Ps 34:14 [15] with wisdom traditions, as reflected in Prov 14:16, where part of this expression surfaces, but more specifically to another wisdom psalm, Ps 37:27, where the exact phrase reappears.

The expression, עֵין יהוה ("the eye of the Lord"), which creates a nexus between Psalms 33 and 34, necessitates a few comments at this point. Psalm 33:18 reads, "Behold, the eye of the LORD [עֵין יהוה] is on those who fear Him, / On those who hope for His lovingkindness." And in a remarkably similar context, Ps 34:15 [16] tells us "The eyes of the LORD [עֵינֵי יהוה] are toward the righteous, / And His ears are *open* to their cry." Apart from Psalms 33 and 34, this particularly anthropomorphism appears just once in the Psalter, in Ps 116:15, with a significantly different meaning. As an expression of compassion, the verse states the pain and compassion in God's eyes (בְעֵינֵי יהוה) when one of his servants falls. Considering this distribution, the expression's appearance in Psalms 33 and 34 suggest a strong motivation for juxtaposing the two compositions, signifying the influence of association.[7]

---

7. Regarding the specific order in which they now appear, one could argue for a logical connection between psalms. After a stated principle, "The eye of the Lord is on those who fear him," the reader faces a practical example; when David fled to the land of the Philistines, God's eye remained on him, and delivered him from the hand of Achish.

Psalm 35

PSALM 35 CONNECTS TO the previous psalm via the simple incipit לדוד ("*A Psalm* of David"). The psalm presents the reader with a visceral complaint to God,[1] regarding an adversary unlike that of the preceding work. Instead of threats from an established enemy, it is a close friend who betrays the psalmist. The opening section, vv. 1–8, calls for God's intervention in the psalmist's situation, requesting that the Lord avenge him with warlike aggression by vanquishing the adversary with spear and shield. In these initial verses, the psalmist depends heavily on jussive forms: "Let those be ashamed. . . . Let those be turned back. . . . Let them be like chaff," etc. Verse 9 opens a new stanza, which extends through to v. 16 and begins with words of hope and trust in God's ability to deliver the afflicted. Such sentiments, however, soon return to complaint as the psalmist adds further details concerning his distress.[2] Within the stanza, the writer compares his integrity and faithfulness to the lack of such qualities found in his betraying friends. Moved with compassion, the psalmist proves faithful to his companions, mourning for them, grieving with them, and praying for them. But in return, the recipients of his compassion repay him by rejoicing at his stumbling, slandering him, and mocking him. The final stanza, vv. 17–28, echoes the first, with respect to the choice of verb aspect, and the psalmist returns to a series of volitive forms: "Stir up yourself" (v. 23); "Judge me" (v. 24); "Do not let them say" (v. 25), etc. Each phrase expresses the speaker's desires, which

---

1. Naturally, it is classified as an individual lament; see Gruber, "Chapter 35," 158, or more precisely as an imprecatory psalm, as VanGemeren, *Psalms*, 328, asserts.

2. His distress, as McCann, "Psalms," 819, claims, is also reflected in the "literary disarray" of the composition.

suggests the author remains in distress waiting for divine intervention. As expected with laments in general, the final verse of the composition expresses the psalmist's promised response if God intervenes and delivers him from his enemy: He will declare the praises of God and proclaim his righteousness. An overall notable feature worth mentioning about this composition concerns the quotes the psalmist inserts into the mouth of both people and inanimate objects: God (v. 3), his enemies (vv. 21, 25), his bones (v. 10) and his supporters (v. 27).

Regarding juxtaposition, the relatively rare expression, "the angel of the LORD" (מלאך יהוה), generates an associative link between Psalms 34 and 35. It appears three times in the book of Psalms, twice in Psalm 35, and once in Psalm 34.[3] In this instance, one could argue, as do Keil and Delitzsch,[4] that the rare phrase influenced an arranger of the Psalter to juxtapose these two works. Examining this lexical connection further, however, raises the possibility that the relationship between the psalms themselves stems from an act of literary borrowing. Two factors, particularly, lend weight to this probability. First, the preponderance of echoes and intertextual allusions that Psalm 35 bears with other biblical texts (see below) suggests the psalmist also borrowed from the preceding psalm. Second, both psalms adopt the phrase, "the angel of the Lord," (מלאך יהוה) with similar intentions, divine protection. In Psalm 34, the angel of the Lord encamps around those who fear him, as a protector and one who shelters God-fearers. Similarly, Psalm 35 reveals the angel of the Lord as one who protects, though the psalmist's portrayal of his role is slightly more aggressive. The angel in Psalm 35 offers a little more than protection of the God-fearer; he actively scatters and disperses those seeking the psalmist's harm, pursuing them as they flee.[5] Thus, one concludes that the borrowed image experiences further development in the hands of the later author. In addition to adopting the "angel of the Lord" imagery, Psalm 35's author intensifies his role.

---

3. Here, I exclude the phrase "Bless the Lord, you his angels" in Ps 103:20 because it fails to reflect the specific figure represented in Psalms 34 and 35.

4. See Keil and Delitzsch, *Psalms*, 1:416.

5. VanGemeren, *Psalms*, 328, pushes the relationship further than just the literary connection of the angel of the Lord. He further asserts thematic associations, including the notion of the poor and the needy reflected in Ps 34:2 [3], 6 [7] and Ps 35:10; and the idea of shame and disgrace linking Pss 34:5 [6] and 35:4, 26. Thematic associations such as these, however, frequently appear as standard elements of the lament genre, so it is hard to assert their influence on an editor's decision to juxtapose psalms.

The volume of shared vocabulary between Psalms 35 and 70 ensures the probability of literary dependence. Below, the table highlights the key areas of commonality.

Psalm 35	Psalm 70
יֵבֹשׁוּ וְיִכָּלְמוּ מְבַקְשֵׁי נַפְשִׁי יִסֹּגוּ אָחוֹר וְיַחְפְּרוּ חֹשְׁבֵי רָעָתִי	יֵבֹשׁוּ וְיַחְפְּרוּ מְבַקְשֵׁי נַפְשִׁי יִסֹּגוּ אָחוֹר וְיִכָּלְמוּ חֲפֵצֵי רָעָתִי
Let those be ashamed and dishonored who seek my life; / Let those be turned back and humiliated who devise evil against me. (v. 4)[6]	Let those be ashamed and humiliated / Who seek my life; / Let those be turned back and dishonored / Who delight in my hurt. (v. 2 [3])
וַיַּרְחִיבוּ עָלַי פִּיהֶם אָמְרוּ הֶאָח הֶאָח רָאֲתָה עֵינֵינוּ	יָשׁוּבוּ עַל־עֵקֶב בָּשְׁתָּם הָאֹמְרִים הֶאָח הֶאָח
They opened their mouth wide against me; / They said, "Aha, aha, our eyes have seen it!" (v. 21)	Let those be turned back because of their shame / Who say, "Aha, aha!" (v. 3 [4])
יָרֹנּוּ וְיִשְׂמְחוּ חֲפֵצֵי צִדְקִי וְיֹאמְרוּ תָמִיד יִגְדַּל יְהוָה הֶחָפֵץ שְׁלוֹם עַבְדּוֹ	יָשִׂישׂוּ וְיִשְׂמְחוּ בְּךָ כָּל־מְבַקְשֶׁיךָ וְיֹאמְרוּ תָמִיד יִגְדַּל אֱלֹהִים אֹהֲבֵי יְשׁוּעָתֶךָ
Let them shout for joy and rejoice, who favor my vindication; / And let them say continually, "The LORD be magnified, / Who delights in the prosperity of His servant." (v. 27)	Let all who seek You rejoice and be glad in You; / And let those who love Your salvation say continually, / "Let God be magnified." (v. 4 [5])

Despite the compelling similarities, the relationship between the two compositions differs from that of Psalm 14's detailed relationship with Psalm 53. Psalms 14 and 53 essentially reflect the same composition that experienced modifications by the hand of different editors from the time of its conception to its present form as two independent psalms. For that reason, the connection between the two represents something more than literary borrowing, and closer to a rewritten or slightly edited version of the same composition.

Focusing on the duplicated material between Psalms 35 and 70, two particularly noticeable characteristics surface. First, Psalm 70 clusters

6. At this point, it is worth mentioning Ps 40:14, יֵבֹשׁוּ וְיַחְפְּרוּ יַחַד מְבַקְשֵׁי נַפְשִׁי לִסְפּוֹתָהּ יִסֹּגוּ אָחוֹר וְיִכָּלְמוּ חֲפֵצֵי רָעָתִי ("Let those be ashamed and humiliated together / Who seek my life to destroy it; / Let those be turned back and dishonored / Who delight in my hurt"). However, more vocabulary similarities appear in Psalm 70.

the shared vocabulary together in consecutive verses. And though the order of duplicated material remains the same in Psalm 35, it appears dispersed throughout this longer composition. Consequently, it reflects an expansion or special development of the same material—or a contraction by the author of Psalm 70, depending on how one views the direction of borrowing. Second, regarding the connection between Pss 35:27 and 70:4 [5], it seems the same words, יאמרו תמיד יגדל יהוה ("let them say continually, 'The LORD be magnified'"), were intended by both authors. Despite the intention, the phrase in Psalm 70 appears with the word אלהים, "God," as opposed to the Tetragrammaton in Psalm 35. The change to אלהים stems from Psalm 70's appearance within the Elohistic Psalter (Psalms 42–83), a known subcollection of psalms that reflects signs of an editorial propensity to substitute the more generic name of God for the divine name.[7] The change from the Tetragrammaton to the word "God" ostensibly suggests Psalm 70 adopted words from Psalm 35. Then at a later stage, the Tetragrammaton in v. 5 underwent redaction to the generic "God," as part of the psalm's inclusion into the Elohistic Psalter. This scenario appears more likely than Psalm 35's author appropriating an expression from Psalm 70 that included the word "God" and subsequently redacting it to the Tetragrammaton. However, the nature of Psalm 35 obfuscates this apparently reasonable assumption. Because Psalm 35 borrows from a wide selection of other biblical texts, Psalm 70 appears to be the earlier source. Consequently, at this stage of analysis, we must surmise that Psalm 35's author gained access to an earlier version of Psalm 70, one that excluded the Elohistic alteration.

At this point, a thematic difference between the compositions with respect to the psalmist and his enemy deserves attention. The presentation of the psalmist's foe in Psalm 35 reflects an extremely intense image of the hostile force. Not only are specifics concerning his attack more forthcoming, together with details of malicious witnesses (v. 11) and mocking grimaces (v. 16), but the enemy's previous relationship to the psalmist, his friend and confidant, further exacerbates the psalmist's hurt. As a result of the heightened intensity, Psalm 35 recalls an extended appeal for God's intervention in vv. 17–24. Here, repeated vocatives addressed to God generate a heightened sense of desperation. The intensity of this enmity between the psalmist and his former friend appears more diluted in Psalm 70, however, and it mitigates the conflict's severity.

7. See Joffe, "The Elohistic Psalter."

At least four further instances of lexical correspondences exist between Psalm 35 and Old Testament literature (see tables below). Ostensibly, each instance may simply reflect a biblical echo, where the psalmist almost unconsciously recalls phrases appearing elsewhere in the Hebrew Bible. However, because each of the intertextual relationships below represents a unique connection between Psalm 35 and a subsequent intertext, it is necessary to reevaluate their relationships. The uniqueness of the common wording suggests an intentional appropriation of known biblical texts. The psalm's first connection to Jeremiah appears in the table below.

Psalm 35:6	Jeremiah 23:12
יְהִי־דַרְכָּם חֹשֶׁךְ וַחֲלַקְלַקּוֹת וּמַלְאַךְ יְהוָה רֹדְפָם	לָכֵן יִהְיֶה דַרְכָּם לָהֶם כַּחֲלַקְלַקּוֹת בָּאֲפֵלָה יִדַּחוּ וְנָפְלוּ בָהּ
Let their way be dark and slippery, / With the angel of the LORD pursuing them.	"Therefore their way will be like slippery paths to them, / They will be driven away into the gloom and fall down in it; / For I will bring calamity upon them, / The year of their punishment," declares the LORD.

In borrowing this phrase from Jeremiah,[8] the psalmist ascribes to himself feelings of betrayal suffered by Jeremiah. Both individuals feel a sense of disloyalty from those who should have provided encouragement and strength. Individuals assumed to be allies become antagonists who betray the innocent. In Jeremiah, the priests and prophets bear responsibility to support the people of Judah, but ultimately, through their treacherous behavior, induce disaster and judgment on the people. Similarly, those closest to the psalmist, to whom he bestowed compassion, betray that trust, and turn to mock and sneer at him. In this way the psalmist compares the actions of his companions to the priests and prophets in Jeremiah's day. Both individuals experience the words of Prov 13:12a, "Hope deferred makes the heart sick." The psalmist's adoption of Jeremiah's words reflects a classic use of allusion, where a writer recalls imagery from a distant location in Scripture to contribute an added dimension and intensity to his work.

---

8. In addition to the underlined words above, two expressions of darkness further connect the texts, חשך in Psalm 35 and אפלה in Jer 23:12.

A further connection appears between Psalms 9 and 35, as seen below:

Psalm 35:7	Psalm 9:15 [16]
כִּי־חִנָּם טָמְנוּ־לִי שַׁחַת רִשְׁתָּם חִנָּם חָפְרוּ לְנַפְשִׁי	טָבְעוּ גוֹיִם בְּשַׁחַת עָשׂוּ בְּרֶשֶׁת־זוּ טָמָנוּ נִלְכְּדָה רַגְלָם
For without cause they hid their net for me; / Without cause they dug a pit for my soul.	The nations have sunk down in the pit *which* they have made; / In the net which they hid, their own foot has been caught.

The desire expressed through the lexical connections above reflects the renowned biblical principle of measure for measure: That which you do to others will return to you as punishment in equal measure. For the author in Psalm 35, his intimate request reflects a desire for retribution against those who attack him personally, that the trap they lay for him turns against them. Psalm 9's author, on the other hand, rejoices in judgment against the nations because they sank into the pit that they had dug and were snared in the net they laid. Instead of an individual instance of measure for measure, Psalm 9 adopts more of a national perspective, where enemies of the nation receive punishment in equal measure to their evil intentions.

A further allusion or echo connects Psalm 35 with a text from the Pentateuch, the book of Deuteronomy:

Psalm 35:11	Deuteronomy 19:16
יְקוּמוּן עֵדֵי חָמָס אֲשֶׁר לֹא־יָדַעְתִּי יִשְׁאָלוּנִי	כִּי־יָקוּם עֵד־חָמָס בְּאִישׁ לַעֲנוֹת בּוֹ סָרָה
Malicious witnesses rise up; / They ask me of things that I do not know	If a malicious witness rises up against a man to accuse him of wrongdoing

Deuteronomy stipulates the required punitive action against a malicious witness (עֵד חָמָס) who arises to testify against another man. Both accuser and accused stand before the Lord, then the priests and judges carefully investigate the allegations. If found guilty, the malicious witness is punished, "Then you shall do to him just as he had planned to do to his brother" (Deut 19:19a). With these words, it appears that the passage in Deuteronomy inspired the psalmist's words. Although the expression

עד חמס appears in Exod 23:1, the context of measure for measure remains absent. By specifically selecting the phrase, "malicious witness," and echoing sentiments of measure for measure, the psalmist apparently pleads to Pentateuchal authority for judgment against his enemy.

Turning now to Psalms 35 and 37, the following similarities appear:

Psalm 35:16	Psalm 37:12
בְּחַנְפֵי לַעֲגֵי מָעוֹג חָרֹק עָלַי שִׁנֵּימוֹ	זֹמֵם רָשָׁע לַצַּדִּיק וְחֹרֵק עָלָיו שִׁנָּיו
Like godless jesters at a feast, / They gnashed at me with their teeth.	The wicked plots against the righteous / And gnashes at him with his teeth.

In Ps 35:16, the psalmist ostensibly draws from a wisdom tradition specifically reflected in Ps 37:12. Ordinarily, the expression, "gnashed at me with their teeth," fails to alert readers of literary borrowing. Biblical literature, after all, echoes the phrase in three other locations.[9] Furthermore, even in English, the concept of gnashing one's teeth in anger constitutes a relatively popular expression. Notwithstanding the incidental nature of this idiom, a case still exists for the author specifically drawing from a particular psalm. One reason to suspect something more than a casual relationship between the psalms concerns the literary setting. As in the case of Deuteronomy 19 above, a similar context between the psalms strengthens their relationship. In Psalm 37, as part of a general wisdom saying, the psalmist states that the wicked schemes against the just and gnashes his teeth at him. The psalmist voices an abstract, perpetual truth without a specific instance in mind, a truth that denounces malicious individuals for plotting against the righteous. This is precisely the situation in which Psalm 35's author finds himself. The wicked, those for whom the psalmist sought to comfort in the past, have plotted against him, a righteous man. Gathering against him when he stumbled (v. 15), they mockingly grimaced at him in his moment of need. Drawing further from Psalm 37, allows the psalmist to take comfort in v. 13, "The Lord laughs at him [the enemy], / For He sees that his day is coming" (Ps 37:13). The corresponding contexts and vocabulary between Psalms 35 and 37 fail to present the reader with an unassailable case for literary borrowing, but the connection nevertheless deserves a mention.[10]

9. See Job 16:9; Ps 112:10; Lam 2:16.

10. The last two intertextual relationships mentioned above represent abstract

The final intertextual association links Psalms 35 and 71, the lexical connections appear in the table below:

Psalm 35	Psalm 71
רָאִיתָה יְהוָה אַל־תֶּחֱרַשׁ אֲדֹנָי אַל־תִּרְחַק מִמֶּנִּי	אֱלֹהִים אַל־תִּרְחַק מִמֶּנִּי אֱלֹהַי לְעֶזְרָתִי [חוּשָׁה] (חִישָׁה)
You have seen it, O LORD, do not keep silent; / O LORD, do not be far from me. (v. 22)	O God, do not be far from me; / O my God, hasten to my help! (v. 12)
וּלְשׁוֹנִי תֶּהְגֶּה צִדְקֶךָ כָּל־הַיּוֹם תְּהִלָּתֶךָ	גַּם־לְשׁוֹנִי כָּל־הַיּוֹם תֶּהְגֶּה צִדְקָתֶךָ כִּי־בֹשׁוּ כִי־חָפְרוּ מְבַקְשֵׁי רָעָתִי
And my tongue shall proclaim Your righteousness / *And* Your praise all day long. (v. 28)	My tongue also will utter Your righteousness all day long; / For they are ashamed, for they are humiliated who seek my hurt. (v. 24)

The closing words of Psalm 35 generate an intertext with Psalm 71,[11] with both compositions utilizing similar terminology expressing the psalmists' constant desire to speak of God's wonderful acts. The specific language of the tongue speaking God's righteousness or beneficent acts all day only appears in these two locations in the Hebrew Bible. Specifically furthering the connection between the two psalms is the phrase, "do not be far from me" (Pss 35:22; 71:12). Although the expression appears elsewhere in biblical literature,[12] this additional connection to Ps 71:24 further solidifies and inculcates the close association between the compositions.[13] Unlike the echoes and allusions mentioned thus far, Psalm

---

concepts from a source transforming into concrete and specific situations relating to an individual.

11. An undeniable relationship exists between Psalms 70 and 71 that partially obfuscates the connections between Psalms 35 and 70. Tate, *Psalms 51–100*, 211, notes that several statements bind Psalms 70 and 71 together.

12. See Pss 22:11 [12] and 38:21 [22] for example.

13. In addition to the common vocabulary mentioned above, the expression לשלם רעה תחת טוב ("to repay evil for good") deserves attention. Even in the English language the phrase represents a relatively common expression, so to argue for an allusion based on these words alone remains difficult to prove. Despite this difficulty, assuming readers of the psalm were well acquainted with the Torah, it is hard to overlook the connection to Gen 44:4. After Joseph frames his brothers for the theft of his silver diviner's cup, he overtakes them and asks why they have repaid evil for good (שלמתם רעה תחת טובה). Although situated in the Joseph narrative, the transfer of this

35 apparently functions as a source for Psalm 71, and not a borrower. Although both psalmists display a propensity to appropriate material from widespread poetic traditions, Psalm 71, overall, reflects an early florilegium, or as Kraus cites, "a collection of quotations."[14] No incontrovertible assurances exist concerning this direction of borrowing, but the probability of Psalm 71 citing from Psalm 35 remains the best solution to the problem at this time.

---

emotion well suits the context of the psalm. The psalmist complains of those who betrayed him and became malicious witnesses. These are the same people with whom he had sympathized and shown genuine concern. They accompanied him as though they were his friends or brothers. Here, the aspect of familial betrayal resonates with the text of Genesis because in Genesis, Joseph's actual brothers betrayed him.

14. See Kraus, *Psalms 60–150*, 71; Tate, *Psalms 51–100*, 211.

Psalm 36

PSALM 36'S TITLE RECALLS Psalm 18's incipit because it includes the designation of a "servant," למנצח לעבד יהוה לדוד ("For the choir director. *A Psalm* of David the servant of the LORD." The psalm consists of two sections, and staunchly resists classification into a single genre as delineated by traditional form-critical methodologies. However, perhaps the most dominant characteristic connects the psalm to Israel's wisdom traditions.[1] Its stereotypical illustration of righteous and wicked behavioral patterns contributes to this categorization, in addition to vocabulary such as להשכיל ("to make wise," v. 3 [4]). The opening section, vv. 1–4 [1–5], depicts the general behavior of the wicked, but the psalm mentions no specific object of the wicked person's actions.[2] In this sense, it differs from the laments discussed thus far, where the psalmists usually receive the taunts and threats of wicked people. The ungodly, according to the psalm, lack the fear of God, speak words of wickedness and deceit, fail to be wise and do good, and plan wickedness on their beds. Contrasting this, the second part of the psalm, vv. 5–12 [6–13], lingers on God's lovingkindness as it extends to the righteous. The critical point of contrast highlighted by the psalmist centers on the blessings God bestows on the righteous. He lets them drink from refreshing streams (v. 9),

---

1. To be sure, the identification of the genre confounds several commentators. McCann, "Psalms," 822, settles on a lament, whereas Craigie and Tate, *Psalms 1–50*, 290, recognize the wisdom and hymnic elements in addition to the lament. Likewise, VanGemeren, *Psalms*, 335, identifies three genres: the hymn, the lament, and the wisdom psalm—though he eventually settles on the final product reflecting a wisdom psalm.

2. Concerning the description of the wicked, Clifford, *Psalms 1–72*, 181, suggests that their portrayal in this psalm is unparalleled in the Psalter.

grants faithful care to those devoted to him, and prevents the foot of the arrogant from treading on them (v. 11 [12]). The final verse returns to depictions of the wicked, lucidly delineating their end: fallen, thrust down, never to rise again. Psalm 36 reminds the reader of Psalm 1's conclusion, which similarly depicts the demise of evildoers.

Concerning echo and allusion, precious little in the way of lexical elements connect Psalm 36 to other biblical texts. The most obvious point of contact relates to the incipit, למנצח לעבד יהוה לדוד, which only appears twice in the Psalter, Pss 36:1 and 18:1. Even this link between the compositions remains tenuous at best because Psalm 18 adds further information to the incipit, "Who spoke to the LORD the words of this song on the day that the LORD delivered him from the hand of all his enemies and from the hand of Saul. And he said . . ." Other than the incipit, no notable shared elements connect the psalms, and all common vocabulary appearing between these psalms frequently appears throughout the Psalter and the Hebrew Bible. It is worth noting, however, that the description of David as "the servant of the LORD" (עבד יהוה) encourages a comparison with other biblical heroes such as Moses (Deut 34:5) and Joshua (Josh 8:33).[3]

Little can be said concerning a juxtaposition rationale between Psalms 35 and 36. The most viable lexical candidate for associating the psalms is the root דחה ("to push/reject"). It is limited to six appearances in the Psalter, and Psalms 35 and 36 contain the only juxtaposed compositions that adopt the root. In both instances, the verb addresses evildoers. In Ps 36:12, these men of iniquity have been thrust down, although no agent is provided for the verb. Psalm 35, however, apparently supplies the missing detail, stating, "Let them be like chaff before the wind / With the angel of the LORD driving them on." Here, it is specifically the angel of the Lord who drives the evil doers away.

---

3. A further connection between these figures appears in Midr. Tehillim 1:2, which compares the five books of the Psalter to the five books of Moses.

Psalm 37

PSALM 37 REPRESENTS ANOTHER acrostic composition that lucidly associates itself with Israel's wisdom traditions; consequently, contemporary scholarship frequently identifies it as a wisdom psalm. Division of the psalm into stanzas presents no shortage of challenges[1] because it constitutes a collection of pithy wisdom phrases that exhort the righteous to continue in faithful service to God, and not concern themselves with the ways of the wicked. Rather than attempt to impose an artificial structure, it seems more appropriate to draw attention to the composition's key themes that coalesce into a unified composition.

One such dominant theme concerns the wicked and their ultimate destruction and demise. They wither like grass (v. 2) and are destined for oblivion (v. 10); they will ultimately perish, being consumed in smoke (v. 20).[2] Detailing their ultimate annihilation goads the righteous to avoid their ways and shun their company. Complementing their future

---

1. This is patently evident from the wide variations of divisions proposed by modern commentators. McCann, "Psalms," 828–30, opts for 1–11, 12–26, 27–29, 30–40; whereas Craigie and Tate, *Psalms 1–50*, 297–99, are guided by the individual verse(s) signified by the letters of the alphabet. VanGemeren, *Psalms*, 341, views it as a wisdom psalm that bears little evidence of logical progression. Kraus, *Psalms 1–59*, 404, echoes a similar sentiment. Brueggemann and Bellinger, *Psalms*, 185, divide the psalm into two sections: 1–11 and 12–20. The first half describes general behavioral patterns about life, and the second section includes more commands. Clifford, *Psalms 1–72*, 187, adopts a similar position. Accepting the composition as a wisdom psalm, McCann, "Psalms," 828, categorizes the composition as a homily addressing the apparent success of the wicked, and links it to other texts addressing theodicy (Psalms 49, 73, and Job).

2. See also v. 28, the unjust destroyed forever, and v. 38, the future of transgressors cut off.

destruction, the psalm devotes time to detailing the behavior of the wicked, and their wrongdoings: plotting against the righteous (v. 12), borrowing and not repaying (v. 21), lying in wait, and killing them (v. 32). As expected from wisdom literature, the depictions reflect abstract concepts as opposed to concrete examples and specific instances of malicious acts performed against the righteous. In addition to detailing wicked and adverse behavior, the psalm reflects on the righteous, their actions, and their destiny. For the righteous, destruction does not await them, but a promise of land, which the psalmist discloses on at least three occasions (see vv. 11, 29, 34). Likewise, the psalmist recognizes the stereotypical behavior of the righteous: they are praised for lending and being generous (v. 26), and their mouths speak wisdom and justice (v. 30). Scattered among the contrasting behavioral patterns of the righteous and the wicked are exhortations to positive actions. The psalm encourages its readers to refrain from worry (vv. 1, 8), trust in God (vv. 3, 5), turn from evil (v. 27), and wait for the Lord (v. 34).

In addition to its focus on people's behavior, the psalmist acknowledges divine action, especially towards the righteous. God sustains them (v. 17), even to the point of holding their hand (v. 24). Moreover, he provides for the just in times of famine (v. 19), keeps the righteous from the hands of the wicked (v. 33), and helps and delivers them (v. 40).

The psalmist's intermittent personal reflections of the righteous and wicked deserves further attention. His understanding of God stems from his personal experience, and from situations he has witnessed. From his experience in v. 25, he declares, "I have been young and now I am old, / Yet I have not seen the righteous forsaken Or his descendants begging bread." Again in vv. 35–36, the psalmist recalls wicked people temporarily flourishing, only to have their end come upon them, leaving no trace of their existence. This type of personal reflection parallels the book of Ecclesiastes, which similarly exhibits the reflections of a wise man ("The Preacher," Eccl 12:10) who proclaims insights from personal life experiences.

Regarding intertextuality, Psalm 37 undoubtedly draws from the deep well of Israelite wisdom tradition. The table below highlights the connection via comparable language between the psalm and the book of Proverbs:

Psalm 37	Wisdom Traditions
אַל־תִּתְחַר בַּמְּרֵעִים אַל־תְּקַנֵּא בְּעֹשֵׂי עַוְלָה	אַל־תִּתְחַר בַּמְּרֵעִים אַל־תְּקַנֵּא בָּרְשָׁעִים
Do not fret because of evildoers, / Be not envious toward wrongdoers. (v. 1)	Do not fret because of evildoers / Or be envious of the wicked. (Prov 24:19)
גּוֹל עַל־יְהוָה דַּרְכֶּךָ וּבְטַח עָלָיו וְהוּא יַעֲשֶׂה	גֹּל אֶל־יְהוָה מַעֲשֶׂיךָ וְיִכֹּנוּ מַחְשְׁבֹתֶיךָ
Commit your way to the LORD, / Trust also in Him, and He will do it. (v. 5)	Commit your works to the LORD / And your plans will be established. (Prov 16:3)
מֵיְהוָה מִצְעֲדֵי־גָבֶר כּוֹנָנוּ וְדַרְכּוֹ יֶחְפָּץ	מֵיְהוָה מִצְעֲדֵי־גָבֶר וְאָדָם מַה־יָּבִין דַּרְכּוֹ
The steps of a man are established by the LORD, / And He delights in his way. (v. 23)	Man's steps are *ordained* by the LORD, / How then can man understand his way? (Prov 20:24)
סוּר מֵרָע וַעֲשֵׂה־טוֹב וּשְׁכֹן לְעוֹלָם	סוּר מֵרָע וַעֲשֵׂה־טוֹב בַּקֵּשׁ שָׁלוֹם וְרָדְפֵהוּ
Depart from evil and do good, / So you will abide forever. (v. 27)	Depart from evil and do good; / Seek peace and pursue it. (Ps 34:14 [15])
פִּי־צַדִּיק יֶהְגֶּה חָכְמָה וּלְשׁוֹנוֹ תְּדַבֵּר מִשְׁפָּט	פִּי־צַדִּיק יָנוּב חָכְמָה וּלְשׁוֹן תַּהְפֻּכוֹת תִּכָּרֵת
The mouth of the righteous utters wisdom, / And his tongue speaks justice. (v. 30)	The mouth of the righteous flows with wisdom, / But the perverted tongue will be cut out. (Prov 10:31)

From the text comparison above one cannot assert conclusively that the psalmist consulted a Proverb's scroll, from which he then wrote his composition, or whether he simply produced his psalm by drawing upon his knowledge of popular wisdom traditions. However, it is notable that of all the intertextual connections above, not a single whole verse from Proverbs was transposed into the psalmist's work; instead, only brief groupings of words and short phrases echoed from Proverbs, which suggests the psalmist operated from a general knowledge of wisdom literature.[3]

Regarding the juxtaposition of the present psalm, Keil and Delitzsch argue that an editor placed Psalm 37 after Psalm 36 because of their similar content.[4] The wisdom elements in the present composition

---

3. The high concentration of wisdom elements in the psalm lends further weight to Kraus's argument for the composition's post-exilic context. See Kraus, *Psalms, 1–59*, 404.

4. See Keil and Delitzsch, *Psalms*, 2:10.

correspond with the faint, but evident, traces of wisdom material in the previous composition. Although the dependence on wisdom traditions differs between the two psalms, their presence may have influenced their juxtaposition because neither Psalms 35 nor 38 contain material connected to Israel's wisdom traditions. Words concerning the fate of evildoers further dictates the specific sequencing of Psalms 36 and 37. Psalm 36:12 [13], the final verse, states that the wicked will be thrust down, never to rise again, and this corresponds with Psalm 37's beginning that discourages anxious concern for the wicked because they will soon fade. The juxtaposition between Psalms 36 and 37 thus reflects the tendency among biblical authors to sequence compositions by placing similar themes together, creating a seamless literary transition.

Psalm 38

PSALM 38 INTRODUCES A new element to the Davidic titles; although it is a psalm of David, the term להזכיר appears, suggesting "for a memorial" or "a memory."[1] The only other time the Psalter records להזכיר as part of an incipit is Ps 70:1, which adopts a slightly varied form, למנצח לדוד להזכיר. That said, neither composition exhibits further clues regarding the relevance of this title to the psalm's contents. If להזכיר means "to remember" or "to remind," the conundrum remains concerning who needs to remember what.

Throughout this individual lament,[2] the primary source of the psalmist's angst concerns God himself, yet the same God also appears as the psalmist's only hope. Like Psalm 37, the present composition resists division into well-defined stanzas.[3] Verses 1–9 [10] predominantly depict the psalmist's personal suffering from an undisclosed physical malady, which removes all soundness from his flesh, leaving him with wounds that stink and fester (vv. 3 [4], 5 [6]). Unlike Psalm 26, the present psalmist recognizes his sin and the role he plays in receiving divine judgment. Undoubtedly, the author realizes his iniquities have overwhelmed him (v. 4 [5]), and they ultimately cause his deteriorating health (v. 5 [6]). Focus on the

---

1. The title may relate to the memorial offering, אַזְכָּרָה, mentioned in Lev 2:2; 24:7, where the prayer apparently augments or replaces the sacrifice.

2. See VanGemeren, *Psalms*, 352; Edenburg, "Chapter 38," 169. Little argument arises concerning the psalm's genre.

3. Probably, this relates to the acrostic structure. Although the psalm fails to convey consecutive letters of the Hebrew alphabet at the start of each line, it comprises twenty-two verses, the same number of letters as the Hebrew alphabet. Various scholars document the difficulty in defining a lucid structural pattern. See, for example, Craigie and Tate, *Psalms 1–50*, 302; and Clifford, *Psalms 1–72*, 192, who further argue that both Psalms 37 and 38 possess a dense logic with respect to structure that is difficult to understand.

psalmist's distress and physical anguish are accentuated in vv. 6–8 [7–9]. Here, the reader learns that he is bent over all day, and suffers a burning in his loins, leading him to groan because of the anguish of his heart. Verses 9–12 [10–13] open a new section that is offset with the vocative, אֲדֹנָי, ("Lord").[4] In this stanza, the psalmist pleads with God concerning his physical suffering, which is exacerbated by his close friends' response: They set traps for him and devise evil plans against him. Creating a more introspective view, vv. 13–17 [14–18] find the psalmist comparing himself to a person lacking the ability to speak and hear, which subsequently leads him to plead his case before God, hoping for divine mercy. In the final verses, 19–22 [20–23], the psalmist again recalls the actions of his enemies, their capabilities, and the vitriol directed toward him. Then, from a position of despair, he utters his final plea for divine assistance: That God would not abandon him, but hurry to save him.

One echo deserving attention appears between Pss 38:12 [13] and 71:24:

Psalm 38:12	Psalm 71:24
וַיְנַקְשׁוּ מְבַקְשֵׁי נַפְשִׁי וְדֹרְשֵׁי רָעָתִי דִּבְּרוּ הַוּוֹת וּמִרְמוֹת כָּל־הַיּוֹם יֶהְגּוּ	גַּם־לְשׁוֹנִי כָּל־הַיּוֹם תֶּהְגֶּה צִדְקָתֶךָ כִּי־בֹשׁוּ כִי־חָפְרוּ מְבַקְשֵׁי רָעָתִי
Those who seek my life lay snares *for me*; / And those who seek to injure me have threatened destruction, / And they devise treachery all day long.	My tongue also will utter Your righteousness all day long; / For they are ashamed, for they are humiliated who seek my hurt.

Ostensibly, the common elements above suggest a purposeful allusion between the psalms, but relevant differences separate the two contexts. In Psalm 71, the utterance "all day long" functions in a positive context, which contrasts the same expression appearing in Psalm 38. The author of Psalm 71 utters God's righteousness all day long, whereas Ps 38:12 [13] recalls the psalmist's enemies devising treachery with their words all day long. Of the three instances in which the expression כל יום הגה ("utter all day") appears in the Psalter (Pss 35:28; 38:12 [13]; 71:24), only Ps 38:12 [13] sets the expression within a negatively framed context.[5] Considering these connections, if literary borrowing were present

---

4. Author's translation.

5. The expression, "seeking my hurt," occurs frequently within individual laments; therefore, one cannot easily present it as a sustainable argument for literary borrowing.

between these psalms, then Psalm 38 probably represents the source text. Despite both psalmists' tendency to reuse wording from other psalms and biblical texts, Psalm 71's author seems more entrenched in this literary practice.[6]

Psalm 38 further connects with Psalm 22:

Psalm 38	Psalm 22
אַל־תַּעַזְבֵנִי יְהוָה אֱלֹהַי אַל־תִּרְחַק מִמֶּנִּי	אֵלִי אֵלִי לָמָה עֲזַבְתָּנִי רָחוֹק מִישׁוּעָתִי דִּבְרֵי שַׁאֲגָתִי
Do not forsake me, O LORD; / O my God, do not be far from me! (v. 21 [22])	My God, my God, why have You forsaken me? / Far from my deliverance are the words of my groaning. (v. 1 [2])
אַל־תַּעַזְבֵנִי יְהוָה אֱלֹהַי אַל־תִּרְחַק מִמֶּנִּי	אַל־תִּרְחַק מִמֶּנִּי כִּי־צָרָה קְרוֹבָה כִּי־אֵין עוֹזֵר
Do not forsake me, O LORD; / O my God, do not be far from me! (v. 21 [22])	Be not far from me, for trouble is near; / For there is none to help. (v. 11 [12])
חוּשָׁה לְעֶזְרָתִי אֲדֹנָי תְּשׁוּעָתִי	וְאַתָּה יְהוָה אַל־תִּרְחָק אֱיָלוּתִי לְעֶזְרָתִי חוּשָׁה
Make haste to help me, / O Lord, my salvation! (v. 22 [23])	But You, O LORD, be not far off; / O You my help, hasten to my assistance. (v. 19 [20])

Although points of resonance appear between Psalms 38 and 22, as demonstrated above, it remains problematic to argue for literary borrowing. The duplicated language suggests a coincidental occurrence rather than an intentional and cognizant adoption of an earlier text. Considering that both compositions reflect the lament genre, such correlation in vocabulary naturally arises without an implication of allusion.[7]

The roots דרש and בקש are frequently used synonymously in poetry, as seen from the expressions דרש רעה and בקש רעה. See Ps 71:13, 24; Prov 11:27.

6. See the discussion on Psalm 35.

7. Keil and Delitzsch, *Psalms*, 2:20, observe that the ending of one psalm provides the impetus for the theme of the following composition, generating the rationale for juxtaposition. Whereas one sees a connection between God delivering the righteous from the wicked in Ps 37:40–41 and the wicked threatening the life of the psalmist in Ps 38:12, 19–20, it is difficult to assert that this connection guided the hand of an arranger to sequence the two works in this order.

Psalm 39

ALTHOUGH PSALM 39'S INCIPIT, למנצח לידותון מזמור לדוד ("For the choir director, for Jeduthun. A Psalm of David"), recalls David's name, like most of the psalms discussed thus far, it further introduces another individual, Jeduthun. According to Chronicles, Jeduthun served in the temple as a prophetic musician, during the days of King David, "Moreover, David and the commanders of the army set apart for the service *some* of the sons of Asaph and of Heman and of Jeduthun, who were to prophesy with lyres, harps, and cymbals" (1 Chr 25:1). Despite his apparent direct connection with David, Jeduthun, as a character in Israelite literary history, only appears in postexilic writings (e.g., 1 Chr 16:38, 41–42; 25:3; 2 Chr 35:15; Neh 11:17). Within the Psalter, only two other compositions bear his name in their title, Psalms 62 and 77.[1]

A similar theme of God as instigator of the psalmist's woes continues from the previous psalm into Psalm 39. The present composition opens with vv. 1–4 [1–5] primarily centered around the psalmist and his behavior as he suffers. First-person verbs and 1cs pronominal suffixes dominate these verses. Within this section, the psalmist expresses a deep desire to restrain his own actions by watching his steps and keeping silent (v. 2). His attempt at stifling his emotions generates an increase of psychological pressure within his heart, a pressure that cannot be contained and ultimately leads him to voice his distress. He expresses his heart's cry in the following section, vv. 5–11 [6–12], which is singled out via an inclusion with the words, אך הבל כל אדם ("Surely every man is a mere breath"). Within these verses, the reader is not confronted with a direct

---

1. Although the psalm title connects these literary units, it is not advisable to assume a purposeful allusion from this evidence alone.

plea for the psalmist's life, but a discourse on his own frailty and the fragility of humanity, as expressed in the phrase generating the inclusion. In comparison to the divine nature, a person's lifetime is just a breath, a moment; therefore, in the psalmist's eyes, humanity deserves mercy to limit their suffering. Throughout the psalmist's depictions of sorrow and grief, he avoids any specific reference to an enemy, or an antagonist who instigates harm. Finally, the last section, vv. 12–13 [13–14] contains the explicit plea for deliverance. In v. 12 [13] he begs, "Hear my prayer . . . and give ear to my cry," and in v. 13 [14] he requests God to turn his gaze from him, to bring him some relief, enabling him to smile once more. The appearance of the divine name in these final verses recalls the opening stanza, the only other place where it appears.

When reading Ps 39:3 [4], it is difficult not to recall Jer 20:9:

Psalm 39:3 [4]	Jeremiah 20:9
My heart [לבי] was hot within me, / While I was musing the fire burned [תבער אש]; / Then I spoke [דברתי] with my tongue.	But if I say, "I will not remember Him / Or speak [אדבר] anymore in His name," / Then in my heart [לבי] it becomes like a burning fire [אש בערת] / Shut up in my bones; / And I am weary of holding it in, / And I cannot endure it.

The prophet Jeremiah, in 20:9, realizes his predicament: caught between a rock and a hard place when speaking out his prophetic message on behalf of the Lord. When he prophesies, those hearing his message ridicule, mock, and even threaten his life, causing him psychological distress. As a natural response, he refrains from speaking (לא אדבר), but the result grants him no release. When he remains silent, God's words burn within his heart like burning fire (והיה בלבי כאש בערת), generating a comparably unbearable state of discomfort. For the psalmist, like Jeremiah, his suffering increases the longer he remains silent; however, a few differences separate the psalmist's situation from Jeremiah's. For our psalmist, withholding a prophetic message is not the source of his distress. While he secures some relief when speaking out his heart, no obvious danger arises from his enemies because he voices his discontent. On a more nuanced note, the psalmist adopts a conciliatory tone in his address to God. Unlike Jeremiah, the psalmist resists chastising God and accusing him of deception.

Despite the unique lexical match between the texts that express deep-seated feelings of internal tension stemming from pent-up words, it is difficult to explain exactly how one author sought to reuse and adapt the other's text. Thus, the connection between the texts probably results from an echo as opposed to purposeful literary borrowing. Even with this determination, aspects of Jeremiah's context still transfer over to the psalmist's context. An example relates to the nature of oppression facing the psalmist. The psalm itself provides scant information, but reading it together with Jeremiah, brings the substance of the prophet's threat to the psalmist's context, thus implying the psalmist's suffering constitutes taunting, ridicule, and mocking.

One can hardly read the words הבל כל אדם ("all men are breath") without thinking of the preacher's words in Ecclesiastes, which employs הבל more times than any other book in the Old Testament: thirty-eight times. More than just the word "breath," however, the overall sentiment of vv. 4–6 [5–7] echoes much of the preacher's musings. Notions of the ephemeral existence of man echo throughout the psalm, and the psalmist painfully reveals his realization of man's brief lifespan with expressions like, "And what is the extent of my days" (v. 4 [5]), and "You have made my days as handbreadths, / And my lifetime as nothing in Your sight" (v. 5 [6]).

The same word, הבל, "breath," and context of the stanza, additionally draws the reader's thoughts to the suffering of Job. As part of Job's initial defense against the words of Eliphaz he declares, "Leave me alone, for my days are *but* a breath [הבל]" (Job 7:16b). With these words, Job, like the psalmist, compares man's lifespan to a breath. They both draw upon humanity's frailty as a reason for God to deliver them from their affliction. Similarly, both individuals suffer from a physical ailment directly attributable to God. Furthering the connection, the psalmist and Job initially remain silent in their sufferings, before voicing complaints to the Almighty. Job sits in silence for seven days and seven nights (Job 2:13) before opening his mouth to curse the day of his birth. Likewise, the psalmist declares that he too initially remained silent during his suffering and held his peace to no avail (Ps 39:2). Pushing the bounds of this intertext further is the presence of an audience in both texts. The psalmist, in v. 1, vows to guard his mouth whilst the wicked are in his presence. Within the context of the psalm, the identity of these individuals remains obscure, but it is clear they remain close to the supplicant. Job's context presents more detailed circumstances, he too sits in the presence of individuals, his three so-called friends, Eliphaz, Bildad, and Zophar.

Regarding both accounts, a sharp contrast arises between the two supplicants' self-perceived moral status. Job views himself as innocent, and not guilty of any action deserving divine disapproval and subsequent punishment. Thus, he perceives that his suffering is unfair. The psalmist, on the other hand, adopts a contrasting approach. He remains fully cognizant of his sin and accepts that he suffers directly because of his transgressions against God.

Turning to the placement of Psalms 38 and 39, the principle of association undoubtedly connects the two works, regarding theme and vocabulary.[2] Both writers suffer as an expression of God's rebuke and discipline. In Ps 38:10–11 [11–12] the author suffers from an unspecified affliction as does the author of Ps 39:10 [11]. His friends consequently reject him, and some acquaintances gossip about his condition to others. As a result, he becomes כאלם לא יפתח פיו ("Like a mute man who does not open his mouth," 38:13 [14]). Within a similar context of suffering, Psalm 39's author sits silently in his affliction, and declares נאלמתי לא אפתח פי, ("I have become mute, I do not open my mouth," v. 9 [10]). Thematically, the source of the remedy for the sufferers' affliction further yokes the two compositions. Despite their physical adversity, both psalmists realize that relief only comes from God, thus they wait on him and him alone (38:15 [16]; 39:7 [8]).[3] Because the word combinations mentioned above solely appear in these two places in the Psalter, it is difficult to maintain that the juxtaposition of the two psalms results from random placement. Despite their genre, they are both laments,[4] the likelihood remains that an arranger positioned the two works next to each other because of the common words and similar content. At this point, the mystery remains why this order was chosen, Psalms 38 then 39, as opposed to reversing the sequence.

2. Clifford, *Psalms 1–72*, 197, similarly recognizes the extraordinary replication of themes and words between the two compositions. Whereas Brueggemann and Bellinger, *Psalms*, 191, simply acknowledge a shared social context for the two works, I would argue that the similarities suggest a more robust relationship.

3. Furthermore, both works adopt the 1cs perfect of אמר to express their plight. However, this instance of repetition falters because the same word appears in many of the surrounding psalms, such as Psalms 32, 40, and 41.

4. See Craigie and Tate, *Psalms 1–50*, 307; Clifford, *Psalms 1–72*, 197.

Psalm 40

PSALM 40'S INCIPIT, למנצח לדוד מזמור ("For the Choir director. A psalm of David"), links it to the previous psalm, despite lacking the reference to Jeduthun. The psalm itself is a somewhat mixed composition, exhibiting elements of thanksgiving together with lament.[1] Unavoidable wisdom vocabulary within the psalm further complicates any final determinations of the genre, especially regarding the expression אשרי הגבר ("blessed is the man"). The psalm opens in vv. 1–3 [1–4] with words of thanksgiving, where the psalmist expresses deep gratitude to the Almighty for an act of past deliverance. The exact nature of the deliverance remains obscure, and the psalmist metaphorically portrays his dilemma as an ensnaring mire. As a result of his rescue, the psalmist proclaims that God has granted him a new song that encourages others to behave as he did, trusting God for their deliverance (v. 3 [4]). From expressions of thanksgiving, the psalmist develops a more introspective nuance in the following section, vv. 4–11 [5–12], concentrating on his own personal goodness and right relationship with God. He declares his lifetime commitment and service to his God (v. 7),[2] and his delight in obeying his will (v. 8 [9]). Furthermore, the psalmist willingly proclaims God's righteousness among the congregation. Upon a foundation of thanksgiving and personal moral uprightness, the psalmist continues in the final section, vv. 12–17 [13–18], with a brief portrayal of his present distress followed by a plea for help. As with many individual laments, the precise

---

1. Most scholars recognize both elements to some degree; see, for example, VanGemeren, *Psalms*, 364; Brueggemann and Bellinger, *Psalms*, 194.

2. Reading the verse as a statement of commitment in light of Deut 15:16–18.

nature of the psalmist's affliction and oppression remains obscure.[3] In this unit, the psalmist juxtaposes curses on his enemies with blessings for those who seek God. For those seeking his life, he prays for their shame and dishonor (v. 14 [15]), but for those seeking the Lord he blesses with rejoicing and gladness (v. 16 [17]). Within this final stanza, the psalmist strategically inserts his primary petitions for deliverance, and the desperate urgency of his cry for help appears particularly noticeable in v. 13b [14b], "Make haste, O LORD, to help me," and then in v. 17 [18], "Do not delay, O my God."[4]

    Echoes of Psalm 40 reverberate through Psalm 149 and into the prophetic literature of Isaiah 42. Each composition reflects the need for a new song, as the table below demonstrates:

Psalm 40:3	Psalm 149:1	Isaiah 42:10
וַיִּתֵּן בְּפִי שִׁיר חָדָשׁ תְּהִלָּה לֵאלֹהֵינוּ יִרְאוּ רַבִּים וְיִירָאוּ וְיִבְטְחוּ בַּיהוָה	הַלְלוּ יָהּ שִׁירוּ לַיהוָה שִׁיר חָדָשׁ תְּהִלָּתוֹ בִּקְהַל חֲסִידִים	שִׁירוּ לַיהוָה שִׁיר חָדָשׁ תְּהִלָּתוֹ מִקְצֵה הָאָרֶץ יוֹרְדֵי הַיָּם וּמְלֹאוֹ אִיִּים וְיֹשְׁבֵיהֶם
He put a new song in my mouth, a song of praise to our God; / Many will see and fear / And will trust in the LORD.	Praise the LORD! / Sing to the LORD a new song, / And His praise in the congregation of the godly ones.	Sing to the LORD a new song, / Sing His praise from the end of the earth! / You who go down to the sea, and all that is in it. / You islands, and those who live on them.

    3. The separate transmission of vv. 13–17 [14–18] in the form of Psalm 70 accentuates the already obvious division between thanksgiving, vv. 1–10 [11] and lament, 11–17 [12–18]. Regarding how these two genres dovetail together, Gruber, "Chapter 40," 176, citing Gunkel, remarks that the writer received deliverance from one crisis only to fall into another, thus explaining the switch from thanksgiving to lament. A further point deserving comment concerns the literary connection to the previous psalm. The theme of thanksgiving beginning Psalm 40 generates an appropriate thematic response to a presumed healing of the sickness reported in Psalm 39 (see VanGemeren, *Psalms*, 364).

    4. Clifford, *Psalms 1–72*, 202, mentions a few shared themes between Psalms 38–41. The expression of intent, "I pray/said" (38:16; 39:1; 40:7 [8]; 41:4); "my cry" links 40:13 to 39:12, and "make haste to help me" connects 40:13 to 38:22. Although notable, such connections probably reflect genre rather than a purposeful editorial attempt to sequence the psalms in this order.

It is unlikely that the common words represent any form of intentional literary borrowing simply because the concept of a new song (שׁיר חדשׁ) signifying a recent act of divine intervention frequently appears in the Hebrew Bible. Furthermore, because the word תהלה ("praise") regularly surfaces in celebratory contexts, its presence is almost expected in Ps 149:1 and Isaiah. Notably, however, Psalm 40 adopts the phrase and concept of a new song in a context different from those in the other compositions above. Isaiah and Psalm 149 employ the phrase as part of an opening, encouraging others to sing a new song in response to God's actions on their behalf. Furthermore, they both frame their respective compositions within a national or communal setting. In Psalm 40, the phrase emerges in a far more personal context: God not only retrieves the psalmist from life-threatening dangers—the metaphorical mire and mud—but additionally puts a new song in his heart. Although probably unintentional, from this intertextual coupling, it is possible to associate the new song granted to Psalm 40's author with the words of praise found in Psalm 149.

In v. 7 [8], the psalmist plainly demonstrates a knowledge of prophetic literature, but in doing so undoubtedly alters or adds certain nuances to his received tradition, assuming his source reflects MT. At various junctures in prophetic literature, God speaks to Israel stressing his rejection of sacrifices when social injustices abound and the rich oppress widows and orphans. Hosea, in his condemnation of Ephraim, the Northern Kingdom (6:6), provides an example of divine rejection on account of social injustice. God explicitly proclaims his desire (חפצתי) for mercy and not sacrifice (זבח), and knowledge[5] of God rather than burnt offerings (עלות). The Northern Kingdom's behavior at that time, unfortunately, contradicted the divine ideals. Isaiah similarly castigates people of the Southern Kingdom for failing to meet the same divine standards of expected behavior. In Isa 1:10–11, he condemns his hearers, pleading with Judah to hear God's instruction (תורת אלהינו), explaining God's lack of appetite for their many sacrifices (רב זבחיהם), rejection of their burnt offerings (עלות) of rams and bulls, and lack of desire (לא חפצתי) for the blood of bulls. Similar verbiage arises in 1 Sam 15:22 and Amos 5:22, and in each instance the prophets highlight the dissonance between the people's behavior and God's desires.

5. Or "obedience," in the words of the JPS.

The present psalmist reworks the context of these words and expressions, removing the negative connotation. He adapts these prophetic words to demonstrate his own perfect obedience to God's will and desires. The psalmist adopts a stance that opposes Israel's and Judah's ignorance of God's deep-seated desires. Because God has revealed his will, the psalmist now knows that the Lord desires neither sacrifice and meal offerings (זבח ומנחה לא חפצת), nor burnt offerings (עולה) and sin offerings. To that end, the psalmist's ultimate desire (חפץ) aligns with divine instruction (תורתך, v. 9). Thus, in the present psalm, the language traditionally employed by the prophets to condemn rebellious communities transforms into expressions vindicating the psalmist's behavior and heart attitude.[6]

The most glaring intertext relating to Psalm 40 concerns its relationship to Psalm 70.[7] The table below compares the two related segments:

Psalm 40:13–17 [14–18]	Psalm 70:1–5 [2–6]
רְצֵה יְהוָה לְהַצִּילֵנִי יְהוָה לְעֶזְרָתִי חוּשָׁה: יֵבֹשׁוּ וְיַחְפְּרוּ יַחַד מְבַקְשֵׁי נַפְשִׁי לִסְפּוֹתָהּ יִסֹּגוּ אָחוֹר וְיִכָּלְמוּ חֲפֵצֵי רָעָתִי: יָשֹׁמּוּ עַל־עֵקֶב בָּשְׁתָּם הָאֹמְרִים לִי הֶאָח ׀ הֶאָח: יָשִׂישׂוּ וְיִשְׂמְחוּ בְּךָ כָּל־מְבַקְשֶׁיךָ יֹאמְרוּ תָמִיד יִגְדַּל יְהוָה אֹהֲבֵי תְּשׁוּעָתֶךָ: וַאֲנִי ׀ עָנִי וְאֶבְיוֹן אֲדֹנָי יַחֲשָׁב לִי עֶזְרָתִי וּמְפַלְטִי אַתָּה אֱלֹהַי אַל־תְּאַחַר:	אֱלֹהִים לְהַצִּילֵנִי יְהוָה לְעֶזְרָתִי חוּשָׁה: יֵבֹשׁוּ וְיַחְפְּרוּ מְבַקְשֵׁי נַפְשִׁי יִסֹּגוּ אָחוֹר וְיִכָּלְמוּ חֲפֵצֵי רָעָתִי: יָשׁוּבוּ עַל־עֵקֶב בָּשְׁתָּם הָאֹמְרִים הֶאָח הֶאָח: יָשִׂישׂוּ וְיִשְׂמְחוּ בְּךָ כָּל־מְבַקְשֶׁיךָ וְיֹאמְרוּ תָמִיד יִגְדַּל אֱלֹהִים אֹהֲבֵי יְשׁוּעָתֶךָ: וַאֲנִי עָנִי וְאֶבְיוֹן אֱלֹהִים חוּשָׁה־לִּי עֶזְרִי וּמְפַלְטִי אַתָּה יְהוָה אַל־תְּאַחַר:

6. The expression "blessed is the man ..." (אשרי/ברוך הגבר/האיש ...) reflects an echo because it often appears in wisdom traditions (Pss 1:1; 34:8 [9]; 94:12; 127:5). Thus, the likelihood of a specific allusion decreases.

7. As already witnessed, the Psalter undeniably reflects instances of duplication; see, for example, Psalms 14 and 53.

Psalm 40:13–17 [14–18]	**Psalm 70:1–5 [2–6]**
Be pleased, O LORD, to deliver me; / Make haste, O LORD, to help me. / Let those be ashamed and humiliated together / Who seek my life to destroy it; / Let those be turned back and dishonored / Who delight in my hurt. / Let those be appalled because of their shame / Who say to me, "Aha, aha!" / Let all who seek You rejoice and be glad in You; / Let those who love Your salvation say continually, / "The LORD be magnified!" / Since I am afflicted and needy, / Let the LORD be mindful of me. / You are my help and my deliverer; / Do not delay, O my God.	O God, *hasten* to deliver me; / O LORD, hasten to my help! / Let those be ashamed and humiliated / Who seek my life; / Let those be turned back and dishonored / Who delight in my hurt. / Let those be turned back because of their shame / Who say, "Aha, aha!" / Let all who seek You rejoice and be glad in You; / And let those who love Your salvation say continually, / "Let God be magnified." / But I am afflicted and needy; / Hasten to me, O God! / You are my help and my deliverer; / O LORD, do not delay.

Concerning the direction of borrowing between these psalms and how their present relationship arose, a few potential explanations deserve attention. First, it is possible that Psalm 40 represents an original work, and a later author adopted the second half of the composition, remolding the words into a new framework and generating a new composition. This possibility represents a minority position among biblical commentators, the most notable of whom are Craigie and Tate, who suggest Psalm 70's author salvaged a portion of Psalm 40 for use in the nonmonarchic era.[8] Second, the likelihood of accidental separation exists as a plausible explanation for the current relationship. As discussed earlier, Psalm 9/10, one composition unified by an acrostic structure, was divided mistakenly to create two individual psalms. In the case of Psalm 40, a similar erroneous division may have birthed Psalm 70 as an independent composition in MT.

Despite the plausibility of the previous ideas, contemporary scholarship predominantly leans towards borrowing in the opposite direction: the shorter Psalm 70 forming the original independent work that a subsequent psalmist redeveloped.[9] Thus, the opening verses of Psalm 40 (vv. 1–12 [13]) reflect an addition to Psalm 70. This version of events garners

8. See Craigie and Tate, *Psalms 1–50*, 314.

9. From a text-critical viewpoint, the natural tendency leans towards textual expansion as time progresses. See Tov, *Text Criticism*, 145. Hossfeld and Zenger, *Die Psalmen*, 252, view Psalm 70 as an independent composition that was reused later, as do Brueggemann and Bellinger, *Psalms*, 304.

endorsements from commentators such as Kraus.[10] Further supporting the possibility of reuse by the composer of Psalm 40 are the additional intertextual connections, in all probability allusions to the biblical texts discussed above. Although inconclusive, evidence suggests Psalm 40's author reused Psalm 70, in addition to other texts, to develop and shape a new composition.[11]

The precise nature of replication between the two textual units, Psalms 70 and 40:13–17 [14–18], therefore, is not, strictly speaking, an allusion, but an independent version of the same composition. Despite this reality, it is prudent to appreciate the differences in wording of the duplicated textual units. The most obvious and expected one concerns the references to God as reflected in both works. Psalm 40:16 [17] employs the Tetragrammaton, and then later in v. 17 [18], the psalmist opts for אדני. Countering this, in the corresponding sections of Ps 70:4–5 [5–6], the author selects the word אלהים. Presumably, the alteration stems from Psalm 70's location within the Elohistic Psalter.[12]

Two other notable differences reflect known textual phenomena related to the copying of biblical manuscripts. The first יָשֹׁמּוּ "let those be appalled" (Ps 40:15 [16]) contrasts יָשׁוּבוּ "let those be turned back" (Ps 70:3 [4]). The differences between the forms concerns the medial wāw—present in Psalm 70, but absent in Psalm 40—and the change between the root letters ב and מ.[13] From a text critical viewpoint, scribes frequently confused the *mêm* and *bêt* while copying manuscripts; consequently, the rendering of יָשׁוּבוּ, "they will return" may have stemmed from the author of Psalm 40 misreading the text.[14] The other difference appears between

---

10. Kraus' approach to the psalm is somewhat unique because he primarily addresses Ps 40:1–12 in his commentary, viewing vv. 13–17 as an independent composition (see Kraus, *Psalms 1–59*, 423). Surprisingly, quite a few commentators remain silent concerning the relationships between the shared material.

11. A variant of the third possibility is that the first half of Psalm 40 existed as an independent composition that a psalmist subsequently merged with Psalm 70.

12. Accepting Psalm 70 as more reflective of the original text, in this instance, assumes it existed in an earlier form that maintained the divine name, and this earlier form was adopted by Psalm 40's author.

13. Evident from Tov, *Text Criticism*, 227–32.

14. Naturally, it is important to acknowledge that his *vorlage* may have reflected a scribal alteration. Alter, *Book of Psalms*, 243, further adduces this change as evidence of a textual development. For him, the reading of ישובו makes more sense than ישמו in Psalm 40. In any event, it is important to note that none of the changes reflect diachronic adjustments.

the words יַחֲשָׁב (40:17 [18]) and חוּשָׁה (Ps 70:5 [6]). Like the previous
example, the similarity between the two forms, especially the repetition
of *ḥēt* and *šîn*, suggests an errant reading. Furthermore, because scribes
and copyists often confused *wāw* and *yôd*, and metathesis exists as a
known phenomenon in textual development, each of the differences can
be explained adequately as scribal developments.

Psalm 41

PSALM 41 REPRESENTS THE last entry in Book I of the Psalter. Although the English translation of the Psalm's title, "For the choir director. A psalm of David," associates it with Psalm 40, the Hebrew word order differs between the two compositions. Psalm 40 reads למנצח לדוד מזמור, whereas Psalm 41 offers a slight change, reading, למנצח מזמור לדוד. This alteration, though slight, represents a degree of discontinuity with the previous psalm.

Like a few psalms already discussed, Psalm 41 resists a firm placement into a basic form-critical category. Characteristics of two genres echo throughout the composition, thanksgiving (vv. 1–10) and lament (vv. 11–17).[1] Within vv. 1–3, the psalmist recalls God's blessing upon those who show compassion to the poor, he heals them when they fall sick and prevents their enemies from overcoming them. As with most wisdom psalms, such blessings are not restricted to the psalmist, but to any who consider the poor. The reader then experiences a theme change in vv. 4–9 [5–10], where the psalmist turns specifically to his personal needs. After a brief confession of sin, the lament begins in earnest as the writer details the persecution he suffers at his enemy's hands. Deceptive people surround him, secretly plotting against him. Adding to the pain,

1. See VanGemeren, *Psalms*, 364. The ordering of thanksgiving then lament is slightly unexpected because laments usually present a petition with the description of the crisis followed by statements of confidence, reassurance, and thanksgiving. Though rare, the present psalm's ordering is not without precedent, as witnessed in Psalm 9/10. Clifford, *Psalms 1–72*, 213, ultimately classifies it as a thanksgiving hymn, as does Gruber, "Chapter 41," 180, who further identifies elements of lament within it. Kraus, *Psalms 1–59*, 430, views it as a prayer song, and Craigie and Tate, *Psalms 1–50*, 319, recognize multiple genres rippling throughout the psalm (wisdom, vv. 2–4; lament, vv. 6–10; prayer, v. 5, 11; and confidence/praise, vv. 12–14); and rather than choosing one, they simply define it as a psalm of illness.

the psalmist recounts that even his close friend, who was expected to support him, has betrayed him (v. 9 [10]). The psalmist's betraying companion visits him with feigned compassion, and subsequently gossips about his sickness when the visit is over (v. 6 [7]), even awaiting eagerly for the day of his death (v. 5 [6]). Throughout this section, the psalm fails to recall physical harm against the psalmist, and the threat remains purely psychological as the writer struggles with threats and slanderous comments directed toward him. Focus switches back to God in vv. 10–12 [11–13], as the ailing psalmist calls to the Lord for mercy. He assures himself, because of his personal integrity, that God will rescue him and permit him to abide in his presence for eternity. The psalm's final verse, in all probability, is not organic to the original composition, but consists of a doxological blessing marking the end of Book I of the Psalter.

Little in the way of significant lexical replication connects Psalm 41 with its predecessor, Psalm 40. Perhaps the most notable instance concerns a term commonly associated with Israelite wisdom traditions, אשרי ("blessed"). Repetition here unlikely reflects literary borrowing, but the presence of the word together with other wisdom elements probably influenced an arranger into juxtaposing the compositions. Regarding how the word אשרי functions in each psalm, it is worth noting that each appearance complements the other, offering alternate sides of the same coin. Psalm 40 blesses the man who seeks refuge in the Lord and disapproves of the proud; whereas, Psalm 41 presents the same sentiment from an alternative angle, lauding the one who regards the poor, as opposed to disregarding the proud.

Another key connection point between the two compositions revolves around a semantic nexus. In the closing words of Psalm 40, the psalmist declares that he is poor and needy (עני ואביון), but despite his lowly position, the Lord considers his life. Following this, the opening words of Psalm 41 (v. 1 [2]) proclaim a blessing on those who consider the poor (דל), where a different Hebrew word appears with the same meaning.[2] This semantic overlap dictates the sequencing of the two compositions. Rather than being influenced by specific words or Hebrew roots,[3] an arranger, apparently, relied on the concept of being impover-

---

2. All three words mentioned here appear synonymously in poetry; see, for example, Pss 72:13; 82:4.

3. The words חפץ, "to delight in" (40:14 [15]; 41:11 [12]), and יחד, "together" (40:14 [15]; 41:7 [8]), represent the only possible candidates for a lexical connection between the compositions. Unfortunately, they are relatively widespread throughout

ished to sequence Psalms 40 and 41, and generate an appreciable degree
of literary continuity.

An unusual number of lexical items connect Psalm 41's doxology
with 1 Chr 16:36. From a comparison of the two texts (see below), the
level of correspondence cannot be attributed to chance.

Psalm 41:13 [14]	1 Chronicles 16:36
בָּרוּךְ יְהוָה אֱלֹהֵי יִשְׂרָאֵל מֵהָעוֹלָם וְעַד הָעוֹלָם אָמֵן וְאָמֵן	בָּרוּךְ יְהוָה אֱלֹהֵי יִשְׂרָאֵל מִן־הָעוֹלָם וְעַד הָעֹלָם וַיֹּאמְרוּ כָל־הָעָם אָמֵן וְהַלֵּל לַיהוָה
Blessed be the LORD, the God of Israel, / From everlasting to everlasting. Amen and Amen	Blessed be the LORD, the God of Israel, / From everlasting to everlasting. / Then all the people said, "Amen," and praised the LORD

That said, the repetition unlikely reflects an instance of biblical
allusion, where an author purposefully sought to connect his composition to another text, intending to transfer meaning from one pericope to
another. The correspondence, in this instance, almost certainly reflects
the repetition of a common doxological formula that developed during
the Second Temple period. Like Psalm 41, the author of 1 Chronicles
16 positioned the doxology in its expected location, at the end of the
composition. Similar doxologies additionally appear at the end of Pss 72
(v. 19), 89 (v. 52 [53]), and 106 (v. 48), marking the division of the Psalter
into five books. The position of the same clause, more or less, at the end of
each composition further solidifies the probability of a common formula
as opposed to a purposeful allusion.[4]

At this point, the word אשרי ("blessed"), which appears in Ps 41:1
[2], deserves attention. Commonly, as discussed earlier, Israelite wisdom
literature and traditions adopts this word to describe the favored status
of those following a righteous path. A remarkable feature, however,
concerns its distribution in Book I of the Psalter: It always appears in

---

the Psalter—the former appearing twenty-seven times and the latter appearing fifteen
times. Clifford, *Psalms 1–72*, 209, draws attention to a cluster of other common words
between the two psalms: לראות as an infinitive construct with *lāmed* (40:12 [13]; 41:6
[7]); אמר as a *qal* 1cs; and בטח (40:3 [4]; 41:9 [10]).

4. Craigie and Tate, *Psalms 1–50*, 319, mention the psalm's similarities with
Psalm 6, but these appear to result more from similar genres than purposeful literary
borrowing.

juxtaposed psalms. The pairing first emerged between Psalms 1 and 2, creating an inclusion, then in Pss 32:2, 33:12, and 34:8 [9], and now in Pss 40:4 [5] and 41:1 [2]. Although the remainder of the Psalter fails to reflect the same arrangement, its presence in Book I at least suggests an editorial preference for the sequencing of these seven compositions.

At this point, it is worth entertaining the notion that an editor specifically composed Psalm 41 to conclude Book I. A unique feature of the psalm concerns the variety of genres lucidly woven into the fabric of a single composition. Clear evidence of wisdom traditions, laments, confidence, thanksgiving, and praise appear within this remarkable psalm. With a little imagination, one can see the flashes of the various genres functioning as a summary of genres reflected in Book I; thus, the final composition connects with each psalm in the collection. The phrase אַשְׁרֵי, previously mentioned, furthers the potential of a specially composed psalm. Its appearance in 41:1 [2], in addition to connecting it to Psalm 40, generates an inclusion with Psalm 1—the beginning and the end of Book I start with the same word. Furthermore, the wisdom component within the present composition seems slightly out of place. Within laments, elements of confidence and thanksgiving frequently appear, but the addition of concrete and identifiable wisdom components are virtually nonexistent. Thus, the presence of wisdom elements in the final psalm point towards a purposeful attempt to generate a composition that forms an inclusion with Psalm 1, encapsulating Book I.[5]

5. Kraus, *Psalms 1–59*, 431, views the book as a relatively late composition, though he offers no firm evidence. Accepting that hypothesis, lends to the idea that a later arranger, or psalmist, composed, or adjusted an extant psalm to forge a more complete ending to Book I.

Afterword

To CLOSE THE DISCUSSION of Book I, attention shifts to a few key observations and comments of particular interest. First, and perhaps most importantly, the principle of association—in the various nuances discussed in the Introduction—patently serves as an influential factor in the sequencing of Book I of the Psalter. An abundance of examples arise where rare words undeniably connect juxtaposed psalms. Among the more prominent examples are the words אשרי ("blessed"), and הגה ("meditate"), unifying Psalms 1 and 2; repetition of the phrase נשא נפש ("lifting up one's soul"), linking Psalms 24 and 25; and the words רבים אמרים ("many are saying") connecting Psalms 3 and 4. Furthermore, although instances were limited, examples of common vocabulary influencing specific sequencing of the psalms should be noted. Psalms 32 and 33 reflect a lucid example, but the juxtaposition technique additionally appears between Psalms 7 and 8. The presence of numerous related themes connecting certain psalms further solidifies the reality of the principle of association in Book I. Notable examples arise with the idea of dwelling in the Lord's house, linking Psalms 23 and 24; as well as the mention of kingship which undeniably link Psalms 20 and 21.

Two psalms deserve further comment because they separate themselves from the other compositions discussed in the present volume: The combination Psalm 9/10 and Psalm 36. Their peculiarity stems from their apparent lack of tangible intertextual or associative connections. Although their presence contradicts principles discussed in the Introduction, their appearance in Book I serves an important purpose. With regard to sequencing and juxtaposition, their lack of clear and obvious connections to their literary neighbors highlights the likelihood and validity of the numerous other connections explored in the present volume. As addressed in the Introduction, their existence within Book I serve as the exceptions that prove the rule. When contrasted with the rationale behind juxtapositional relationships in the remaining psalms, the absence of a concrete literary connection between them highlights the reality of the Psalter's editors and arrangers exhibiting a tangible inclination to juxtapose psalms in a purposeful and logical order when they could.

From the examination of Book I, firm identification of inner-biblical allusions and scriptural reuse proved an elusive but nevertheless fruitful endeavor. Undoubtedly, purposeful inner-biblical allusions exist at numerous points throughout Book I, such as Psalm 4's development of the Aaronic blessing in Num 6:25–26, and Psalm 8's use of the creation account. However, numerous problematic allusions frequently complicate the overall profile of Book I, one example being Psalm 15's undeniable connection with Isa 33:14–16. Without question, one author knew of the other's work in one form or another. However, the specific direction of the allusion remains somewhat uncertain. Although the present volume speculatively engages in discussions concerning the direction of borrowing, it needs to be said that conclusive irrefutable evidence regarding who borrowed from whom ultimately remains elusive at this time. Further obfuscating firm identification of vectors of allusion were the copious appearances of common stock phrases—common reusable expressions known by many psalmists—and duplicate compositions.

Stepping back and considering all the purposeful sequential relationships supports the probability of some psalmists also functioning as editors/arrangers, composing psalms with the specific intent of complementing an existing psalm. Perhaps the best example of this phenomenon appears with Psalms 1 and 2. With Psalm 2 reflecting the later of the two compositions, the author of Psalm 1 apparently composed his work with Psalm 2 in mind, writing specifically to create a companion to the second psalm in the Psalter. This seems the most acceptable explanation for the similarities between the two compositions. It is unlikely that the two psalms were independently written and yet coincidently shared such a vast number of literary and thematic features. Another example of the phenomenon appears between Psalms 20 and 21, both of which focus on God's relationship with the king. Psalm 20 reflects a request for the king's protection before battle, and Psalm 21 serves as a direct response to this request. Concerning the relationship between the psalms, it again seems unlikely that they were composed independently of each other.

Logically, the likelihood remains that Psalm 21's author knew of Psalm 20 and sought to create a literary companion. Alternatively, a single author may have composed both songs intending them to appear together in a larger collection. Although only two instances of this phenomenon appears in Book I, the remaining books of the Psalter may feature additional instances.

Most allusions discussed in the present work fall into the more classical category of biblical allusion. Psalmists are frequently drawn to associating their compositions to well-known biblical texts with the intention of enriching themes and images in their own songs. By leading a reader to a known text via lexical or thematic markers, psalmists further enhance or evoke additional emotion to statements appearing in their psalms. Psalm 4's use of the Aaronic blessing falls into this category, along with Ps 17:8's allusion to Deut 32:10–11. While the books of the Pentateuch form the most common target for psalmists, there are clear allusions to prophetic literature and the Writings, especially with regards to the wisdom literature in Proverbs, as well as other compositions in the Psalter itself.

From our examination of Book 1, a few intriguing questions remain for future study of the remaining books of the Psalter. Regarding juxtaposition strategies, a further investigation could potentially reveal new rationale for the juxtaposition of psalms, or additional evidence for rarer strategies such as liturgical organization, the least attested strategy. Concerning biblical allusions, further analysis of the remaining books of the Psalter may shed additional light on preferred sources employed by psalmists. For instance, are certain books of the Hebrew Bible specifically targeted by psalmists more than others, and conversely, are any books avoided, and if so, why? With questions such as these still in the air, this closing discussion at the end of the analysis should not so much be viewed as an end, but as a platform to expand and continue into the remaining books.

Bibliography

Allen, Leslie C. *Psalms 101–150*. Edited by David A. Hubbard and Glen W. Barker. WBC 21. Waco, TX: Word, 2002.

Alter, Robert. *The Book of Psalms: A Translation with Commentary*. New York: Norton, 2009.

Avishur, Yitzhaq. "Chapters 1–17, 19–21, 23–24, 29." In *Tehillim א: 'Olam HaTanak*, edited by Gershon Galil, 26–76, 84–94, 105–11, 127–38. Tel Aviv: Divrei Hayamim, 1999.

Beentjes, Pancratius C. "Inverted Quotations in the Bible: A Neglected Stylistic Pattern." *Biblica* 63 (1982) 506–23.

Berger, Yitzhak. "The David-Benjaminite Conflict and the Intertextual Field of Psalm 7." *JSOT* 38.3 (2014) 279–96.

Berlin, Adele. "Psalms." In *The Jewish Study Bible*, edited by Adele Berilin and Marc Zvi Brettler, 1275–446. Oxford: Oxford University Press, 2004.

Booij, Th. "Psalm 144: Hope of Davidic Welfare." *VT* 59.2 (2009) 173–80.

Botha, P. J. "Psalm 5 and the Polarity between Those Who May Stand before Yahweh and Those Who May Not." *HTS Teologiese Studies/Theological Studies* 74.1 (2018) 1–7.

Briggs, Charles Augustus. *A Critical and Exegetical Commentary on the Book of Psalms*. Edited by S. R. Driver et al. Vol. 1. ICC. Edinburgh: T. & T. Clark, 1970.

Brueggemann, Walter, and W. H. Bellinger. *Psalms*. New Cambridge Bible Commentary. New York: Cambridge University Press, 2014.

Carr, David. "Method in Determination of Direction of Dependance: An Empirical Test of Criteria Applied to Exodus 34, 11–26 and Its Parallels." In *Gottes Volk am Sinai: Untersuchungen zu Ex 32–34 und Dtn 9–10*, edited by Matthias Köckert and Erhard Blum, 107–40. Gütersloh: Gütersloher Verlagshaus, 2001.

Cassuto, Umberto. "The Arrangement of the Book of Ezekiel." In *Biblical and Oriental Studies*, translated by Israel Abrahams, 277–40. Jerusalem: Magnes, 1973.

———. "The Sequence and Arrangement of the Biblical Sections." In *Biblical and Oriental Studies*, translated by Israel Abrahams, 1–6. Jerusalem: Magnes, 1973.

Childs, Brevard S. "Psalm Titles and Midrashic Exegesis." *JSS* 16.2 (1971) 137–50.

Clifford, Richard J. *Psalms 1–72*. Edited by Patrick D. Miller. Vol. 1. Abingdon Old Testament Commentaries. Nashville: Abingdon, 2003.

Clines, David J. A. *Job 1–20*. Edited by David. A Hubbard and Glen Barker. WBC 17. Dallas: Word, 1989.

———. *On the Way to the Postmodern: Old Testament Essays, 1967–1998*. 2 vols. JSOTSup 292–93. Sheffield: Sheffield Academic Press, 1998.

Cohen, A., ed. *The Psalms: With Hebrew Text, English Translation and Commentary*. Soncino Books of the Bible. London: Soncino, 1945.

Cole, Robert. "An Integrated Reading of Psalms 1 and 2." *JSOT* 98 (2002) 75–88.

Craigie, Peter C., and Marvin E. Tate. *Psalms 1–50*. Edited by John D. W. Watts et al. 2nd ed. WBC 19. Waco, TX: Word, 2004.

Creach, Jerome F. D. "Like a Tree Planted by the Temple Stream: The Portrait of the Righteous in Psalm 1:3." *CBQ* 61.1 (1999) 34–46.

Dahood, Mitchell S. J. *Psalms I*. AB 16. Garden City, NY: Doubleday, 1965.

Edenburg, Cynthia. "Chapter 38." In *Tehillim א: 'Olam HaTanak*, edited by Gershon Galil, 69–172. Tel Aviv: Divrei Hayamim, 1999.

Emanuel, David. "The Elevation of God in Psalm 105." In *Inner Biblical Allusion in the Poetry of Wisdom and Psalms*, edited by Mark J. Boda et al., 49–64. Library of Biblical Studies 659. London: T. & T. Clark, 2019.

———. *From Bards to Biblical Exegetes: A Close Reading and Intertextual Analysis of Selected Exodus Psalms*. Eugene, OR: Pickwick, 2012.

Etheridge, John Wesley. *The Targums of Onkelos and Jonathan ben Uzziel on the Pentateuch: With the Fragments of the Jerusalem Targum from the Chaldee*. London: Green, Longman and Roberts, 1862.

Fishbane, Michael. *Biblical Interpretation in Ancient Israel*. Oxford: Clarendon, 1985.

Futato, Mark D. *Interpreting the Psalms: An Exegetical Handbook*. Handbooks for Old Testament Exegesis. Grand Rapids: Kregel 2007.

Garr, W. Randall, and Steven Fassberg, eds. *A Handbook of Biblical Hebrew: Periods, Corpora and Reading Traditions*. Vol 1. Winona Lake, IN: Eisenbrauns, 2016.

Gordis, Robert. "Psalm 9–10: A Textual and Exegetical Study." *JQR* 48.2 (1957) 104–22.

Goulder, M. D. "The Fourth Book of the Psalter." *JTS* 26.2 (1975) 269–89.

Gruber, Mayer. "Chapters 25, 32–37, 40–41." In *Tehillim א: 'Olam HaTanak*, edited by Gershon Galil, 111–14, 149–69, 176–81. Tel Aviv: Divrei Hayamim, 1999.

Hayes, John H. *Dictionary of Biblical Interpretation*. 2 vols. Nashville: Abingdon, 1999.

Hays, Richard B. *Echoes of Scripture in the Letters of Paul*. New Haven: Yale University Press, 1989.

Hendel, Ronald, and Jan Joosten. *How Old Is the Hebrew Bible: A Linguistic, Textual, and Historical Study*. New Haven: Yale University Press, 2018.

Ho, Peter C. W. "The Design of the MT Psalter: A Macrostructural Analysis." PhD diss., University of Gloucestershire, 2016.

Hossfeld, F.-L., and E. Zenger. *Die Psalmen: Psalm 1–50*. Die Neue Echter Bibel: Kommentar Zum Alten Testament Mit Der Einheitsübersetzung. Würzburg: Echter Verlag, 1993.

———. *Psalms 2*. Edited by Klaus Baltzer. Translated by Linda M. Maloney. Hermeneia. Minneapolis: Fortress, 2005.

Howard, David M. *The Structure of Psalms 93–100*. Biblical and Judaic Studies 5. Winona Lake, IN: Eisenbrauns, 1997.

Hurvitz, Avi. *A Concise Lexicon of Late Biblical Hebrew: Linguistic Innovations in the Writings of the Second Temple Period*. VTSup. Leiden: Brill, 2016.

Hutton, Rodney. "Cush the Benjaminite and Psalm Midrash." *HAR* 10 (1986) 123–37.

Jacobs, Jonathan. *Measure for Measure in the Bible Story*. Alon Shebot: Tebonot, 2005.

Joffe, Laura. "The Elohistic Psalter: What, How, and Why." *SJOT* 15.1 (2001) 142–66.

Johnson, Vivian L. *David in Distress: His Portrait through the Historical Psalms*. T. & T. Clark Library of Biblical Studies 505. London: T. & T. Clark, 2009.

Keener, Hubert James. *A Canonical Exegesis of the Eighth Psalm: YHWH's Maintenance of the Created Order through Divine Reversal*. JTISup 9. Winona Lake, IN: Eisenbrauns, 2013.

Keil, Carl Friedrich, and Franz Delitzsch. *Psalms*. Translated by James Martin. 3 vols. Commentary on the Old Testament 5. Grand Rapids: Eerdmans, 1982.

Kim, Hee Suk. "Exodus 34.6 in Psalms 86, 103, and 145 in Relation to the Theological Perspectives of Books III, IV and V of the Psalter." In *Inner Biblical Allusion in the Poetry of Wisdom and Psalms*, edited by Mark J. Boda et al., 36–48. Library of Biblical Studies 659. London: T. & T. Clark, 2019.

Klaus, Nathan. "Chapter 18." In *Tehillim א: 'Olam HaTanak*, edited by Gershon Galil, 76–83. Tel Aviv: Divrei Hayamim, 1999.

Kraus, Hans-Joachim. *Psalms 1–59: A Commentary*. Translated by Hilton C. Oswald. Minneapolis: Augsburg, 1988.

———. *Psalms 60–150: A Commentary*. Translated by Hilton C. Oswold. Minneapolis: Augsburg, 1988.

Leonard, Jeffery M. "Inner-Biblical Interpretation and Intertextuality." In *Literary Approaches to the Bible*, edited by Douglas Mangum and Douglas Estes, 97–142. Bellingham, WA: Lexham, 2017.

Leslie, Elmer A. *The Psalms: Translated and Interpreted in the Light of Hebrew Life and Worship*. New York: Abingdon-Cokesbury, 1949.

Levine, Baruch A. *Numbers 1–20: A New Translation with Introduction and Commentary*. AB 4. New York: Doubleday, 1993.

Liebreich, Leon J. "The Position of Chapter Six in the Book of Isaiah." *HUCA* 25 (1954) 37–40.

Malul, Meir. "Chapters 22, 26–28, 30." In *Tehillim א: 'Olam HaTanak*, edited by Gershon Galil, 94–105, 114–27, 138–42. Tel Aviv: Divrei Hayamim, 1999.

McCann, J. Clinton, Jr. "Psalms." In vol. 4 of *NIB*, edited by Leander E. Keck, 641–1280. Nashville: Abingdon, 1994.

Meek, Russell L. "Intertextuality, Inner-Biblical Exegesis, and Inner-Biblical Allusion: The Ethics of Methodology." *Biblica* 95.1 (2014) 280–91.

Milgrom, Jacob. "The Alleged 'Hidden Light.'" In *The Idea of Biblical Interpretation: Essays in Honor of James L. Kugel*, edited by Hindy Najman and Judith H. Newman, 41–44. SJSJ 83. Leiden: Brill, 2004.

Miller, Glenn. "Psalm 15." *Interpretation* 65.2 (2011) 186–88.

Miller, Patrick D, Jr. "Trouble and Woe: Interpreting the Biblical Laments." *Interpretation* 37.1 (1983) 32–45.

Oancea, Constantin. "Psalm 2 im Alten Testament und im frühen Judentum." *Sacra Scripta* 11.2 (2013) 159–80.

Parunak, H. Van Dyke. "Transitional Techniques in the Bible." *JBL* 102.4 (1983) 525–48.

Pope, Marvin H. *Job: Introduction, Translation, and Notes*. AB 15. New Haven: Yale University Press, 2008.

Robertson, O. Palmer. *The Flow of the Psalms: Discovering Their Structure and Theology*. Phillipsburg, NJ: P&R, 2015.

Rofé, Alexander. "The Arrangement of the Laws in Deuteronomy." *ETL* 64.4 (1988) 265–87.

———. *Introduction to the Literature of the Hebrew Bible.* Jerusalem: Carmel, 2006.

Ross, Allen P. *A Commentary on the Psalms.* Vol. 1, *Psalms 1–41.* Kregel Exegetical Library. Grand Rapids: Kregel, 2011.

Schwartz, Sarah. "Bridge over Troubled Waters: Psalm 147." *JSOT* 42.3 (2018) 317–39.

Schonfield, Jeremy. "Psalms 113–18: Qualified Praise." *EJ* 50.2 (2017) 147–57.

Seitz, Christopher R. "Psalm 34: Redaction, Inner-Biblical Exegesis and the Longer Psalm Superscriptions—'Mistake' Making and Theological Significance." In *The Bible as Christian Scripture: The Work of Brevard S. Childs,* edited by Christopher R. Seitz and Kent Harold Richards, 279–98. Atlanta: Society of Biblical Literature, 2013.

Skehan, Patrick W. "A Liturgical Complex in 11QPsa." *CBQ* 34.2 (1973) 195–205.

Sommer, Benjamin D. "A Little Higher Than Angels: Psalm 29 and the Genre of Heavenly Praise." In *Built by Wisdom, Established by Understanding: Essays on Biblical and Near Eastern Literature in Honor of Adele Berlin,* edited by Maxine L. Grossman, 129–53. Bethesda, MD: University Press of Maryland, 2013.

———. *A Prophet Reads Scripture: Allusion in Isaiah 40–66.* Stanford: Stanford University Press, 1998.

Stec, David M. *The Targum of Psalms: Translated, with a Critical Introduction, Apparatus, and Notes.* The Aramaic Bible 16. Collegeville, MN: Liturgical, 2004.

Tanner, Beth L. "Allusion or Illusion in the Psalms: How Do We Decide?" In *Inner Biblical Allusion in the Poetry of Wisdom and Psalms,* edited by Mark J. Boda et al., 24–35. Library of Biblical Studies 659. London: T. & T. Clark, 2019.

———. *The Book of Psalms through the Lens of Intertextuality.* Studies in Biblical Literature 26. New York: Lang, 2001.

Tate, Marvin E. *Psalms 51–100.* Edited by John D. W. Watts et al. WBC 20. Waco, TX: Word, 2000.

Thomas, Marlin E. "Psalms 1 and 112 as a Paradigm for the Comparison of Wisdom Motifs in the Psalms." *JETS* 29.1 (1986) 15–24.

Tov, Emanuel. *Textual Criticism of the Hebrew Bible.* 3rd ed. Minneapolis: Fortress, 2012.

Trible, Phyllis. "The Book of Jonah: Introduction, Commentary, and Reflections." In vol. 7 of *NIB,* edited by Leander E. Keck, 461–530. Nashville: Abingdon, 1994.

VanGemeren, Willem A. *Psalms.* The Expositor's Bible Commentary 5. Grand Rapids: Zondervan, 2008.

Waltke, Bruce K. "Ask of Me, My Son: Exposition of Psalm 2." *Crux* 43.4 (2007) 2–19.

———. "Psalm 3: A Fugitive King's Morning Prayer." *Crux* 44.1 (2008) 2–13.

Watson, Wilfred G. E. *Classical Hebrew Poetry: A Guide to Its Techniques.* JSOTSup 26. Sheffield: JSOT, 2001.

Weiss, Meir. *The Bible from Within: The Method of Total Interpretation.* Jerusalem: Magnes, 1984.

Whiting, Mark J. "Psalms 1 and 2 as a Hermeneutical Lens for Reading the Psalter." *EQ* 85.3 (2013) 246–64.

Williamson, H. G. M. "Isaiah 62:4 and the Problem of Inner-Biblical Allusions." *JBL* 119.4 (2000) 734–39.

Wilson, Gerald H. *The Editing of the Hebrew Psalter.* SBLDS 76, Chico, CA: Scholars, 1985.

———. "Shaping the Psalter: A Consideration of Editorial Linkage in the Book of Psalms." In *The Shape and Shaping of the Psalter*, edited by J. Clinton McCann, 72–82. JSOTSup 159. Sheffield: JSOT, 1993.

Yarchin, William. "Were the Psalms Collections at Qumran True Psalters?" *JBL* 134.4 (2015) 775–89.

Young, Ian, and Robert Rezetko. *Linguistic Dating of Biblical Texts: An Introduction to Approaches and Problems.* Vol. 1. London: Equinox, 2008.

Zakovitch, Yair. *And You Shall Tell Your Son.* Jerusalem: Magnes, 1991.

———. *An Introduction to Inner-Biblical Interpretation.* Even-Yehuda: Reches, 1992.

———. "Juxtaposition in the Abraham Cycle." In *Pomegranates and Golden Bells: Studies in Biblical, Jewish, and Near Eastern Ritual, Law, and Literature in Honor of Jacob Milgrom*, edited by David P. Wright et al., 509–24. Winona Lake, IN: Eisenbrauns, 1995.

———. "On the Ordering of Psalms as Demonstrated by Psalms 136–50." In *The Oxford Handbook of the Psalms*, edited by William P. Brown, 214–28. New York: Oxford University Press, 2014.

Scripture Index

89:52 [53]	188
92:7 [8]	47n3
92:12–13 [13–14]	28n21
93	132
94:1	42n7
94:4	47n3
94:12	155n6, 182n6
95–99	132
95	29n3, 111n6
96	132
96:3	151n9
96:7	133
98	87
98:7	113
99:9	39n12
101:8	47n3
102:3	83n3
103:20	158n3
104	98
104:15	42n7
105–7	6n12
105	6
106	6
106:8	110
106:48	188
111–17	6n12
111	28n22
112	28
112:1	28
112:10	28, 163
113–18	8
114:1–2	150n7
115:9	151
115:10	151
115:11	151
116:15	156
118:27	42n7
119:64	151
119:135	42n7
127:5	155n6, 182n6
139:12	42n7
139:20	117
142:1	83
143	126
143:3	52
143:7	129, 138–39
143:8	119n2
144:3	58

146–50	6n12
146:10	134n5
147:10	101n3, 149
147:11	151
148	98
149	180–81
149:1	180, 182

Proverbs

1:8	22n8
3:1	22n8
3:19	98
5:7	155n6
7:2	86
7:9	86
7:24	155n6
8:32	155n6
10:31	170
11:27	174n5
13:5	155
13:12a	161
14:16	156
14:32	155
15:28	155
16:3	170
20:20	86
20:24	170
24:16	155
24:19	170
34:14 [15]	170

Ecclesiastes

12:10	169

Isaiah

1	27n20
1:10–11	181
30:27–28	91n5
31:1	101
33:10	68
33:14–16	77, 79, 191
33:15	78
38:18	138
42:10	180
59:3	26n18
59:4b	52